'For more than a decade Shaun has [...] of the *Baptist Times* what it means to pract[...] [H]e has shown how this ancient wis[...] the distraction, stress and anxi[...] [i]n his own life while pastorin[...] [dr]awing us to God.

'This book represen[ts...] [le]arned as he has explored Christian mindfu[lness...] [i]r depth. As such it has the power to enable any[one...] [u]p a mindful spirituality wherever they are, whatever t[hey are d]oing. Prepare to slow your breath, smell the coffee – and onc[e] again experience the closeness of God.'
Paul Hobson, Faith & Society Coordinator, Baptist Union of Great Britain; editor/writer

'What a rich, deep dive into mindful practice. Shaun offers such wisdom in this handbook for the mindful pilgrim. As someone who really wants to practise the presence of God and who also values intentional community, I know this book will be a treasured gem not just on my bookshelf but also as a tool for life-changing practices. A must read for anyone who is even slightly interested in mindfulness and essential reading for any Christ followers.'
Ruth Rice, Director, Renew Wellbeing

'At a time when mindfulness dominates much of the secular self-help landscape, Lambert offers a thorough-going framework for mindful formation in the Christian life. The subtitle does not over-promise – in chronicling his own spiritual liberation, Lambert illuminates this ancient pathway for Christians today.'
Dr Amy Oden, Adjunct Professor of Early Church History and Spirituality

'Dr Lambert is ten years ahead of me in this field and has generously supported me in my journey. My personal "aha" moment, which set me on the path, came when I embarked on a secular Mindfulness Based Stress Reduction (MBSR) course and all I could "see" in the material was the presence of God! This work gives language to much of what I've been engaged with for this past six or seven years.

'It is a brilliant book. Shaun has done a great job of marrying together the academic with the accessible. The auto-ethnographical method of telling his story is powerfully evocative and, rightly, critiques a world where sending a child away at six is "normal". It comes with a trigger alert. If you've suffered trauma of any kind, but especially childhood trauma, then you will undoubtedly find resonances. Speaking from a therapist's perspective, reading this book may act as the stimulus required to seek healing. Seek it. Personally, I found Shaun's vulnerability, honesty and intimacy opened up something in me which enabled God to minister to old wounds.

'I believe that people probably need a "dark night of the soul" experience before they can truly engage on a mystical/spiritual level with the mindfulness of God. The harsh reality is that most of us have had them.

'This is a book for Christians open to learning that mindfulness is as deeply rooted within the Christian tradition as it is in Buddhism; but it is also for "secular" mindfulness practitioners who are open and curious about the connections with the Christian faith.

'I love the idea of having an explicit, rather than implicit, "mindful rule for living", and I particularly connected with this: "The three points of light that illumine mindful awareness of self are awareness, regulation and transcendence. I take the log out of my own eye; I do not let the sun go down on my anger, and I transcend the anxious and wounded parts of my self."'

'Thank you, Shaun!'

Karen Openshaw, co-author of Mindfulness as Mission Gift *and* Mindful Devotions

'This is an intensely personal, and at times raw, story of an ongoing pilgrimage to wholeness. Shaun draws on his psychotherapy training, along with engaging creatively, analytically and theologically with the Bible and a variety of Christian traditions. He also affirms the insightful wisdom of secular mindfulness, including addressing the suspicions some Christians hold towards mindfulness.

'I was particularly moved to read of the way in which the

Christian Community of Scargill House has been such an integral part of Shaun's journey towards restoration. Drawing on this experience, he offers some profound and practical insights on how embracing a mindful rule of life could enable any of us to live in less painful and more life-giving ways.

'American Professor Brené Brown says this: "Owning our story and loving ourselves through that process, is the bravest thing we'll ever do." That's exactly what Shaun has done in this book. In order to experience the liberation to which he points, you'll need to savour the contents by reading it mindfully, and using the invitations at the end of each chapter to apply the insights he shares.'

Bishop Chris Edmondson, Former Chair of the Council of the Scargill Movement

'*Mindful Formation* is a beautiful, inspiring and challenging read. Shaun shares his own journey with vulnerability and openness and reveals how his journey into Christian mindfulness has been a pilgrimage into wholeness and into the spacious love of God. Shaun shares generously his extensive research as well as his story, and encourages us to reflect deeply on our own story. This book is thoroughly biblical, and it inspires us to be open to the Holy Spirit and to rediscover the contemplative life, living in the present, mindful of God. Shaun's life embodies this book and I wholeheartedly commend it to you.'

Rev Canon Phil Stone, Director, Scargill Movement

'Shaun has written a deeply personal book, drawing on his own experiences as well as a wealth of knowledge from a variety of complementary fields. Shaun's wisdom surrounding the cultivation of a mindful awareness of both God and self is clear as he guides the reader, encouraging them in a journey through the liberation of attention, enabling "moments of meeting" with the Lord and equipping them to detach from the "cultural web" that surrounds us and so often unconsciously entraps us.

'Shaun's experience is particularly powerful in his vulnerability and authenticity, sharing from his own experience of processing past trauma, the reperceiving, recognition, reclaiming and redeeming of our own experience in order to rediscover our true self when we may be misperceived by others. His careful articulation of how our past can overwhelm our ability to truly connect in the present is powerful, and he gently guides the reader along a path of listening to their own self, beginning a narrative that brings healing, even from experiences that are literally unspeakable, that defy attempts to be put into words. He models the use of art and poetry as well as mindful meditation to assist this journey, awakening our minds and guiding us to rediscover our identity as "a word spoken by the light to be light". This is a beautiful book, carefully and compassionately written, with hope on every page.'

Rev Dr Kate Middleton, Director of Mind and Soul Foundation

MINDFUL FORMATION

A PATHWAY TO SPIRITUAL LIBERATION

Shaun Lambert

instant apostle

First published in Great Britain in 2024

Instant Apostle
104A The Drive
Rickmansworth
Herts
WD3 4DU

Copyright © Shaun Lambert 2024

The author has asserted his rights under Section 77 of the Copyright, Designs and Patents Act, 1988, to be identified as the author of the work.

All rights reserved. No portion of this book may be reproduced or transmitted in any form or by any means, electronic or mechanical, including photocopying and recording, or by any information storage and retrieval system, without permission in writing from the publisher.

Unless otherwise indicated, all Scripture quotations are taken from the Holy Bible, New International Version® Anglicised, NIV® Copyright © 1979, 1984, 2011 by Biblica, Inc.® Used by permission. All rights reserved worldwide.

Scripture quotations marked 'NKJV' are taken from the New King James Version®. Copyright © 1982 by Thomas Nelson. Used by permission. All rights reserved.

Every effort has been made to seek permission to use copyright material reproduced in this book. The publisher apologises for those cases where permission might not have been sought and, if notified, will formally seek permission at the earliest opportunity.

The views and opinions expressed in this work are those of the author and do not necessarily reflect the views and opinions of the publisher.

British Library Cataloguing-in-Publication Data

A catalogue record for this book is available from the British Library.

This book and all other Instant Apostle books are available from

Instant Apostle:

Website: www.instantapostle.com

Email: info@instantapostle.com

ISBN 978-1-912726-81-3

Printed in Great Britain.

Cover image: Tom Denny's LIGHT Three from the Ivor Gurney Windows, Gloucester Cathedral. Used with permission of the artist.
Photograph by James O Davies and Rebecca Lane; cropped with permission.

Acknowledgements and dedication

'Slowly but surely' could be the motto of the pilgrimage of writing this book, whose beginnings go back nearly twenty years to a providential encounter with Simon Barrington-Ward, former Bishop of Coventry. My mindful family, Clare, Zac, Amy and Coco the dog, have loved me along the way. I am grateful to my places of learning over the last twenty-five years: Roehampton University, London School of Theology (LST) and The Mindfulness Network. I would like to thank my supervisors at LST, Steve Motyer and Janet Penny, who oversaw my PhD research on which this book is based. I am also deeply grateful to Phil Stone and my friends at the Scargill Community (so many of you, although special mention to Mike and Alison Leigh) for all your affection, friendship and playfulness. I have also appreciated very much the suggestions and wise proofreading of this book by the poet and breadmaker extraordinaire Helen Brocklehurst. I dedicate this book to the community at Scargill Movement.

About the author

Shaun Lambert is a writer, psychotherapist, mindfulness researcher, Baptist minister, and honorary mindfulness chaplain to the Scargill Movement. He is currently pursuing a training pathway in mainstream mindfulness with The Mindfulness Network, with a particular focus on interpersonal mindfulness. He loves flat whites, newts, walking and the idea of wild swimming, and lives in Hampstead with his family when not in Yorkshire with the Scargill community.

Contents

1. Introduction 13
2. The crisis of attention 26
3. Some underlying theory 48
4. Reclaiming our present moments 62
5. Retrieving mindfulness of God 90
6. The influence of Mark's Gospel 105
7. Reclaiming My present moments through a creative fusion with secular mindfulness 111
8. A reflection on spiritual senses 132
9. Three models for liberating our present moments 137
10. Who am I in the present moment? 145
11. Liberating the past through mindfulness of God 154
12. A spiral learning approach to trauma 162
13. Listening to your own self 170
14. Liberating the future through mindfulness of God 184
15. The application – the foundation of a mindful rule 204
16. Other dimensions to the mindful rule 224
17. The mindful rule 235
18. Coming home 241
19. Finding a theological home 248
20. The onward journey 256

Bibliography 270

1
Introduction

Suddenly an angel touched me, through these words…

> Fix your eyes…
> Fix your eyes on the depths of your heart…
> With an unceasing…
> With an unceasing mindfulness of God…
> I was fragile, breaking.
> The touch held me together…[1]

Closing the wound within attentively

'Attention equals Life' is the wisdom equation that has helped me most.[2] When that attention is focused on God that equals fullness of life. I say this having been broken and glued back together by the attentive grace of God. But more than that I have been mindfully reformed by God's gracious remaking. I think many others know what it is like for their lives to fracture but are not sure how to remake their world. So, this is a book

---

[1] An allusion to Elijah being touched by an angel in 1 Kings 19:5. A poetic rendering of the words that launched my research, Diadochus of Photike, Gnostic Chapters, 56 (SC 5 bis. p. 117), quoted in Olivier Clement, *The Roots of Christian Mysticism*, 7th edition (London: New City, 2002), 204.

[2] Attributed to dance critic and poet Edwin Denby by Frank O'Hara in *Standing Still and Walking in New York*, edited by Donald Allen (Bolinas, CA: Grey Fox, 1975), 184, quoted in Andrew Epstein, *Attention Equals Life: The Pursuit of the Everyday in Contemporary Poetry and Culture* (OUP: 2016), 2, Kindle.

about graced mindful formation. At the heart of mindful formation lies paying attention.

However, our most important capacity, attention and awareness is held captive by the virtual world. We need to learn to reclaim our attention from the Web. As somebody said, 'When it comes to the Web, we think we're spiders, but really we're flies.'[3] Oxford philosopher and former Google executive James Williams says, 'The liberation of human attention may be the defining moral and political struggle of our time.'[4] Freedom for me came when I learned to pay attention.

What I realised on this personal journey of reaching the end of my own self is that emptiness can be the pathway to a new thing. A process of being formed in a new way. What has helped me in that process is intentional mindful formation alongside God's hidden work. Mindfulness is our God-given capacity for awareness and attention, and mindful formation happens through what we pay attention to – if it is unhelpful then it is mind*less* formation. If it is helpful and intentional, then it is mind*ful* formation. From a Christian perspective, mindful formation occurs when we pay attention to God.

What I want to offer in this book is the wisdom contained within contemplation and mindfulness. I trained for three years at Bible college between 1994 and 1997 but realised I needed to continue to seek wisdom. My first quest was to seek relational wisdom, and between 1998 and 2010 I pursued counselling and psychotherapy training at Roehampton University. During that time in 2006 I came across Christian contemplative practices and mainstream mindfulness. I have been mining the wisdom of these strands ever since, completing a PhD in 2022 looking at mindfulness of God.

---

[3] Frances Ward and Richard Sudworth, 'Introduction', in *Holy Attention: Preaching in today's church*, eds Frances Ward and Richard Sudworth (Norwich: Canterbury Press, 2019), 63, Kindle.
[4] James Williams, *Stand Out of Our Light: Freedom and Resistance in the Attention Economy* (Cambridge: Cambridge University Press, 2018), xii.

It is this accumulated wisdom I share in this guide to mindful formation.

Holistic contemplation

When thinking of our attention and awareness I find it helpful to think of my awareness as the ground (like the background of a 3D visual puzzle) and the figure as something that emerges from that background when my attention is stretched towards something. Gestalt psychology conceptualised the idea of figure and ground (*back*ground) as something that can be seen in visual perception. Gestalt therapy took up the idea of figure as that 'which is most relevant or meaningful to the person', and the meaningful need emerges from the background of our awareness.[5] But it can also be used as a metaphor for how attention draws a figure (object of attention) out of the background of awareness. As Lucy Alford puts it, 'The ability of human perception to isolate objects (whether material or conceptual) from the general surrounding flux is attention's principal and most primal task.'[6] I want to extend the metaphor to say we can create intentional ethical figures that can be attentively recollected from the flux of our memory. These are the metacognitive propositions that have ethical value that I expand on later.

I also like the visual example of our inner frontstage and backstage. When I pay attention to something it appears on my frontstage. These concepts can be applied to our lives. For example, I make sure that having a hand-crafted cup of coffee is a figure in my daily life (if possible). The same is true of eating regularly, having a shower, drinking enough water. I've created the internal conditions that these necessary (or desired) things

---

[5] Petruska Clarkson, *Gestalt Counselling in Action*, 4th edition, updated by Simon Cavicchia, Sage Counselling in Action Series, series editor Windy Dryden (London: Sage, 2014), 242, Kindle.
[6] Lucy Alford, *Forms of Poetic Attention* (New York: Columbia University Press, 2020), 12, Kindle.

emerge out of the ground of my life as figures. I'm arguing in this book that the process of mindful formation is a necessary figure in our daily life, and that we need to create the conditions for it to emerge as a figure and not merely stay a background intention. It is so important it should feature in the frontstage of our life. This is easier said than done.

I've tried to make prayer a figure that emerges out of the background of my life for nearly forty years. More recently I've expanded that to the idea of mindful formation, a holistic contemplation that involves the whole of me – it needs to be a central figure in my life that constantly emerges into awareness. One of the things I'm asked is, 'How long should I spend in contemplation?' When I was running a church, I would make spending half an hour to an hour in prayer a priority and the first thing I would do – after making a cup of tea. Try to catch that early morning light!

As I've moved into a role where I lead retreats, I try to follow a rhythm I picked up at Scargill House, a Christian community and retreat centre. At Scargill there is a rhythm of praying three times a day, half an hour in the morning, fifteen minutes at lunchtime and fifteen minutes at teatime. This spiralling back to tune in again to God is what I recommend now. However, cultivating mindful awareness of God can be done at any time, whatever you are doing. So, I also cultivate mindful awareness when I am drinking a cup of coffee, or walking the dog, or washing up. The aim, of course, of Christian contemplation is a continuous awareness of God.

This holistic contemplation is not just sitting down: it can be walking, running, gardening, looking at a sunset while opening your awareness to the spiritual as well as physical dimension. It might be using simple body movements to indicate opening yourself up to the Holy Spirit. I am trying to learn sign language for concepts like sorry, forgive, welcome, breath, heart, as well as the signs for Holy Spirit, Jesus, Father and so on. Try to find different ways of moving into your body that work for you. This can be noticing your feet on the ground, or coming to your breath, or allowing sounds to come to you.

In mindful contemplation I am trying to move into a place of stillness, or open awareness. By focusing on one element of our body that can be an anchor I am simplifying the way my mind normally works, as it tries to juggle many things all at once. I believe multitasking is a myth. Focusing on one thing and doing it well refreshes the mind rather than tires it. The focused attention allows the emergence of an open awareness, a move into a spacious place in our minds. We can allow ourselves to move back and forth with our attention from a narrow beam of light to a wider spotlight. This wider spotlight enables the emergence of our witnessing self where we perceive or reperceive what is coming or going in our minds, bodies and emotions.

As I train to teach mainstream mindfulness one to one via an accredited path, at the heart of being a teacher is having a personal practice. That means I also practise secular mindful awareness practices each day, although God can drop in on these as well! The challenge to the Church comes around this domain of practices. On secular mindfulness training or retreats I have often spent three to four hours a day in practice. In the Church, the emphasis is on information and knowledge rather than transforming practices. We need to redress the balance.

In a holistic pathway to contemplation, returning to the body whenever we can, moving out of our heads, is essential. This is because the body is always in the present moment and the present moment is home in mindfulness of God. It is also important because, as Alister McGrath says, 'It is merely to assert that for human beings in this world the transcendent is accessed and the spiritual life is expressed exclusively through the medium of our material bodies.'[7] This is my own experience and forms part of my argument that our natural senses, when inhabited by the Holy Spirit, become spiritual senses, receptive to the presence of God. A good question to ask ourselves is,

---

[7] Alister E McGrath, *The Open Secret: A New Vision for Natural Theology* (Oxford: Blackwell Publishing, 2008), 82.

'Why should I as a Christian pay attention to my body?' It's a question I hope to answer in part in this book. One of the answers is that Jesus came to live in a body to show us how to live in a body! I think many Christians are dissatisfied with their spiritual life because it is a disembodied spirituality.

As we learn to pay attention, we find that other things pull us away from what we are trying to focus on or be aware of. For me it was mainly anxiety. At other times, and I think this feeling is created by our virtual world inhabitation, it is restlessness. Sometimes it might be cravings for things that will bring us emotional comfort. Often these distractions are automatic reactions which we need to become aware of – so that we can choose wise responses instead.

The structure of this book

In Chapter Two I expand on the crisis of attention that we need to intentionally address. The key task is reclaiming our attentional capacities from their cultural captivity to our virtual world. Mindful formation occurs through intentionally training our attentional capacities to be aware of God. Paying attention to God is distinctive of Christian mindfulness. Going deeper into contemplation requires us to keep spiralling back to God through our spiritual practices. What we pay attention to in mindfulness of God is crucial. As we do this, we may experience epiphanies or moments of meeting with God. We cannot be mindful of God unless we first understand what mindfulness is and so I address this by drawing on secular or mainstream mindfulness which works with our innate capacities for attention and awareness. Secular mindfulness as a cultural phenomenon is an act of resistance. Paradoxically, if we are to become aware of God, others and creation, we need to cultivate self-awareness – we need to examine our own self. This reflexivity is an attentive act of resistance. There are some key formational questions that need to be asked, which I outline in this chapter. The process of mindful formation is a quest, a journey and a pilgrimage. I invite you to join me on it.

Running through the book are some shorter, more academic but accessible chapters which bring in some insights from my PhD research. In Chapter Three I introduce some of the theory underpinning the book. To understand mindfulness, we need to utilise contextual theology, which engages with personal experience, theology and wider culture. I add some further reflections on autoethnography and how it can help us observe our participation in mindfulness of God. There are key themes in the book which are introduced in this chapter: remembering, reperceiving, recognition, reclaiming and redeeming. I outline the idea that Christian mindfulness has an ethical dimension, how to live by our values. I outline a way of being introspective without being narcissistic. I also introduce the importance of embodied incarnational spirituality (sometimes called kataphatic). An important question to ask is how can we represent our contemplation of God, what sort of language can we use? I emphasise the importance of creative, poetic language that is symbolic as we walk at the edge of language in contemplative experience.

In Chapter Four I share how reclaiming our present moments is central to mindful formation, as the present moment is where we find our home in God. I write about some of the epiphanies or moments of meeting I have had that have generated wisdom. Many of our present moments are lost and so identifying the charged moments when life changes is a crucial first step in reclaiming our here and now. I articulate these through eight windows that explore my participation in mindfulness of God and secular mindfulness. Tom Denny, the stained-glass artist, provides inspiration for those creative reflections through his work at Gloucester Cathedral in the Ivor Gurney windows. These reflections include the learning from painful and vulnerable experiences.

In Chapter Five I trace and recontextualise the contemplative historical strand of mindfulness or remembrance of God, particularly in relation to the Jesus Prayer and the Benedictine monastic tradition. This chapter presents an informed position on this important but neglected strand. I address the suspicions of some Christians towards mainstream mindfulness, establishing that it is our God-given capacity for attention and awareness. I outline theologically what is God's part and what is our part in mindfulness of God and the mindful turns we need to make in our spiritual formation. I emphasise the importance of embodied or incarnational spirituality.

In Chapter Six I outline the importance of Mark's Gospel for living by our values. This is through an informed reading of commentaries, articles and narrative criticism, but also through emphasising the significance of Mark for devotional reading, that intentionally leads us by the hand into transformation. The watchfulness commended in Mark's Gospel bears a family resemblance to mindfulness.

In Chapter Seven my theme is how I reclaimed my present moments through a creative fusion of secular mindfulness with mindfulness of God. I had realised that most of my present moments were overwhelmed by anxiety. The pathway to liberation is accessible to all. I address the problem of the present moment, and how often we are in mental time travel and not fully present to the here and now, which is reality. This is a problem faced by most people in our age of distraction. This means much of the time we are not living by our values. I begin to develop a theology of the present moment and how we can live by our values. This includes the theoretical underpinning for the idea that much of our relationship with God lies out of our awareness. These insights came out of a pilgrimage walk I undertook in northern Spain. As well as exploring anxiety as something that keeps us out of the present moment through mind wandering, I begin to explore the role of shame. I return to mindful theory about how we can cultivate self-awareness and learn to regulate the anxiety and shame we often feel in a way that liberates us.

In Chapter Eight I offer another strand of informed reading with a short reflection on the doctrine of the spiritual senses. My discovery is that my natural senses when inhabited by the

Holy Spirit become spiritual senses. I engage briefly with Balthasar's doctrine of spiritual senses which offers theological support for my discovery. This embodied, incarnational spirituality is called kataphatic in the contemplative tradition.

In Chapter Nine I expand on three models for liberating our present moments and leading us into mindful formation. The first is about how to live by our values in each ethical moment of choice, the second enables us to understand our relationship with God in time, especially when we doubt God's presence, through noticing moments of meeting with the divine. The third is the adaptation of the Jesus Prayer and *Lectio Divina* (slow meditative reading of Scripture) as attentional training tools that enable us to inhabit all of our being, including the embodied.

In Chapter Ten I ask, 'Who am I in the present moment?' This is another chapter based on my informed reading, drawing on the idea from Logos theology that each of us is a word spoken by Christ (the Word/Logos) to be light to the world. I also draw on recognition theory which argues how fundamentally important it is for our wellbeing to be recognised as who we are. In Christian terms that is who we are in Christ. This recognising has an important relational and ethical dimension. I also touch on the impact on us when we are misrecognised and how mindfulness can help us recognise others as they truly are.

In Chapter Eleven I suggest that if we are to reclaim our present moments to be mindful of God, we also need to address the shadow of the past which may hang over our present. For me this was the trauma of being sent to boarding school at a young age. Freedom in the present moment comes from integrating every part of us into our conscious awareness. I begin to discuss the importance of trauma theory, especially in the age of trauma in which we live.

In Chapter Twelve, in a short, accessible chapter I offer some further informed reading around trauma theory as I spiral back to it to help deepen our understanding of it. There have been important developments in trauma theory which I address here. How the unspeakable nature of trauma can be represented creatively is touched on.

In Chapter Thirteen I come back to the theme of self-awareness and self-examination by offering ways to listen to the different parts of our self, especially those parts that may have been pushed to the margins of our lives. One way is to simply do a self-interview. I offer personal examples. I have found this helps us live in an integrated way, all of our being becoming transparent to our witnessing self. This includes listening to our past and the voices that bring the past to life, liberating ourselves from internalised and distorted narratives.

Liberating our present needs some examination of our past. However, it can also enable us to liberate our future through mindfulness of God. This is the focus of Chapter Fourteen. We can gaze at the future with realism and hope as we make this pilgrimage, once we are able to perceive a God-formed narrative for our life. One way we can do this is to look at the past through a symbolic lens, without our normal negative bias, and find what has been redemptive and graced in the past. This interaction with key symbols in our life can redress the balance and lessen the gravitational pull of negativity bias on our thought life.

In the final section of the book, beginning in Chapter Fifteen, I begin to apply what we have discovered. The wisdom of intentional Christian community says that if we are to live by our values we need a rule of life, pathways that are incarnate values. I lay out the foundation of a mindful rule of life that enables this congruent way of life where we choose the values of God over our culturally derived values. This enables us to live relational lives that are mindful of others and recognise the image of God within them. As well as drawing on the wisdom of intentional community I utilise psychological theory around healthy relationships and how to avoid distortions and handle fractures within them. Confession and drawing on the creativity of our moral imagination is also part of the foundation of the mindful rule.

In Chapter Sixteen I develop some other dimensions to the mindful rule. If we are to be transformed through mindfulness of God, we must find an inner motivation and will to fuel our intention. This can be found through stories, humour, symbols that become lamps that guide us. Another dimension is that the mindful rule is participatory and can be adapted for each person's context. I outline how we can cultivate a wise remembering of the rule. The rule begins with a mindful confession of both our strengths and those elements of our life that get in the way of a relationship with God.

Chapter Seventeen outlines the short mindful rule. It draws on the wisdom that has directed the rest of the book. It is made up of the distilled wisdom of the fusion of Christian mindfulness and secular mindfulness – propositions that enable us to be self-aware and self-regulating, transcending our automatic self-focus. For example, one proposition in it says, 'I aim to recognise and lay down negative critical unhelpful judgements about my own self, and others and cultivate a compassionate reperceiving.'

In Chapter Eighteen I also consider if there is an 'overriding directional image' to my journey.[8] I identify that overriding directional image of the journey – as coming home. I explore this briefly in a wider cultural context. This theme is amplified in Chapter Nineteen when I reflect on the theologies I have found a home in, whose commonality is that they are open, spacious and aware theologies. They enable us to adapt our spiritual perceiving to grasp the Light in a dark world.

In the final chapter I offer a summary of the distilled wisdom that has helped me and that I hope will be a guide to others in this book. I reflect on the generous God I have met. I use David Brown's theology of interaction between natural symbols, human unconscious, human creativity and God as a sign of the

---

[8] David J Leigh, *Circuitous Journeys: Modern Spiritual Autobiography* (New York: Fordham University Press, 2000), 1, Kindle.

generosity of God.[9] This symbolic interaction can be a pathway to God for others and I outline ways this might be possible.

I see this symbolic interaction as a sign that creation is sacramental. This idea has come to me in fragments. I briefly outline this journey of discovery. For example, in conversation at Worth Abbey, a Roman Catholic Benedictine monastery, as I explained how creation spoke to me, a guest said, 'Oh, you are talking about creation as sacramental!' James K A Smith, the Christian philosopher, defines a sacramental view of nature as meaning 'that the physical, material stuff of creation and embodiment is the means by which God's grace meets us and gets hold of us'.[10] This makes sense to my embodied, incarnational mindful spirituality. God speaks to me through nature. My application of creation as sacramental is to see our God-given mindful capacities as sacramental, full of created goodness. This means secular mindfulness that works with these created capacities has a sacramental element.

Summary

Mindful formation has a framework that explains why we are doing what we are doing (metacognition). There is an intentional act of remembering our values (God-given) and choosing them over the worldly culturally conditioned values jostling for our attention. In other words, at the heart of mindful formation is an ethical stance.

I am remembering how to be mindful of God. The practices of remembering are developed in this book. As I am mindful of God, I begin to reperceive God, myself, others and creation. I

---

[9] David Brown, 'God and Symbolic Action', in *Divine Action: Studies Inspired by the Philosophical Theology of Austin Farrer*, eds Brian Hebblethwaite and Edward Henderson (Edinburgh: T& T Clark, 1990), 113-117, and David Brown, *Divine Generosity and Human Creativity* (London: Routledge, 2017), 5.

[10] James K A Smith in *Desiring the Kingdom: Worship, Worldview, and Cultural Formation* (Grand Rapids, Michigan: Baker Academic, 2009), 141.

have reclaimed a historic strand from Christian contemplation which is about mindfulness (remembrance) of God. I have recontextualised that historic strand using the language, theory and practices of secular or mainstream mindfulness.

The present moment is home in mindfulness of God and so I must reclaim my present moments (the here and now) from cultural captivity to the virtual world. Although I can reclaim them through intentional attentional training, remembering my values and recognising how I relate to God in time (mostly unaware), only God can redeem my present moments.

As I begin to reperceive on this pathway to spiritual liberation I start to recognise my God-given identity – my true self, created by Christ. I am also graciously enabled to recognise others, God and the world, and as I do this, I begin to change my self-centred, judgemental attitudes. I am helped in this formation through a mindful rule of life.

2
The crisis of attention

In this book I introduce a wide range of theory and practice that has informed and guided me. It might feel overwhelming, but we will keep circling back to these central concepts. Wisdom is not easy and straightforward; it takes time and effort to acquire. It takes time and often we feel like we are walking in the dark with only just enough light to illumine a few steps ahead. One of the central pieces of wisdom I want to share is about reclaiming our attentional capacities.

The problem is our attentional capacities are held captive by the virtual world and media technologies. The Web lures us in like a Venus flytrap lures in a fly. For example, N Katherine Hayles critiques the wider digital nature of our culture which channels us into 'hyper-attention, a cognitive mode that has a low threshold for boredom, alternates flexibly between different information streams, and prefers a high level of stimulation'.[11] I see this in myself when I go on retreat and put my phone away, and experience immediate boredom and the desire to search for the different information streams my phone provides. It may be that the intuitive turn towards mindfulness in the same culture is a form of tacit searching for the antidote to this cultural stream of hyper-attention and digital media.

The other phrase that Hayles uses as the opposite of hyper-

---

[11] N Katherine Hayles, *How We Think: Digital Media and Contemporary Technogenesis* (Chicago, London: The University of Chicago Press, 2012), 12.

attention is 'deep attention'.[12] This is the ability to sustain attention. This is now a rare commodity in our society. We live in an attention economy and reclaiming our attention is our number one task in mindful formation. We do that by mindfully training our attentional capacities. I offer models for doing this in this book.

What are we doing when we pay attention to God? I am suggesting that, as in the Jesus Prayer ('Lord Jesus Christ, Son of God, have mercy on me, a sinner'),[13] we pay attention to Jesus Christ, the incarnated Son of God. We pay attention to Scripture through *Lectio Divina* (the slow meditative reading of the Bible). We examine our own self and pay attention to others and creation. These practices simplify what we are paying attention to: very often we have too many tabs or windows open in our mind.

We pay attention to the ordinary, to the margins of our lives, to the symbolic. It is the virtual world that now shapes our everyday life. Because we are shaped by what we pay attention to it is the media and communication technologies that we conform to. None of this is new, but because of the cultural captivity of our attentional capacities our ability to truly pay attention is flabby and anaemic. The models I offer alongside the attentional training in this book are important additional and neglected steps to mindful formation. The spirituality we develop through these processes is incarnational and embodied, not virtual. It is not just the external world that we need to liberate ourselves from; we need to learn to deal with the tangled webs of anxiety and stress within.

I think we are often, unknowingly, trying to practise a disembodied spirituality. We can move our bodies in unaware, habitual ways with a limited range of how our physicality is used. We can have a body that we do not inhabit in an aware way. For

---

[12] Hayles, 12.

[13] The Jesus Prayer is an ancient Christian contemplative prayer, a good introduction is Simon Barrington-Ward, *The Jesus Prayer: A Way to Contemplation* (Boston, Massachusetts: Pauline Books & Media, 2011).

example, it took me a long time to realise that I held stress, difficult emotions and tension in my shoulders, neck and lower back. I have learnt through working with a chiropractor what movements are helpful and safe to maintain flexibility and strength.

Within Christianity we don't have a systematic practice of working with the body; what we have is fragments out of which we can make a whole. Knowing what movements are difficult for you is helpful to know. Now I have difficulty in lifting my right arm up to the sky because of a muscle that is tight and isn't responding quickly to treatment. If I bend down, I bend down with my knees, rather than bending over, to protect my lower back. Learning to move and inhabit our bodies in an aware way is an important part of our mindful formation. In doing this we can work out if we are not inhabiting our bodies because we feel ambivalent about them.

My contemplative life story has been a meeting point between my intuitive impulse for healing and transformation and the cultural phenomenon of mindfulness. It led to a recognition of a pathway to mindful formation. My moment of need coincided with a cultural moment of great importance – the rise of mindfulness and a turn towards contemplation. This is an act of resistance because, as we learn to free our attentional capacities, we liberate our internal and external worlds. It's a convergence that many others have experienced. One stream that enters this convergence that differentiates my story is the impulse to explore mindfulness of God. This makes it a unique pathway to mindful formation. In this book I retain an emphasis on personal story, theory, theology and cultural engagement.

As I researched mindfulness of God, I realised that I kept returning to the key concepts because I didn't understand them completely the first time I examined them. The same was true for the academic methods I looked at and utilised, or complex subjects like trauma theory. I also realised that mindfulness and contemplative practices used this circling back in a process of deepening repetition. This intuitive process of circling back has been discovery-based and iterative, a deepening spiral of transformation. Mindful and contemplative formation happens through a revisiting of key concepts and practices and building on them, which fits with spiral learning theory. There are many subjects that cannot simply be reduced to something that is understandable immediately – some subjects need a pattern of returning to them that leads to a deeper understanding as this process is followed.

The architect of spiral learning theory was Jerome Bruner back in 1960, and it can be summarised as 'the encounter and the revisit of specific content, e.g., concepts at stages in a course – but where the revisit includes a step up in rigour or depth'.[14] This spiral process of repetition, remembering or iteration enables us to be slowly formed in spiritual terms. Mindful formation or any spiritual formation or discipleship takes time. It needs the benefits of a spiral learning approach which Harden outlines as 'reinforcement', a 'move from simple to complex' and 'deepening levels' of knowledge.[15] I introduce some key concepts as we go along and then spiral back to them. These include mindfulness theory, representation in writing, trauma theory, spiritual senses and types of spirituality.

Ultimately this process is rewarding. It can be approached from another angle. Margaret Koehler, in her study of attention in eighteenth-century poetry, writes about walking the same route again and again as a poetic act of attention: 'A circumscribed area of terrain gets deeper and deeper, sharper and sharper, more and more familiar, over repeated

---

[14] Russell Woodward, 'The Spiral Curriculum in Higher Education: Analysis in Pedagogic Context and a Business Studies Application', *E-Journal of Business Education and Scholarship of Teaching* 13, no.3 (2019): 15. See Jerome S Bruner, *The Process of Education* (Harvard University Press, 1960), particularly chapter three.

[15] R M Harden, 'What is a spiral curriculum?', *Medical Teacher* 21, no. 2 (1999): 142, accessed 28th September 2023, dx.doi.org/10.1080/01421599979752.

considerations.'[16] In this consideration we are paying attention carefully over a long period of time. In mindfulness of God, we need to expose ourselves to 'repeated considerations' of the theory, practice and lived experience. That is why it is a pilgrimage.

This approach, with its revisiting of core concepts, which are applied in different contexts, led to three quest questions. The first was, 'What is mindfulness of God, and how might we cultivate it?' My lived experience suggested my home was in the present moment with God. The problem of the present moment was that I was unable to be present in the here and now because of anxiety. This led to a second question, 'How can we reclaim our present moments from anxious rumination to be mindful of God?' You may be taken out of the present moment by other afflictive thoughts and emotions. However, I also found the roots of my anxiety lay in the trauma of childhood separation from my family. I discerned through this experience of complete aloneness that I had to find my home in my own body. I recognised I did not live in all the rooms of my own being, and so discovered a deeper related question, 'How could we be fully aware of and at home in our whole embodied self, to further reclaim our present moments?' This is about life in all its fullness. This alienation from our bodies is a wider cultural issue because of the virtual world we live in. These quest questions are archetypal and need to be articulated for many.

Epiphanies and moments of meeting

This book has been influenced by the accessible methodology of autoethnography (AE), which came out of ethnography. Ethnography is a key methodology in anthropological research and is based on participant observation in and of a group of

---

[16] Margaret Koehler, *Poetry of Attention in the Eighteenth Century* (London: Palgrave Macmillan, 2012), 187.

people.[17] In a brilliant turn of phrase Tedlock outlines the key turn from ethnography to AE: 'Beginning in the 1970s, there was a shift in emphasis from participant observation to the observation of participation.'[18] In this way she distinguishes between ethnography as participant observation and AE as the observation of participation. However, for it to be true AE it needs to be the observation of one's own participation in culture and society. I am, therefore, *locating* my journey as autoethnographic because I am observing my own participation in mindfulness and culture. Mindful formation requires us to examine our place in culture and how it has shaped us. That is why AE is a helpful methodology in keeping us intentionally focused on culture and our relation to it. This also enables me to share out of my contemplative experience and practice, which is also a mainstream mindfulness principle, and the way early contemplatives shared their teaching.

Another AE principle that has helped me to focus my thinking is the idea of examining epiphanies.[19] Epiphanies are moments of recognition about your own life, others or God. I am also calling them 'moments of meeting', to signal these are the key times I had insights or moments of heightened awareness of God.[20] These epiphanies or moments of meeting momentarily free us from the gravitational pull of our culture; they are an antidote to our crisis of attention.

---

[17] Paul Atkinson, et al, 'Editorial Introduction', in *Handbook of Ethnography*, eds Paul Atkinson et al (Los Angeles, London: Sage, 2001), 5.

[18] See Barbara Tedlock, 'From Participant Observation to the Observation of Participation: The Emergence of Narrative Ethnography', *Journal of Anthropological Research* 47, no. 1 (1991): 69.

[19] Focusing on epiphanies is highlighted in Carolyn Ellis, Tony E Adams and Arthur P Bochner, 'Autoethnography: An Overview', *Forum: Qualitative Social Research* 12, no. 1 (2011): 347, accessed 26th August 2016, doi.org/10.17169/fqs-12.1.1589.

[20] See The Boston Change Process Study Group, *Change in Psychotherapy: A Unifying Paradigm* (New York, London: W W Norton & Company, 2010), 5-7, for the idea of moments of meeting in implicit relationships.

A key epiphany was the realisation that if I wanted to be mindful of God, I needed to reclaim my present moments, which were often overwhelmed with anxiety. This meant my original quest question, 'What is mindfulness of God, and how can we cultivate it?' which needed to start with historical retrieval led to a related more present moment focused question: 'How can we reclaim our present moments from anxious rumination to be mindful of God?' I am aware that God is mindful of me, but in this question I want to establish my part: 'How am I to be mindful of God?'

Some of my epiphanies have been positive realisations or insights that came out of my brokenness and vulnerability. This is another key focus of AE; through researching autobiographical impulses, the self becomes visible and vulnerable 'in research and in writing'.[21] To acknowledge vulnerability is not weakness but facing reality, being real. It isn't just an academic exercise; it is something we need to do in our spiritual journey.

Secular mindfulness – a response to the crisis of attention

A near breakdown in 2006 was like an unmaking of my sense of self, through stress, anxiety and burnout. This resulted in an impulse to explore secular mindfulness which I had encountered in my counselling and psychotherapy training at Roehampton University. Secular mindfulness is generally mindfulness for mental health, and I was able to draw on it to manage my anxiety and stress. The pioneering mindfulness-based approaches were Mindfulness-Based Stress Reduction followed by Mindfulness-Based Cognitive Therapy for recurrent depression. Mindfulness has emerged as a response to

---

[21] Leon Anderson and Bonnie Glass-Coffin, 'I Learn by Going', in *Handbook of Autoethnography*, eds Stacy Holman Jones, Tony E Adams and Carolyn Ellis (Walnut Creek, California: Left Coast Press Inc, 2013), 71.

the crisis of attention and our inability to live aware and wakeful lives.

Secular (or, as it is sometimes called, mainstream) mindfulness defines mindfulness essentially as 'awareness itself, an entirely different and one might say, larger capacity than thought, since any and all thought and emotion can be held in awareness'.[22] This is a simple but profound definition of mindfulness as awareness which can hold our thoughts, emotions and bodily sensations in present moment consciousness. Awareness, and therefore mindfulness in this definition, is a universal human capacity. I cannot talk about my capacity for awareness without talking about attention, which is where I direct my awareness. Attention is, according to Tim Lomas, 'awareness stretched *toward* something'.[23] This interconnection between awareness and attention is underlined in the definitions provided by Brown and Ryan: '*Awareness* is the background "radar" of consciousness' which scans the environment, and attention 'is a process of focusing conscious awareness'.[24]

Another central definition has helped me steer my course to mindfulness of God. It is this central summary of mindfulness by Jon Kabat-Zinn: 'paying attention in a particular way: on purpose, in the present moment, and non-judgementally'.[25] Shapiro et al take this definition and break it down into key

---

[22] J Mark, G Williams and Jon Kabat-Zinn, 'Mindfulness: Diverse Perspectives on its Meaning, Origins, and Multiple Applications at the Intersection of Science and Dharma', in *Mindfulness: Diverse Perspectives on its Meaning, Origins, and Applications*, eds J Mark, G Williams and Jon Kabat-Zinn (London: Routledge, 2013), 15.

[23] Tim Lomas, *Masculinity, Meditation and Mental Health* (London: Palgrave Macmillan, 2014), 100-101.

[24] Kirk Warren Brown and Richard M Ryan, 'The Benefits of Being Present: Mindfulness and its Role in Psychological Well-being', *Journal of Personality and Social Psychology* 84, no. 4 (2003): 822-848, accessed 18th September 2017, dx.doi.org/10.1037/0022-3514.84.4.822.

[25] Jon Kabat-Zinn, *Wherever You Go, There You Are: Mindfulness Meditation for Everyday Life* (New York: Hyperion, 1994), 375.

elements, and here I come back to her theme of reperceiving. These key elements are to intentionally practise mindfulness, train your attention and change your attitude. As you do this there is a 'shift in perspective' where you 'reperceive' reality.[26] Through reperceiving you can '*reflectively* choose what has been previously *reflexively* adopted and conditioned'.[27] This has implications for wanting to live consciously by my values: 'Reperceiving may also help people recognise what is meaningful for them and what they truly value.'[28] I use these key elements to shape intentional reflection at the end of each chapter. An important element of mindful formation is consciously living by our values. Our culture and the power of the virtual world make it very difficult to live by our values; rather, we live by the values of a materialistic world that wants us to over-consume without awareness.

Attention itself has a range of capacities. What we need to learn to exercise is our muscle of attention. Instead of my attention being held captive, for example, by social media, I can learn to regulate my attention.[29] I can focus my attention on Scripture, or chocolate, or my breath, or a bird of the air. What happens next, according to the muscle of attention, is that my mind will wander, and that is indeed my experience.[30] I have this

---

[26] Shauna L Shapiro, et al, 'Mechanisms of Mindfulness', *Journal of Clinical Psychology* 62, no. 3 (2006): 374, accessed 18th July 2014.
[27] Shapiro, et al, 'Mechanisms of Mindfulness', 380.
[28] Shapiro, et al, 'Mechanisms of Mindfulness', 380.
[29] Scott R Bishop, et al, 'Mindfulness: A Proposed Operational Definition', *Clinical Psychology: Science and Practice* 11, no. 3 (Autumn 2004): 232.
[30] See Wendy Hasenkamp, et al, 'Mind Wandering and Attention During Focused Meditation: A Fine-grained Temporal Analysis of Fluctuating Cognitive States', *Neuroimage* 59 (2012), 751, accessed 18th November 2015, dx.doi.org/10.1016/j.neuroimage.2011.07.008. Daniel Goleman calls these steps the muscle of attention see, Daniel Goleman, 'Meditation: A Practical Way to Retrain Attention', November 2013, accessed 18th November 2015, available at www.mindful.org/meditation-a-practical-way-to-retrain-attention.

beautiful capacity called meta-awareness, where I notice that part of my mind has wandered to a meeting I am worried about tomorrow. Through the self-regulation of my attention, I can switch my attention back to what it is I am focusing on.[31] This enables me to sustain my attention.[32] With practice I am able to both sustain a focused attention and inhabit an open awareness to thoughts, feelings and bodily sensations as they appear in awareness.[33] This can be described in different ways and has important implications not only for wellbeing but also for my awareness of God's presence.

When I was first married, we went to ballroom dancing, but gave up after the first lesson owing to my lack of rhythm. Recently, as part of the community at Scargill House, during an entertainment evening I mentioned this lack of rhythm, and someone offered to teach me some dance moves, which they proceeded to do. I find it helpful to talk about mindfulness as consisting of several moves as in a dance. Mark Williams outlines a helpful concept of how our mind works, principally through two modes, 'conceptual (language-based) processing versus sensory-perceptual processing'.[34] This has also been called our narrative self and experiential self.[35] I will expand on this as I show how I applied this map to my wellbeing and spirituality. Put simply, my narrative self is where I live most of

---

[31] Bishop, et al, 232.

[32] Bishop, et al, 232.

[33] Bishop, et al, 232.

[34] J Mark, G Williams, 'Mindfulness and Psychological Process', *Emotion* Vol. 10, no. 1 (2010): 2.

[35] See Farb, et al, 'Attending to the present: Mindfulness Meditation Reveals Distinct Neural Modes of Self-Reference', *Social Cognitive and Affective Neuroscience (SCAN)* 2 (2007): 313-322, accessed 13th March 2019, dx.doi.org/10.1093/scan/nsm030, 313-314. See also D J Siegel, 'Mindfulness Training and Neural Integration: Differentiation of Distinct Streams of Awareness and the Cultivation of Well-being', *Social Cognitive and Affective Neuroscience* (SCAN), 2, no. 4 (2007), 261, accessed 12th March 2022, dx.doi.org/10.1093/scan/nsm034, for a witnessing or observing self that holds the narrative and experiential self.

the time, telling stories, often negative ones. My experiential self is my body, breath and senses.

Mark Williams introduces another aspect of our being when he says in a summary statement, 'Attentional training in mindfulness programs cultivates the ability to shift modes as an essential first step to being able to hold *all* experience (sensory and conceptual) in a wider awareness that is itself neither merely sensory or conceptual.'[36] In mindful experience it is essential to shift to this wider, more open awareness that holds all our experience in conscious awareness. It is in this place of open awareness, as we expand our bandwidth of conscious experience, that we can also become more aware of God's presence. In my experience, the same attentional capacities are at work in mindfulness of my anxious thoughts as are at work in mindfulness of God. This awareness has also been called the 'observing self'.[37] Just as the phrase 'seeing clearly' can be critiqued from a disability consciousness perspective, so 'participant observer' can be critiqued from the perspective of sensory ethnography.[38] The participation in sensory ethnography is conceptualised through the wider idea of perception, drawing on all the senses.[39] I prefer the term 'witnessing self', or perceiving self.[40] Having outlined these three aspects of self – narrative, experiential and witnessing – I can then show the moves that I make in mindfulness.

The first move is to navigate from my narrative self, my

---

[36] Williams, 'Mindfulness and Psychological Process', 2.
[37] See for a full-length exploration of this idea. Arthur J Deikman, *The Observing Self: Mysticism and Psychotherapy* (Boston, MA: Beacon Press, 1982). Siegel, 'Mindfulness training and neural integration', for delineating the witnessing or observing self holding narrative and experiential selves, 261.
[38] Sarah Pink, *Doing Sensory Ethnography*, 2nd edition (Los Angeles, London: Sage, 2015), 95-96.
[39] Pink, 95-96.
[40] Shapiro, et al, 'Mechanisms of Mindfulness', 379. Shapiro also uses the term witnessing and says reperceiving allows an 'intimate observing or witnessing, not a detached one'.

head, into my experiential self – my body, my senses, my breath. This is important because in doing this I shift into the present moment; my body, breath and senses can never be at any other point of time.[41] In my head I can be at any point in time, as I worry about the morning prayer I am doing tomorrow or imagining reactions to the sermon I preached last Sunday. It is a move I can make without conscious awareness through having natural ways to find a calm state of mind when I am stressed, for example, by taking the dog for a walk. If I can learn to make this move intentionally and with conscious awareness, then I move out of mind wandering and my distorted stories. Within this I am using my witnessing self to tell a bigger narrative, one that can hold the distorted narratives within me. As a graced response, as God transforms my awareness, I want to rewrite my story, in my mind and body, not just on the written page.

However, there is another move, and that is into my witnessing self, where I can hold both my narrative self and my experiential self in conscious awareness. It is in this place that I learn to relativise my distorted thoughts and stories as just thoughts, not facts. But for my purposes it is also in this place of awareness that I can sense God's presence. In this place I am also in the present moment, and here my experience is that I am more likely to find God. The theology of the present moment is also something that I develop further.

Just as modern discipleship is often disembodied, we are not often taught how to deal with our afflictive thought life. I offer one central way in the relativising of our thoughts. It is there in the Christian tradition, and one helpful verse is, 'take captive every thought to make it obedient to Christ' (2 Corinthians 10:5). This is not every thought but the afflictive ones. We cannot take captive what we are not aware of, and so implicit in this verse is the idea that we can witness our thoughts from a larger self. Again, another challenge for Christian discipleship from mainstream mindfulness is the time and effort to become

---

[41] Mark Williams and Danny Penman, *Mindfulness: A Practical Guide to Finding Peace in a Frantic World* (London: Piatkus, 2011), 197-198.

aware of one's state of mind in the practice. I don't think significant transformation is possible without this self-work. I emphasise the importance of embodied living and awareness of thoughts and emotions in mindful formation.

Evagrius Ponticus (345-399), an early Christian contemplative, emphasised the importance of becoming aware of our thoughts and feelings. Bamberger calls this 'psychology of a practical, experiential kind'.[42] We see the examination through self-reflection: 'Let him keep careful watch over his thoughts. Let him observe their intensity, their period of decline and follow them as they rise and fall.'[43] It was to be a non-elaborative awareness with the aim that you catch the first thought as it appears, before a whole train of thought takes your attention away.[44]

These definitions make a statement that is anthropological; they raise a central, if neglected, part of our incarnated being – the importance of awareness and attention, and the different aspects of self we can inhabit. Mindfulness definitions also recognise other mindful capacities that we all have. These have been called 'self-awareness', 'self-regulation' and 'self-transcendence'.[45]

Vago defines these three aspects of mindfulness as:

> meta-awareness of self (self-awareness), an ability to effectively manage or alter one's responses and impulses (self-regulation), and the development of a positive relationship between self and other that transcends self-

---

[42] Evagrius Ponticus, *The Praktikos: Chapters on Prayer*, translated by John Eudes Bamberger OCSO (Spencer, Massachusetts: Cistercian Publications, 1970), lxviii.

[43] Evagrius Ponticus, *The Praktikos*, 29.

[44] Mary Margaret Funk, *Tools Matter for Practicing the Spiritual Life* (New York: Continuum, 2004), 53.

[45] David R Vago and David A Silbersweig, 'Self-Awareness, Self-Regulation, and Self-Transcendence (S-ART): A Framework for Understanding the Neurobiological Mechanisms of Mindfulness', *Frontiers in Human Neuroscience* 6 (2012): 4.

focused needs and increases prosocial characteristics (self-transcendence).[46]

I need to transcend my anxious self, my wounded boarding school self, through self-awareness and the regulation of the anxiety that takes up so much of my inner space. These capacities can be enhanced through mindful awareness practices.

Mindfulness theory distinguishes between mindfulness-based therapies like Mindfulness-Based Stress Reduction (MBSR) and mindfulness-incorporating therapies like Acceptance and Commitment Therapy (ACT). I also draw on the ideas of experiential avoidance, cognitive fusion, and acceptance from ACT in my map of mindfulness. Experiential avoidance is quite simply 'the process of trying to avoid your own experiences' as a way of regulating them.[47] Acceptance is the way to step out of avoidance: we accept the reality we face in the moment, without avoiding it.[48] In cognitive fusion I become the difficult thought or feeling.[49] In my experience of anxiety I was trying to avoid the difficult thought, not accepting it and often fused to it. I must learn to 'defuse' from my anxious thought, to witness that thought and not be a victim of it.

Each chapter will have a reflection space to do some self-work. It will ask you to work on something intentionally that the chapter talks about. It will ask you to train your attention in a way that helps you be mindful of God. There will be an opportunity to examine your attitudes which are unhealthy. I will also ask you to see if there is an element of your life or the world or another person you can reperceive, see more clearly. There are other definitions of mindfulness that we will pick up

---

[46] Vago and Silbersweig, 2.
[47] Steven C Hayes, *Get Out of Your Mind & Into Your Life: The New Acceptance & Commitment Therapy* (New Harbinger Publications, Inc, 2005), 30, 58.
[48] Hayes, 45.
[49] Hayes, 58.

later and spiral back to.

By examining my life, I had the vulnerable epiphany that the cultural 'making of me' at boarding school had created an identity that fractured under extreme pressure, because it was self-sufficient, emotionally avoidant and, therefore, avoidant of the body. At my boarding school, unquestioning loyalty was encouraged rather than awareness, exploration and curiosity. Mindfulness turned me towards an aware inhabiting of my body, emotions and awareness. As it did so it brought spiritual life. This slow turn to incarnational living was followed by a spiritual epiphany, a moment of meeting that was brief but has stayed with me ever since. Mindful formation is a turn to incarnational spirituality. This pattern of not inhabiting our bodies and emotions is mirrored in our virtual culture.

A spiritual impulse in 2006 led to the discovery of mindfulness of God and the foundational epiphany for my contemplative formation. One phrase from my contemplative reading has been a second-person guide to me since 2006 when it first sounded in my awareness. It has led me by the hand into a lived experience of its intention. Olivier Clement translated an original Greek phrase from fifth-century Greek Bishop Diadochus of Photike, a pioneer of the Jesus Prayer, as, 'Let us keep our eyes always fixed on the depths of our heart with an unceasing *mindfulness* of God.'[50] These words were a summary statement, a theological fragment, that became the cornerstone of my research. This phrase struck my heart, as if my heart was a bell, and I still ring with it today. It was a spiritual defibrillator that shocked me into awareness, my body and emotions. It was more than words on a page; it was something sensed spiritually in my embodied being. The energy of that moment has never left me. I have asked myself why. I think the phrase caught the

---

[50] My italics, Diadochus of Photike, Gnostic Chapters, 56 (SC 5 bis. p. 117), quoted in Olivier Clement, *The Roots of Christian Mysticism*, 7th ed (London: New City, 2002), 204.

'attention of my heart'.[51] That is, there was an emotional connection that motivated me to examine this phrase year after year. Even when my heart was burnt to ashes. This emotional magnetism provided me with the fuel for my intention to study mindfulness of God.

The paradoxical mutual indwelling of the physical and spiritual in me in that moment of meeting with God helped shape the rest of this quest. The original phrase could be translated as remembrance of God, and this element of remembering has become important to my concept of mindfulness of God.

Reflexivity as attentive resistance

An important question to ask in a journey of mindful formation is how to critically examine our own experience. The critical gaze I use to uncover the implicit and observe my own self experience to gain some critical distance is mindful awareness. This use of mindful awareness as reflexive self-awareness is essential in mindful formation. Scripture encourages us to examine ourselves and to allow ourselves to be examined by the Holy Spirit (Psalm 139:23; Lamentations 3:40). If we do not become self-aware, we cannot change into Christlikeness. It is in this way we can move from being flies in a cultural web to those who become liberated to transcend it. We are equipped to resist our cultural captivity.

Mindfulness also has an anthropological stance in its emphasis on awareness as the central aspect of the good life. This is a critical gaze when directed towards Western culture and its emphasis on information and the mind. Williams and Kabat-Zinn in the context of critiquing Western culture make the point, 'While we get a great deal of training in our education systems in thinking of all kinds, we have almost no exposure to the cultivation of intimacy with that other innate capacity of

---

[51] Cynthia Bourgeault, 'Centering Prayer and Attention of the Heart', *Cross Currents* 59 no. 1 (2009), 23.

ours that we call awareness.'[52] This critical gaze and anthropological stance can be used not only to examine my boarding school self, and other cultural shaping, but also to critically examine my experience within a specific charismatic church culture.

Within my discovery process I grasped that my participative approach led me to read scriptural and mindfulness texts in a distinct way. I wanted to apply theory to this way of reading, and the best way to describe it is as one articulated by Peter Candler, that is I read 'manuductively', allowing the text to 'lead you by the hand'.[53] I have done this with Scripture, but also with the mindfulness self-help texts and some key contemplative texts. This is a helpful devotional form of reading that I spiral back to, to develop it further.

As a young man, not yet a Christian, I was drawn to the charismatic movement because of its lively embodied worship. However, my immersion in secular psychology as a psychotherapist provided another critical gaze. I felt that much of the practice of charismatic worship had not been reflected on, that it was not an aware or particularly self-reflective movement. This was especially highlighted when I began to explore mindful theory and practice. I was looking for more introspective, meditative practices in my own spirituality. This led me to historic Christian contemplation, which can also be used as a critical gaze on charismatic worship, because of its contemplative emphasis on silence, solitude and meditation on Scripture. However, there was still something missing, and I did not know what that was until I discovered mindfulness theory and practice.

In charismatic worship I did not fully inhabit awareness, but

---

[52] Williams and Kabat-Zinn, 'Mindfulness: Diverse Perspectives on its Meaning', 15.
[53] See Peter M Candler Jr, *Theology, Rhetoric, Manuduction, or Reading Scripture Together on the Path to God* (London: SCM Press, 2006) for this idea of manuduction, texts that are written to lead you by the hand towards God, 1-20.

in Christian contemplation I felt I was practising a disembodied platonic spirituality. Mindfulness theory and practice, with its emphasis on the cultivation of mindful awareness, a clear seeing of reality, became the new critical gaze for me. Although I am critiquing my experience of charismatic worship, I still identify as belonging to a charismatic spirituality, in believing in the person and presence of the Holy Spirit as the transforming presence of God. However, that charismatic spirituality has required a new anthropological understanding of my mindful and embodied capacities that are inhabited by that divine presence.

Journey, quest and pilgrimage

This retrieval of the phrase 'mindfulness of God' from contemplative history led me on both personal and academic journeys, both a quest and a pilgrimage. Two central metaphors of pilgrimage and quest will help shape the journey of mindful formation in terms of its representation and wider resonance as there are archetypal elements to both ideas. I saw that mindfulness itself as a cultural phenomenon could be described using pilgrimage language.

I began to make connections between mindfulness and pilgrimage after reading Jill Dubisch's autoethnographic book on pilgrimage to a Greek island. A common factor between pilgrimage sites and mindfulness as a cultural phenomenon, as I observe it, is that both have 'spiritual magnetism'.[54] Mindfulness has personally attracted me, and it is a widespread cultural phenomenon in the West in terms of numbers of people practising, the rise of self-help books, the new therapies incorporating mindfulness and the emergence of mindfulness gurus. Traditionally it is places that have spiritual magnetism. On pilgrimage one is drawn to a place that has spiritual

---

[54] Jill Dubisch, *In A Different Place: Pilgrimage, Gender and Politics at a Greek Island Shrine* (Princeton, New Jersey: Princeton University Press, 1995), 35.

magnetism. Certain sites even within secular psychology could be said to have become must-go-to pilgrimage places, like Jon Kabat-Zinn's hospital in Massachusetts, or Mark Williams' Oxford Centre for Mindfulness.

It is not just 'places' that attract pilgrims; 'Pilgrimage may also center around a sacred person.'[55] Mindfulness in secular psychology has its 'saints' and gurus that have spiritual magnetism. People flock to hear the main mindfulness speakers. In the virtual world we now live in, with internet connectivity, we do not have to physically go to a site any more to make a pilgrimage. Mindfulness can be accessed via the online world, as well as in the physical world.

People who are in pain are attracted to pilgrimage. People who are in pain are attracted to mindfulness. Mindfulness research shows that mindfulness can help alleviate chronic pain.[56] On pilgrimage people hear stories of healing and transformation. Mindfulness books tell stories of healing and transformation as people give testimony in them.[57] We can ask the question here as to why mindfulness has become so popular.

Regarding mindfulness, I believe it is something to do with the search for wellbeing and wisdom, and an intuitive response to a culture inimical to health, as well as a desire for self-transcendence which is something mindfulness offers. It is also a pathway to liberation from a distracted life.

Another helpful methodology that can help develop self-awareness is the heuristic approach, which has a clear process for working with lived experience, involving a personal

---

[55] Dubisch, 35.
[56] See Dubisch, 111, and for mindfulness stories Vidyamala Burch and Danny Penman, *Mindfulness for Health: Relieving Pain, Reducing Stress and Restoring Wellbeing* (London: Piatkus, 2013), 27-35.
[57] See Dubisch, 72, and Burch and Penman, Mindfulness for Health, 27-35, where both authors tell story of terrible injuries leaving them in chronic pain, and page 2-11 for reference to the efficacy of mindfulness in reducing pain.

'immersion' in a quest. After immersing yourself in the quest you might have a period of 'incubation' where you allow your thinking to grow intuitively. You might experience an epiphany or 'illumination' before everything is put together in a 'creative synthesis'.[58] These are archetypal experiences in learning and creativity. A heuristic approach can, therefore, transcend an academic methodology and be a conscious, intentional *process* for contemplative and mindful formation.

The initial question was 'What is mindfulness of God, and how can it be cultivated?' Although my discovery was built on a moment of meeting with God, I was not aware that I did not inhabit fully most of my present moments. As the journey progressed, I realised that if I wanted to be more mindful of God, I needed to reclaim my present moments from being overwhelmed by anxious thoughts. I was also aware that anxiety is a symptom; I had recognised that my anxiety came from automatic boarding school narratives that operated out of my awareness, with anxiety being their symptom. In this sense the past is always in the present and I knew I had to also see if I could rewrite these scripts through engagement with scriptural propositions.

Paradoxically, it was secular mindfulness that helped me be more mindful of God, by allowing me to be more mindfully aware in the present moment. I realised that the theory, practice and anthropological insights of secular mindfulness were a key foundation in my practice of mindfulness of God.

A brief summary

I am on a quest to discover a culturally congruent form of mindfulness of God, how I can cultivate it and how it can be offered to others. The form of mindfulness of God I have created is an integration of secular mindfulness and mindfulness of God becoming an original pathway to kataphatic spirituality

---

[58] Clark Moustakas, *Heuristic Research: Design, Methodology and Applications* (London: Sage, 1990), 9, 28.

leading to mindful formation. My personal journey shows God is to be found in the present moment. If I am to be mindful of God I need to be in the present moment. I have identified that the 'problem' of the present moment is that I am often not in the present moment owing to anxiety. This anxiety stems from my childhood experience of boarding school. I need, therefore, to reclaim my present moments to be more mindful of God. I also recognise I need to reclaim the past to reclaim my present moments. Although I can reclaim my past to some extent using mindfulness and other theory, again, as with the present moments, only God can redeem my past. These insights are true for others.

What emerged unexpectedly with the creation of this mindful spirituality was the existence of symbolic interaction between my unconscious self and God that had been hidden in my childhood, an interaction that was continuing as an adult. This included a symbolic aspect of that self through which God was able to redeem my interpretation of the past. Although the aim of mindfulness of God is a continuous awareness of God's presence, through the creation of another analogical conceptual model I am seeking to open myself to multiplying moments of meeting with God as a form of scaffolding on the way to continuous awareness. Moments of meeting with God are to be valued. My own experience in the foundational epiphany of this research shows that one moment of meeting with God can transform the direction of a whole life. Enabling this is ethical mindful awareness, a form of remembrance of God in the present moment.

Reflection

Intention
We live in a crisis of attention. We are the flies in the web, not the spiders. What in the virtual world holds you captive? Intentionally resolve to reduce the time you give to the world of media. How often are you in the present moment?

Attention
What absorbs you outside of the virtual world, which could be a pathway to freedom? For me, for example, it is walking in nature. To train your distracted and captivated attention, find other pathways that absorb you.

Attitude
What is your attitude when you read something you don't understand straight away, that requires focused attention? Resolve not to give up on more difficult pastimes. Perhaps read some poetry that requires effort.

Reperceiving
Have you had any epiphanies that have helped you reperceive the world or yourself? Meditate on Luke 5:1-11 where in a small detail the disciples wash their nets every day. If they didn't, their nets would deteriorate. Our minds and bodies are our nets and need to be washed daily in spiritual and mindful practices. Use the model of the disciples to strengthen your intention to practise daily.

3
Some underlying theory

A contextual approach

My professional context as a Baptist minister, secularly trained psychotherapist and mindfulness researcher also converged with the cultural shift to mindfulness in recent years. This led me to notice that although secular mindfulness and Buddhist mindfulness dominate the marketplace, Christian mindfulness, whose intention is mindfulness of God, barely features. This led me into the area of contextual theology. The Church has not engaged substantially with the context of mindfulness. Contextual theology reflects theologically on our cultural context and enables us to engage thoughtfully with cultural phenomenon like mindfulness, avoiding the pitfalls of myths and prejudicial misunderstandings.

There are different models of contextual theology. Stephen Bevans defines five key models, recognising that these can be synthesised. Like AE (my PhD methodology) contextual theology acknowledges that a theologian must engage with human experience of self and culture but adds the dimensions of Scripture and tradition.[59] A spiritual AE can add these dimensions. One of the models of contextual theology that overlaps with mindfulness and contemplation is the transcendental model. The starting point for transcendental contextual theology is not to begin with gospel, tradition or

---

[59] Stephen B Bevans, *Models of Contextual Theology* (Maryknoll, New York: Orbis Books, 1992), 2.

culture but 'with one's own religious experience and one's own experience of oneself'.[60] This is how the contemplative tradition has developed and is passed on. Another key presupposition is the idea that my subjective experience can resonate with others, that others can identify with my experience.[61] A further point of contact with a sideways look at my spiritual experience is the idea that 'The only place God can reveal Godself truly and effectively is within human experience.'[62] AE is an academic method that can help examine our human experience in ordinary life or academic research in an intentional process, and contextual theology helps us have a theological perspective on what we experience in culture.

Part of mindful formation is learning to observe or witness our lived contemplative experience, and AE allows us to stay on track with this. So, this journey is more than autobiographical; it engages with culture. I am observing through mindful awareness, although I expand my perceiving beyond that of observing. AE is like contemplation in the observation of one's participation in a phenomenon. Although AE is an academic methodology it can be used as a way of life, a method of examining and writing about one's contemplative journey that gives it shape and rigour. It also transcends its academic roots as it grew out of observed lived experience and again offers an intentional, phased way of mindful formation. This is how I use key elements of it in this book.

Five key themes

I outline the emergence of five key themes in my journey, namely remembering, reperceiving, recognition, reclaiming and redeeming. These are the spine of mindful formation and are archetypal themes and so might resonate with you. I begin with the importance of remembering. My intention is to remember

---

[60] Bevans, 98.
[61] Bevans, 99.
[62] Bevans, 99.

God, to be mindful of God in each moment, and to cultivate an 'ethical mnemonic awareness'. I build on and refine this idea of ethical mnemonic awareness throughout the book. It is an important dimension of our mindful formation. I foreground its genesis and meaning here because of its use as a summary statement in mindful formation.

I define this awareness, paraphrasing Mark 8:33 as 'having in mind (being mindful of) the things of God and choosing them over the human things jostling for my attention'. This is both an intention to do this – 'having in mind' – and also an experience – I have done it. Through an immersive reading of the Gospel, I made an associative logical connection with Mark 8:33, that having in mind the things of God and choosing them in each ethical moment of choice was an element of being mindful of, remembering God. Interestingly in the New King James Version (NKJV) of this verse, the phrase is, 'For you are not *mindful* of the things of God, but the things of men.' This is my emphasis and I use this version, although it is not gender inclusive, for the use of the word 'mindful'. My felt sense was if I am to have in mind, in the present moment, the things of God, that I need a mnemonic awareness that holds those things of God.

This felt sense is part of experiencing Mark 8:33 as 'manuductive'. I was invited to participate in the ethical spiritual reality this verse describes or commends. The verse led me by the hand. I chose the word 'mnemonic' because it has an important symbolic meaning to me. The phrase 'mindfulness of God' is *mnēmē theou* in the Greek.[63] I carry that through into the phrase ethical 'mnemonic' awareness to remind myself of the origin of the idea for me.

Dreyfuss criticises secular mindfulness for not emphasising

---

[63] Cliff Ermatinger, *Following the Footsteps of the Invisible: The Complete Works of Diadochus of Photike*, Vol. 239 (Collegeville, Minnesota: Liturgical Press, 2010), 32.

the 'mnemonic' element within mindfulness.[64] He links this element to 'working memory, the ability of the mind to retain and make sense of received information'.[65] From a Buddhist perspective he argues that 'if mindfulness is to distinguish wholesome from unwholesome mental states, it must be explicitly cognitive and evaluative'.[66] However, in my experience of using secular mindfulness there is an implicit evaluative and mnemonic element where I am being asked to evaluate my thoughts as just thoughts.

This can be seen in a key element of Teasdale's Interacting Cognitive Subsystems theory.[67] In this theoretical framework Teasdale distinguishes between 'metacognitive propositions' and 'metacognitive insights'.[68] For example, the metacognitive proposition that 'thoughts aren't facts' has 'little "saving" power in protecting … from the effects of depressive thought patterns'.[69] However, if 'negative self-critical thoughts are experienced with metacognitive insight as "events in the mind"' rather than as propositions that are seen as 'reflections of reality', then those thoughts lose their power to depress.[70]

I took this idea of metacognitive propositions needing to become metacognitive insights as I had experienced this in my own life and created a new practice of meditating on scriptural propositions until they became insights held in mnemonic awareness. In Christian discipleship we are trying to live by our

---

[64] George Dreyfus, 'Is Mindfulness Present-Centred and Non-Judgmental? A Discussion of the Cognitive Dimensions of Mindfulness', in *Mindfulness: Diverse Perspectives on its Meaning, Origins, and Applications*, eds J Mark, G Williams and Jon Kabat-Zinn (London: Routledge, 2013), 43.
[65] Dreyfus, 46.
[66] Dreyfus, 45.
[67] John D Teasdale, 'Metacognition, Mindfulness and the Modification of Mood Disorders', *Clinical Psychology and Psychotherapy* 6 (1999), 146-155.
[68] Teasdale, 'Metacognition', 147-148.
[69] Teasdale, 'Metacognition,' 146.
[70] Teasdale, 'Metacognition', 153.

values. Through them I would be able to choose the things of God over the human things jostling for my attention in each moment of ethical choice (Mark 8:33). I also refer to these propositions as ethical 'figures' that we intentionally place in our memory.

This idea of metacognitive propositions and insights is worth staying with. The idea that 'thoughts are not facts' is a proposition about the way we think, and that is what makes it metacognitive. For it to become an insight we need to have an 'aha' moment about our own thought life. This is a theory that we will return to.

As I engage with mindfulness, I begin to reperceive. I have taken the term from mindfulness theory, where Shapiro et al define it as:

> through the process of mindfulness, one is able to disidentify from the contents of consciousness (i.e., one's thoughts) and view his or her moment-by-moment experience with greater clarity and objectivity.[71]

I have experienced this 'shift in perspective' with my anxious thoughts. However, the word has also taken on a symbolic significance for me, with a wider spiritual meaning. The aim of my mindfulness of God is to see clearly to reperceive myself, God, others and creation. This reperceiving is to perceive in the way God wants me to perceive. If I am to do this, I recognise that I need to reclaim my present moments from anxiety which is a distorted form of perceiving, a way of not seeing. As I reclaim my present moments it becomes possible for God to redeem them, for me to have moments of meeting with God. In reperceiving I begin a journey of recognition.

What started as a personal journey found its way to the theory of recognition, which helped shape my ethical view on

---

[71] Shapiro, et al, 'Mechanisms of Mindfulness', 377.

life.[72] In recognition theory I treat people with respect because they are persons not just individuals.[73] This recognition, or seeing clearly of others, comes out of the reperceiving that mindfulness enables. In mindfulness of God, I come home to the present moment to reperceive God, myself and others; in reperceiving I recognise our essential relational reality. I talk to many people who feel ignored, not recognised by others. It is an existential need within us to experience recognition.

Introspection and the contemplative

In asking the question, 'What is mindfulness of God, and how can we cultivate it?' I am talking about my mindfulness of God which is dependent on God's mindfulness of me (Psalm 8:4). One congruent methodology for examining one's own consciousness of God is introspection, a first-person method.

This methodology bears a family resemblance to the way early Christian contemplatives examined their own experience. The traditional historic way this has happened within Christian contemplation is for the contemplative to pray '*in recto* while at the same time observing themselves *in obliquo*, as it were photographing their own transcendence', to help others also contemplate God.[74] In other words, I am being mindful of God directly in the moment, while also observing that contemplation with a sideways (*in obliquo*) look. In introspection I am examining my participation in contemplative practices. This is first-person research.

---

[72] See Maijastina Kahlos, Heikki J Koskinen and Rita Palmen, 'Introduction', in *Recognition and Religion: Contemporary and Historical Perspectives*, eds Maijastina Kahlos, Heikki J Koskinen and Rita Palmen (London: Routledge, 2019): 1, for a summary of recognition theory around recognising the other as a person through respect, esteem and friendship.

[73] Kahlos, Koskinen and Palmen, 1.

[74] Hans Urs von Balthasar, *Prayer*, translated by Graham Harrison (San Francisco, California: Ignatius Press, 1986), 117.

Kataphatic spirituality

One of the terms that I have used to describe my mindful spirituality as it became apparent in my mindful formation is kataphatic. Kataphatic spirituality can be defined as the possibility that 'human persons may mystically experience the presence of God in and through creation and incarnation'.[75] As the term kataphatic is a useful summary statement of my spirituality, which has been shaped by mindfulness to be embodied and aware of creation, I begin with this simple definition. As my understanding of my spirituality matured, I continued to be influenced by Ruffing's definition, and as she develops it elsewhere, as well as by Hans Urs von Balthasar's writings on the spiritual senses. I spiral back to kataphatic spirituality and develop a more rounded understanding as the journey unfolds.

Kataphatic spirituality is often understood in contrast with apophatic spirituality. One such contrast is in the terms themselves, '"kataphatic" in Greek means with images while "apophatic" means without form or images'.[76] One is mediated; the other is not. Although these two spiritualities are seen as 'opposite', the relationship 'between these two spiritual paths has often been asserted to be one of progression'.[77] In this progression one moves from the kataphatic 'mediated path to God' for the 'self-emptying, knowing of unknowing' of the apophatic pathway.[78] Janet Ruffing, who conducted her own qualitative research into kataphatic spirituality, points out, 'Very little research has been done on what people's actual religious experience is, even less has been done on Christian religious

---

[75] Janet Ruffing, 'Kataphatic Spirituality', in *The New SCM Dictionary of Christian Spirituality*, ed Philip Sheldrake (London: SCM Press, 2005), 393.
[76] Ruffing, 'Kataphatic Spirituality,' 393.
[77] Ruffing, 'Kataphatic Spirituality,' 393.
[78] Ruffing, 'Kataphatic Spirituality,' 393.

experience.'[79] This book hopes to redress this in part.

There are two other theological influences on the shape, structure and representation of my book that I wish to briefly outline here. The natural and intuitive shape to my model of mindful formation resonates with a four-fold model of theology outlined by David Ford. This is a 'wise and creative theology' that can be defined as 'trying to do justice to scripture and tradition while also exploring new ways of conceiving the truth'.[80] I engage with Scripture and the contemplative tradition while drawing on the wisdom of secular mindfulness with the aim of arriving at a wise and creative synthesis.

The four elements of this 'wise creativity' include '*ressourcement,* a return to sources that can nourish theology and life now'.[81] Ford defines this as 'wise and creative retrieval'.[82] I have retrieved the strand of mindfulness of God from Christian contemplative history. This then needs his second step, which is 'bringing up to date' what you have retrieved.[83] I have recontextualised this strand of mindfulness of God through an integration with secular mindfulness. The third step is 'wise and creative thinking'.[84] I see this as using my thinking, imaginative and mindful capacities. Finally, Ford argues for accessible 'wise and creative expression', for as Ford points out, 'Theology often does not read well.'[85] I want my writing to be creative and accessible. I expand on this in the next section.

---

[79] Janet K Ruffing, 'The World Transfigured: Kataphatic Religious Experience', *Studies In Spirituality* 5 (1995): 234-5, accessed 7th December 2020, dx.doi.org/10.2143/SIS.5.0.2004170.
[80] David F Ford, *The Future of Christian Theology* (Chichester, West Sussex: Wiley-Blackwell, 2011), 6.
[81] Ford, 12, 13.
[82] Ford, 13.
[83] Ford, 15.
[84] Ford, 17.
[85] Ford, 20.

Symbol, representation, and poetics

I sensed that mindfulness, symbolically, was pregnant waters. Within this metaphor of pregnant waters can be placed the representation of my writing. Representation is how we write, the style and the influences. I have been influenced by AE thinkers who observed the strange absence of emotions, the body and the 'literary and aesthetic' in research and emphasised a more integrated and holistic approach to research involving the whole person.[86] This is where my interest in mindfulness overlaps with AE as the importance of the body and emotions is emphasised in mindfulness. Within my context of describing spiritual experience, and accessing the unconscious and symbolic, I need to be able to represent the journey poetically, symbolically and in narrative form. This turn to the literary, evocative, embodied and emotional has been called a 'crisis of representation'.[87] I believe all writing, including contemplative, should involve the whole person and be accessible.

This emphasis on creativity, the evocative, embodied and imaginative writing could be called the poetics of AE. Poetics understood simply is a technical term for the theory and practice of writing poetry or other creative writing. Heather Walton, a practical theologian, has written about poetics in theology.[88] Walton expands the meaning of the term 'poetics' beyond 'writing as a creative act'.[89] My interest in poetics is how it helps us understand the nuts and bolts of writing, but also as something that theology can engage with – a theopoetics. This

---

[86] Tony E Adams, Stacy Holman Jones and Carolyn Ellis, *Autoethnography: Understanding Qualitative Research* (Oxford: Oxford University Press, 2015), 10-11.
[87] Nicholas L Holt, 'Representation, Legitimation, and Autoethnography: An Autoethnographic Writing Story', *International Journal of Qualitative Methods*, 2, no. 1, (March 2003): 19, 24, accessed 22nd December 2021, doi.org/10.1177/160940690300200102.
[88] Heather Walton, *Writing Methods in Theological Reflection* (London: SCM Press, 2014), 135-136.
[89] Walton, *Writing Methods*, 133-136.

is a complex idea, but my working definition is that theopoetics is the use of creative and poetic language in theology.[90]

Just using logical, propositional writing to do theology has been likened to 'trying to put lightning in a matchbox'.[91] Poetics can be a complex idea along with theopoetics and I've returned to it in the spiral form of learning alluded to earlier. Paying attention is difficult, I have found. Paying attention to difficult things is even harder! However, it is worth it, and the way I've made sense of things is to keep returning to the concept (in this spiral way) – and each time I return I make more sense of it. I commend this approach to anything in this book that is hard to grasp at first.

This crisis led to new ways of representing research, including the rise of reflective self-narrative and what has been called 'evocative' AE, a way of writing that provokes a response in the reader. The term evocative became, then, a term to describe a completely different way of approaching academic research. The evocative and vulnerable aspects of this book are an important step of authenticity in our culture.

My own journey into the poetic began with being taught to read at the age of three by my mother. My favourite subject at school was English, I did English A Level and my first degree was in English Literature at Leeds University (1981-84). The love of lyrical and poetic language is part of my ontology of being. I include poetry and narrative or prose in my understanding of lyrical language. I was drawn to AE because of its capacity to represent research in more evocative, poetic and story-telling form.

---

[90] Walton's book *Writing Methods* is a very useful conversation partner if you want to explore this further.
[91] A N Wilder, *Theopoetic: Theology and the Religious Imagination* (Minneapolis, MN: Fortress Press, 1976), 41, quoted in Ronald T Michene, 'Theological Turns Toward Theopoetic Sensibilities: Embodiment, Humility, and Hospitality', *Evangelical Quarterly: An International Review of Bible and Theology* 89, no. 1 (2018): 23, accessed 22nd November 2023, doi.org/10.1163/27725472-08901002.

I first came across a more intentional use of the poetic in AE through the work of Richard Furman. He makes a distinction between poetry and research poems, calling research poems 'quasipoetic forms'.[92] Representing our lived experience poetically is important without getting stuck on the aesthetics of it all. Peter Willis makes a similar point about using 'poetic forms' in phenomenological research. In his article entitled 'Don't Call it Poetry', he prefers the term 'poetic reflections'.[93] These are helpful distinctions in bringing the 'expressive approach' into the hands of all.[94] In this book an expressive approach is taken. I cite these examples because I believe that we need to embrace the poetic in this less-elevated style. In an age of artificial intelligence (AI), it is what distinguishes us as human.

I also use the term 'awakened language', which is what the poet Seamus Heaney calls poetry, to describe how I am representing the journey of mindful formation.[95] Heaney describes poetry as 'awakened language' and I wish to take that term and use it in a wider sense to describe expressive writing, whether poetic, narrative or prose. I see awakened language as what happens when someone writes or speaks with their whole incarnated being, with their God-given creative word at the core of their being awakened within them. I believe part of mindful formation is awakening our language of creativity within, which is different for each person but central to living life in all its fullness.

However, I also have a specific rationale for using this form

---

[92] Rich Furman, 'Poetic Forms and Structures in Qualitative Health Research', *Qualitative Health Research* 16, no. 4 (April 2006): 560, accessed 14th June 2018, dx.doi.org/10.1177/1049732306286819.

[93] Peter Willis, 'Don't Call it Poetry', *The Indo-Pacific Journal of Phenomenology* 2, no. 1 (April 2002): 1, accessed 8th May 2018, dx.doi.org/10.1080/20797222.2002.11433869.

[94] Willis, 'Don't Call it Poetry', 1.

[95] Seamus Heaney, *The Redress of Poetry* (London: Faber & Faber, 2006), 10.

of expressive writing. I am using poetic and creative-expressive writing, both in research poems and other forms, to access what is dissociated – those parts of me that are hard to reach through reason and deductive logic. I use the word dissociated through the influence of Joy Schaverien's book, *Boarding School Syndrome: The psychological trauma of the privileged child*. She argues that dissociation is part of the 'hidden trauma' of boarding school experience.[96]

The phrase that is particularly evocative for me and describes my experience of dissociation is when Schaverien writes, 'There are times when the *broken attachments* have been *so unbearable* that they have been repressed and the emotions are *beyond conscious recall*.'[97] So in dissociation I repress a traumatic memory so that I cannot consciously remember it. This is a necessary defence.

My first experience of trauma was being separated from my parents just before my seventh birthday. It was an unbearable experience. I spiral back to trauma later in the book and describe helpful ways I found to deal with it. I've experienced trauma in different settings and tell the story of the impact of searing and sustained verbal assaults during the Covid-19 pandemic that left me with panic attacks, severe chest pains, constant shaking and an inability to continue working.

How to express the inexpressible is explored later in the book. The poetic and creative-expressive use associative logic and the symbolic in a way that enables what is hidden to be expressed.[98] This is the specific rationale. By accessing the symbolic in all our lives, any one of us can begin to access the hidden, marginalised parts of our own self.

Jesus' parables take us out of automatic habits of thinking.

---

[96] Joy Schaverien, *Boarding School Syndrome: The psychological trauma of the privileged child* (London, New York: Routledge, 2015), 113-123.
[97] Schaverien, 9. My italics.
[98] Carol Gilligan and Jessica Eddy, 'Listening as a Path to Psychological Discovery: An Introduction to the Listening Guide', *Perspectives on Medical Education* 6, (2017): 79, accessed 16th February 2019. dx.doi.org/10.1007/s40037-017-0335-3.

Mindfulness talks about how we are often on autopilot and live much of our lives out of our awareness. The culture we live in wants us to live like automatons without questioning our cultural captivity. This is why living attentively is so important.

Representation has been a central concern in Christian contemplation since the beginning of Christianity. Contemplative language is not propositional but paradoxical, playful and poetic.[99] In utilising the poetic and creative-expressive in my writing I am seeking to express my spiritual experience in this way. My poetic turn is a necessity because I am trying to express something that needs a spiritual reperceiving of the ordinary details of my life, as well as the epiphanies. I am also representing my relationship with God as implicit, with much of God's interaction with me being out of my awareness. There are other words I will use that try to convey this liminal realm of divine-human interaction. I am especially drawing on nature writers, who also try to express what is almost inexpressible.

From a mindful formation perspective, it is important to work not just from a thinking mode, but from all the dimensions of our embodiment: mind, emotion, body, awareness, self-awareness and relational awareness of the world(s) in which we are embedded.

I am also aware from a mindful perspective that reality is complex and multi-layered. Langer calls the appropriate response to this complexity 'mindfulness'.[100] I am using her definition from mindful learning theory, which is different from mindfulness meditation. She defines mindfulness as 'the continuous creation of new categories; openness to new information; and an implicit awareness of more than one perspective'.[101] Critical realism as defined by Wright also

---

[99] Mark A McIntosh, *Mystical Theology: The Integrity of Spirituality and Theology* (Blackwell Publishing, 1998), 125.
[100] Ellen J Langer, *The Power of Mindful Learning* (Reading, Massachusetts: Addison-Wesley Publishing Company Inc., 1997), 4.
[101] Langer, *The Power of Mindful Learning*, 4.

recognises that reality is 'pluriform and stratified', and because of that we can 'provide multiple explanatory accounts of the same object'.[102] In this book I don't try to hide the complexity of life but engage with it. Part of that complexity is about living in the present moment, which is what I engage with next.

Reflection

Intention

The journey of contemplation is an intentional pilgrimage. You might start it for different reasons. Why might you consider undertaking that pilgrimage?

Attention

As you go forward, pay attention to your context. What are the origins of your spirituality? In what contexts did you grow up? What are your other contexts relationally? Try to use mindful awareness as a critical friend to interpret those contexts.

Attitude

As you examine your contexts, try to have an open awareness that allows you to see your contexts as they really are, without defensiveness or unnecessary criticism.

Reperceiving

Do any epiphanies or moments of reperceiving come to mind?

---

[102] Andrew Wright, *Christianity and Critical Realism: Ambiguity, truth and theological literacy* (London, New York: Routledge, 2013), 11.

4
Reclaiming our present moments

Introduction – the ordinary world

Mindfulness is self-work, enabling us to cultivate self-awareness, regulate our emotions and become aware of moments of meeting with God, our own self and others. It liberates us from the addiction of social media and cultural captivity to the virtual world. In this way we begin to be mindfully formed. Mindfulness shows us how many moments are lost to distraction, stress and anxiety. My story is one of lost moments and found moments. However, we need to notice the importance of one moment before we can understand the importance of all moments. It is through a spiral of God-aware moments that we are mindfully formed.

In the ordinary world I have had brief conversations that have stayed with me and become small confessional or conversational tales, shining as points of wisdom for me in my life. They have been moments of meeting that have helped me learn to value and savour the present moment. As a moment of self-reflection, can you think of such moments in your own life? I present some key epiphanic moments below that have happened in my ministerial role, personal life, counselling training or study. Sometimes it's easier to show the power of these moments by recreating them, rather than just talking about them. Pay attention to any associations with these stories that emerge for you.

'Most conflicts happen in church life because the person running the church doesn't know how to relate to people.' I probably heard this said in 1996 while I was training to run a church. I have always joked that this was a heretical statement. But it stayed with me.

'Christian theology is all about relationship. God is a loving community and calls us into a loving community.' I heard this about the same time at Bible college. It stayed with me. My intuition pulsed. I followed the impulse and began relational training as a counsellor and psychotherapist in integrative and relational counselling, alongside my role as a Baptist minister.

'It's no wonder you're struggling as an adult; you were sent to boarding school at a young age.' It seemed like a throwaway remark, spoken by the counsellor sitting opposite me. I cried. The remark stayed with me like a piece of grit in my intuition. I began to search for psychological books or articles on boarding school life. I read a book by Nick Duffell about boarding school with the ironic title *The Making of Them*.[103] I had been made. I was being unmade. It was 2006.

'Shaun, come with me, you look grey.' My lecturer took me into her study. It was my study day at Roehampton University. I was studying integrative and relational counselling and psychotherapy. It was 2006 and I was struggling. She sat there and didn't say anything, but her presence drew something out of my inner being.

'I feel like I'm falling apart and there's nothing I can do about it,' I said.

'And yet you haven't fallen apart.'

I felt held by the remark in my fragmentation. But her presence held me together until I was able to hold myself together. Mindful presence of another. In her presence I was able to be vulnerable and visible in my vulnerability. Mindful formation is also relational and happens in community.

'People and texts have guided me.' By texts I mean books and articles. And impulses. Spirit-led homing impulses. I don't remember the exact text in which I read the word mindfulness.

---

[103] Nick Duffell, *The Making of Them: The British Attitude to Children and the Boarding School System* (London: Lone Arrow Press, 2010).

I know it was in 2006 at Roehampton. Why do some words hook us? This word hooked me. It invited me to explore it. It became a quest.

'Let us keep our eyes always fixed on the depths of our heart with an unceasing *mindfulness* of God.' In the moment this phrase rang me like a bell. It was a guide in a book; just one sentence, but it changed my life. The words spoke to me like the first words in a conversation that has not yet ceased. This was another pebble causing ripples in the pond of 2006.

'Oh, but mindfulness is Buddhist! When you meditate, you are trying to empty your mind. You're inviting the demonic in.' I have heard this comment so many times in my church culture. I was reluctant in the beginning to let people know I was practising and researching secular mindfulness. It seemed even mindfulness of God was suspect for some, those guardians of evangelical purity. The suspicion was automatic, the minute I used the words mindfulness or meditation. I address this concern later.

'Get behind Me, Satan! For you are not *mindful* of the things of God, but the things of men' (Mark 8:33, NKJV, my emphasis). I once had a dream where I saw words in the Bible raised up in gold and silver lettering and I knew these words were significant for me. I had a similar experience when I first read this verse in Mark's Gospel. I immediately associated it with the idea of being mindful. It was only later I came across this translation of the verse. It is a verse I keep revisiting in a spiral process. Sometimes we need to listen to what has been called the logic of association as it emerges in our own lives.[104]

I was examining my own experience of mindfulness. Much like the early Christian contemplatives. But there were no people in my church culture who knew about mindfulness of God (that I knew). Christians didn't feature in the marketplace

---

[104] Mechtild Kiegelmann, 'A Conversation with Carol Gilligan: Making Oneself Vulnerable to Discovery', *Forum for Qualitative Social Research* Vol. 10, no. 2 (2009): 13, accessed 3rd June 2020, doi.org/10.17169/fqs-10.2.1178.

of mindfulness. The texts on mindfulness became my guide, my mentors.

'Welcome to Gloucester, Shaun. Thanks for agreeing to talk to us. I thought I'd let you wander around Gloucester Cathedral before I take you home for supper.' On 11th October 2019 I was taken to Gloucester Cathedral. I was unaware that stained glass artist Tom Denny had created the Ivor Gurney Window, consisting of eight LIGHTS, panes that tell the story of the First World War poet and songwriter. The moment I saw the windows, I had to just sit with them. I was moved to tears. They told aspects of my story.

Sometimes it is things outside our own self that speak to us. In this case it was the art of stained-glass windows that told a story, a true story that resonated with my story.

Out of this moment I had a creative epiphany about how I could partially represent these epiphanies. In the way the windows and poetic fragments of Gurney's writings spoke to me, I wanted to create the possibility of that resonance for others reading my words or looking at my images. In this age of AI writing for us in a way that dehumanises us, it is by paying attention to the real stories of individual people with their own individuated voice that we are rehumanised.

I had an experience of identifying with the archetypal, symbolic themes of each window. Ivor Gurney is sometimes called the poet of mental health, and the story and representation of his pain in his poems resonated with me. However, he was also wrestling with God. The repeated symbol of walking, the bodily postures and colours of the figures in the scenes echoed in my story. The insight I received was to represent my story in eight similar windows, drawing inspiration from Denny and Gurney, with a creative-expressive telling of aspects of my story with each window. My own windows appear on the inside cover of this book. It is the creative process that matters, not the outcome – although we are taught the opposite in our culture. In part this is a guide to inspire others to enter their creative process. Here also I allowed the logic of association to flow. As you read this chapter, write down the associations that emerge for you.

My poetic imagination was stirred even further when I read a small booklet by Denny, published by Gloucester Cathedral, telling the story of his creative interaction with Gurney, the First World War poet who was later incarcerated in an asylum. The fragments of poems quoted led me to create my own distilled Haiku-like poems for each window, summarising the key epiphany infusing each pane.[105] I place the painted windows together, as if they were a stained-glass representation, and the evocative narratives also follow that order throughout this chapter.

I do this to enable you as the reader to engage with the margins of your own life, where the poetic, dreams, images, are displaced. From the very beginning of the book this has been a key process. This is an insight pioneered by psychoanalytic theory, sometimes called depth psychology. Mary Watkins summarises this idea that depth psychologies (think Freud, Jung and their developers) 'attempt to have us listen into the margins of our experience for thoughts, images and bodily knowings that hold alternative perspectives and insights'.[106] These alternative perspectives can be windows into our true self, because, as Watkins adds, our ego, which is our 'habitual point of view', is suspect.[107] Our ego has an automatic self-focus and lives for self-interest.

---

[105] Tom Denny, *Gloucester Cathedral: Stained Glass Windows* (Chapter of Gloucester Cathedral, 2016). See David Cobb, ed, *The British Museum: Haiku* (The British Museum Press, 2002), 1-7 for an introduction to Haiku, which is a three-line poem of five/seven/five syllables, often with a catch in the last line.

[106] Mary Watkins and Helene Shulman, *Toward Psychologies of Liberation* (London: Palgrave Macmillan, 2008) is a helpful introduction to the idea of exploring the margins. This quote is Mary Watkins, 'Seeding Liberation: A Dialogue Between Depth Psychology and Liberation Psychology', in *Depth Psychology: Meditations in the Field*, eds D Slattery and L Corbett (Daimon Verlag, 2001), 206.

[107] Watkins, 2001, 206.

I found boarding school trauma pushed to the margins of my life. I conceptualise this crisis of unmaking as the first key window into my world. Paradoxically it was the earlier making of me in my childhood schooling that was to be my unmaking. *My windows are not numbered sequentially, because life is not nice and ordered.* Mindful formation is intentionally reforming yourself with God's help. But first, we need to be self-aware, we need to notice our fragility and brokenness – gather the moments of wisdom in our lives that have guided us, as I have done.

I invite you to use these creative reflections on archetypal themes to see what emerges from the margins of your life, to see if there are resonances within your own experience. I will encourage you to do this in each of the windowed reflections I present.

My painted Windows read left to right: one, five, seven, four; two, three, six, eight. You can read the descriptions below with the image on the inside cover.

Window one: The making of him

> I dissolve within
> From trauma a sinkhole forms;
> I fall unknowing.

As I look at Denny's LIGHT ONE, *Glimmering Dusk*, I first find a place of open awareness to take it all in.[108] The light of dusk was gathering for me back in 2006, with night about to fall suddenly as in the tropics. On the road of Denny's scene are dark holes. I recreate these in my Window as symbolic of my journey. Out of my awareness a sinkhole was forming. I was heading for a breakdown and would fall unknowing into it.

Intuitively I have used camouflage colours, chameleon shades, in my painting because they represent a hiding from

---

[108] *Glimmering Dusk* is the title of an Ivor Gurney poem, Ivor Gurney, *Rewards of Wonder,* ed George Walter (Manchester: Carcanet Press, 2000), 93, quoted in Denny, 4. Title used by permission of Carcanet Press.

reality. I hid my vulnerability and distress backstage. On my frontstage I appeared well. The sinkhole broke through from my backstage into the frontstage. I was a Christian, a Baptist minister and had been intentionally living a Christian life for twenty years.

The 'making' of me at boarding school was de-formation; it was not mindful. How have you been 'made' in your childhood? What was your formation? Take a mindful moment to reflect on these questions.

Part of my formation led to these scripts. 'I don't know how to ask for help. I need to sort things out myself. It's also not safe for me to show my feelings.' In the moment of needing help and yet not being able to ask for help I am overwhelmed with anxiety. This script was written in heavy type, it was hard to rub it out. Although for most of my life I had not known this was my script. I recognised it was my script through reading Duffell's book on boarding school survival. That book became a guide. Knowing your hidden automatic scripts from a distorted narrative self is an important first step to freeing yourself from them. Spend some mindful moments seeing if you can identify any.

'Shaun, I'm suffering from recurrent depression. My doctor has said try mindfulness. Someone in the church says don't touch it with a bargepole. I'm in so much pain.' I began to help those in pain because I've suffered pain.

Window five: The pain of others

I have used the motifs of quest and pilgrimage to describe this journey. I am on a pilgrim journey, but it is not linear. It is more a making, an unmaking, a remaking, a breaking, a remaking. The journey remains unfinished. I think it is more congruent to acknowledge the fragility, vulnerability and brokenness of our lives while seeking a wholeness.

Denny's LIGHT FIVE is called *Pain*. It takes Gurney's words of the 'pain continual' of the battlefield as its inspiration.[109] It is grey, unrelenting grey, with shades of mustard – perhaps symbolically indicating the gas that may have been present. The figures are indistinct as if they have lost all sense of self and personhood. The poem is not just about his pain, but about the pain of others.

My Window five is called 'The pain of others'. The background colour is a more hopeful blue, but grey and red colours of trauma bleed into the reality of goodness and wholeness. Some of our cultural traumas are written into the window: stress, anxiety, depression, chronic pain, eating disorders, cancer, trauma and Covid-19, symbolically represented. Our culture tries to teach us to avoid pain, and so when we experience pain we have a very small window of tolerance for it. The window of tolerance is a term that Daniel Siegel uses to describe an 'internal zone' where we can hold pain or difficulty. It can be used as a way to ensure 'people aren't exceeding how much they can handle'.[110] In mindful formation we turn and face the pain but in a safe way. We can learn to stretch our window of tolerance. We also recognise that calm, still, mindful states of mind exist and can be accessed:

> As the people cry help,
> At culture's toxicity
> A mindful door opens.

An important question is, 'Why now for mindfulness?' It is a turn towards health and wellbeing, but also an intuitive turn towards the incarnational and embodied world as a reaction to the virtual disembodied world we live in. I believe it is a turn inspired by God working in culture, as the Church was

---

[109] Ivor Gurney, *Severn & Somme and War's Embers,* ed R K R Thornton (Manchester: Carcanet Press, 1997), 50, quoted in Denny, 6. Reprinted by permission of Carcanet Press. Title of poem is 'Pain'.
[110] David A Treleaven, *Trauma-Sensitive Mindfulness: Practices for Safe and Transformative Healing* (New York, London: W W Norton & Company, 2018), 88, Kindle.

inattentive and focused on information rather than embodied transformation.[111] For me it was because I had lost my present moments, although I was unaware of that, or their importance.

My pain brought me into contact with others who were in pain. Writing about my trauma brought others to me crying, 'Help!' I am not comparing my trauma of childhood separation or anxiety or breakdown to the trauma of the First World War, but I can document the trauma caused by our toxic culture in the twenty-first century. As I look at the grey of Denny's LIGHT FIVE, I am aware of how dead I was to my senses, how grey was my perceiving of the world – as if colour had fled. It was mindfulness that woke me to my senses, with its incarnational focus on reality and what is, and the perceiving of body, emotions and thought life in a clearer way. This was a graced response, made possible through the presence of God. As I immersed myself in my physical senses, and the sense of what was going on in my body, and the sense of what I was thinking and feeling, and the sense of what others were thinking and feeling, I became spiritually alive.[112] I entered the present moment through the back door. I was being mindfully formed and learning about fullness of life.

There is still breaking and remaking. During lockdown I experienced a blow, a searing assault that set off a traumatic response in me. There was nothing I could do about it. A wise guide said to me, 'Shaun, with these people, there is no defence with which you can defend yourself.' It was my body that showed the trauma, with chest pains, shaking, difficulty breathing. Unable to fight, to flee, to freeze – I just fell. Where is your pain?

---

[111] See the critique of James K A Smith in *Desiring the Kingdom*, 43.
[112] See Daniel Siegel, *The Mindful Brain* (New York: W W Norton & Company, 2007), 121-123, for his view that we have eight senses, not five; the sixth sense knowing what is going on in our body, the seventh sense knowing something of our thoughts and feelings, and the eighth sense picking up other people's thoughts and feelings.

Window seven: Turn and face the shadow

In Denny's LIGHT SEVEN he draws on a poem by Gurney called 'To God', written in the asylum where the poet spent much of his adult life.[113] The figure is sitting, grey, bowed and barefoot.

The line that I identified with, which describes the agony of mental health distress, was, 'Gone out every bright thing from my mind.'[114] The figure of the poet looks like a shadow of his former self. This time the window creates associations for me about facing my shadow.

It was the summer holidays 2008. I was reading Ursula Le Guin's *A Wizard of Earthsea*. I identified with the main character who must turn and face a shadow he released into the world.[115] I felt hunted by anxiety. I realised that I had to turn and face my shadow, which was anxiety. I had been running away from it.

> Turn and face and face,
> Face, face reality
> Turn and face the shadow.

You face the shadow in the present moment. I revisit the shadow of my boarding school past in an intentional piece of self-work. I want to foreshadow some of the pain in this section. I especially want to foreground finding the words for something for which I had had no words. What I write here may help you find your own shadow and decide whether you are ready to face it – or that perhaps you need to find a wise counsellor to travel the journey with you.

---

[113] Ivor Gurney, *Collected Poems of Ivor Gurney*, ed. P J Kavanagh (Manchester: Carcanet Press, 2004), 197, quoted in Denny, 7. Reprinted by permission of Carcanet Press.
[114] Gurney, *Collected Poems of Ivor Gurney*, 197, quoted in Denny, 7. Reprinted by permission of Carcanet Press.
[115] Ursula Le Guin, *A Wizard of Earthsea* in *Earthsea: The First Four Books* (London: Penguin Books, 2016), 120.

Finding the words for the emotions

As part of my self-work, I have been reading Joy Schaverien's book about boarding school syndrome. I avoided and circled around the book for some years after buying it. I bought it as part of my PhD research. As I read her first chapter it told my story in words that are empirical, psychological and exact, but evocative beyond words for me. I had no words of my own for my experience and the depth of my trauma, but she gave me the exact words as if she was there with me. I had avoided the difficult emotions as a way of coping. Mindful formation offers a different way of dealing with them by facing them and accepting they are the reality you face in that moment.

I give them here in the order they appeared, like words written in fire on the page. Each word seared truth into the present moment:

> 'early boarding *ruptured* their primary *attachments*' and 'as children ... learn to *hide* their *emotions* ...' – also left '*unable* to *talk* about his *feelings*'.
> 'suffered from living *without* their *families* and *without love*'.
> 'the experience ... literally unspeakable.'
> 'homesickness is reframed as bereavement ... and yet the child is ashamed to complain.'
> '*cut themselves off* from *compassion* for their own predicament'.
> 'It is the *depth* of the trauma that may be missed.'[116]

I realised for the first time how deep the trauma of being sent to boarding school went. The next insight was about how I could both access and represent this trauma which is 'beyond [my] conscious recall'. I realised that if I genuinely wanted to reclaim my present moments more fully, I had to deal with not only present anxiety but the roots of it as well.

Trauma isn't just about big catastrophic events in our lives; there are many hidden traumas. Being able to name something

---

[116] Schaverien, 2, 4, 6, 9, 10, 11. My italics.

as traumatic can be very helpful, as it was for me with my boarding school experience. Is there something traumatic in your past? I'm not asking to you retell it in detail; I don't want you to retraumatise yourself. Trauma theory does emphasise that we don't have to explore our traumatic past, especially if we are not in a place of security and safety in our present life, otherwise we might retraumatise ourselves.[117] Remember it doesn't have to be what has traditionally been seen as trauma. Don't minimise the pain you have experienced. Do you need to see a trauma specialist? I will come back to the helpful insights from trauma theories.

Window four: Looking for the Light

In Denny's LIGHT FOUR the scene is sunset; a figure looks out of the shadows at the River Severn and the willow trees. Gurney's phrase that inspired Denny is from the poem 'Song (Severn Meadow)', 'And who loves joy as he/That dwells in shadows?'[118]

In my Window the panes are half in shadow, half in light. A small dark figure reaches out to the light from the shadow. I was not looking for joy; in fact, I avoided joy and happiness. At boarding school, because of the pattern of term and holidays, any joy I felt in the holidays was quickly taken away when I returned to school, and so in the end I did not let myself feel it. I lived on the edge, in shadow but looking for light, afraid to step out. In this way I missed the bright moments of my life. However, I was looking for light:

---

[117] See Babette Rothschild, *The Body Remembers:* Volume 2: *Revolutionizing Trauma Treatment* (New York, London: W W Norton & Company, 2017), 16, for the importance of having well-informed professional help to create safety and stability if you suffer from trauma, and revisiting the trauma is not necessary.

[118] Ivor Gurney, *Severn & Somme and War's Embers,* ed R K R Thornton (Manchester: Carcanet Press, 1997), 36, quoted in Denny, 5. Reprinted by permission of Carcanet Press.

> In the dark looking
> For unceasing light
> Mindfulness of God.

Intuitively I have chosen the word dark to symbolise the being of my life.

I have already begun to outline some key elements of mindfulness of God. Trying to understand and practise mindfulness of God became a quest. The genesis of the quest, however, remains childhood trauma of separation.

I was first sent to boarding school at the age of six and three-quarters. It is part of my biography, my life narrative that cannot be separated from my self-examination. Through boarding school, I lost my body, I lost my emotions, I lost awareness, I lost control of my present moments because of anxiety. My personal journey tells me that it is in the present moment that I meet God. Written on my body and the emotions that inhabit it are different texts: personal, familial, boarding school, cultural, evangelical, charismatic – in this sense my body is like a lost palimpsest which I need to find to read these different layers of text. However, a new text can be written in and on my embodied wholeness; the text written by the practice of mindfulness of God. The text that is mindful formation.

Not only did I need to turn and face the past, but I had an inkling that I needed to reclaim my present moments, that I was losing them to anxiety. The epiphanies in the present moment and windows of insight led me to an intuitive impulse that an extended piece of walking would help centre me in the moment. I have found walking and formal mindful walking meditations enable me to be embodied and to process emotion. It was a strong impulse and so I followed it. I knew the Camino pilgrimage walk was very popular. I decided to walk a section and record my thought life. *This was a form of intentional self-listening which is a theme I return to as part of our mindful formation.* You are listening to the stream of consciousness within without trying to curate it. As I show this journey as it happened, with its turn from anxiety to peace, how does it resonate with your journey?

An intuitive impulse and the Camino
I walked for a week in 2017 and realised my impulse was right; I felt restored and refreshed. In 2018 I set out a deliberate piece of self-work which I detail more fully later. I briefly summarise here what I did. I recorded samples of my present moment experience walking the Camino on my phone. I wrote up the transcript in the evening after each day's walking, as a sample of my stream of consciousness. I later analysed it using adapted qualitative methods. It is something anyone could do, and I present a simplified but profound way to do it later. Here it is standing alone as an evocative piece of reality. My hope is that you identify with it in some way.

Day One: Tuesday 29 May 2018 – the epiphany around reclaiming my present moments
I spend my first night in historic Santiago, at the Hotel Pazos Alba, before setting off early in the morning the next day to Negreira, a walk of some 22 kilometres.

I normally rely on Clare, my wife, to do the directions when we are travelling, so having to take responsibility is both good for me and triggering for my anxiety. I feel self-conscious as I record my first thoughts on the walk. My mood matches the overcast, humid, slightly oppressive morning. I wonder if I can trust the cleanliness of my CamelBak watercarrier I first used last year. I know from last year that drinking so much water leads to needing some wild wee stops. I feel self-conscious about that. I am worried about getting lost.

I am filled with anxious thoughts about my fitness and my back, which is often problematic. I feel stiff and wish I had stretched my muscles. As I walk, though, I am swamped by the scent of the eucalyptus trees. As I have this private time, on my own, in silence and solitude, I am aware of the shame that is often cast at me as a minister in the public domain. Again, the worry about getting sick from drinking from my water pack intrudes. I know that people who love me do not shame me. The verse from Mark's Gospel I have been meditating on intentionally pops into my head, 'Whoever wants to save their life will lose it' (Mark 8:35).

I keep a look out for any water points that I can also drink from. Fleetingly I sense that this pilgrimage walk also offers spiritual water. What am I trying to save myself from through my anxious thoughts? I am trying to save myself from exposure to judgement, to unfair criticisms, to projections, but end up losing my life. I am not exposed here, as I walk, unknown to any fellow travellers, completely anonymous. I get a rush of gratitude that I am here in Spain, physically well and able to walk the Camino. I hope I can walk all day. Every now and then the sun breaks through the cloud and I can feel hot spots on my back. Little bursts of shame flicker into my consciousness. Suddenly I place the reason why. I think I have committed a micro-offence with someone, and it triggers a huge wave of shame and anxiety. The birdsong breaks in through my hearing. I think of Clare and Zac, Amy and Coco the dog at home. I realise that I have forgotten the athlete's foot cream which I might need; I feel self-conscious for recording that. I hear fellow walkers behind me and resent their closeness. I decide to slow down so they can walk past, and I can return to my solitude and silence. I see a dog and smile: Coco would love this walk, all the smells and sights.

There is an intersection ahead; I see people consulting maps and phones for directions. I begin to doubt myself. I see a yellow arrow and realise I am still on the way. I want to be on the Way, not in my head. I am fed up with being in my head. The birdsong breaks through again. I feel the soles of my feet against the earth. The familiar sound of dogs barking soothes me. I listen to the crunching of my steps on the path. I see so many houses have their own vegetable patch, chickens, dogs sitting in the yard. Flitting across my mind is the thought I'd like a little vegetable patch (and someone to cultivate it).

I feel slightly less shame. Does the fire of God burn shame? Again, the scent of the trees wafts through my senses carried by the breeze. The birds are still singing. I notice my breathing; it is deep and steady. Suddenly I pray in tongues. Am I afraid of exposure because I have a monstrous ego, or because I was shamed as a child at boarding school, with no one to turn to? A friend of mine says we have a shame basement, full of the dank water of shame, and that the smell of it pervades our whole being. I feel that. But I wonder if walking like this drains the basement, wicks it away like my shirt wicks away sweat. I see everything through a fence. I pray, 'I let go of the desire to change anything.' I feel peace. I walk past a storehouse for maize; I recognise God has given me storehouses of ancient wisdom in mindfulness and contemplation. My mind travels forward, and I feel excited about going to speak at Exeter Cathedral. I would like a little house. Like the swallows that flit around me laughing with joy.

I realise that this walk can be part of my spiritual story, a modern-day confessional tale of trying to 'follow the footprints of the Invisible One'.[119] Every hour I have set an alarm to record a little summary review – its ringing catches me by surprise. I must have been in the present moment. I realise I have not thought of coffee. I look around for the swallows, but they have gone for the moment.

Shame is a dip in the ground that catches you unawares, a step that moves on a staircase as you are about to trust it with your weight. I've packed my croissant and ham and cheese from the hotel breakfast. In taking it with me is that stealing? I finally stop for coffee and food. I wonder if the little café does goulash. There's one person who's sitting at a table of four chairs; there are no other tables available. Can I sit with him, I anxiously ask myself? I make myself sit.

The coffee gives me a high. I start paying attention. I am training my attention and awareness on this walk. After six hours walking, I feel like I've got my wind and my legs. The swallows, the path, the weather all speak to me symbolically. I think God uses these created things as natural symbols and

---

[119] This is how Diadochus of Photike describes the spiritual life, see Cliff Ermatinger, *Following the Footsteps of the Invisible*, 50.

speaks to us through them. The joy of the quest and the pilgrimage, how to be mindful of God, floods through me. I'm a symbolist, and each symbol fills me with some self-awareness or awareness of God.

This was a walk to clean every room in my head, heart, body and soul. This was a walk to cleanse my awareness. The Ananias Prayer comes into my head unprompted:

> May the love of Christ take hold of me,
> May the light of Christ shine in my heart,
> May the love of Christ flow through me like a river.[120]

I'm climbing a hill. Even shame gets left behind on this hill. I think shame and anxiety lead to self-focus. In that way I lose my life if life is with others. My family pop into my mind. I will ring them tonight. It will be nice to see their faces. What is mindful symbolism? Thank You, Lord. Thank You, Lord. Gratitude fills my soul. There's a beautiful old bridge I walk across. Maybe mindfulness is a bridge you can only walk across physically; you cannot get there technologically. Mindful symbolism is walking in awareness and allowing whatever is around you to speak to you. I'm grateful to the second-person guides I have met in books… like the apostle Mark, the early Christian contemplatives like Diadochus and Evagrius. The secular mindfulness guys. I face the pain. That's the mindful thing to do. Pain that comes and goes at the end of the walk. It doesn't stay; it moves around. Pain in the sole of my right foot, left knee. Achilles tendons on both ankles hurt. Mindfulness weighs nothing but can hold heavy experience.

Gentle heat of the sun breaking through the clouds, birds still singing, cars in the distance. A stream. Open awareness. I've expanded into a bigger space. Elation. Joy. I think I've reached Negreira. Relief, happiness. I am no longer fizzing. I lose my ego as I walk. A leaky drain. I probably don't smell nice either.

---

[120] This is a prayer of compassion that I created as a spiritual mindful awareness practice.

Anxiety says there's a 98 per cent chance of rain on a cloudless day. I wasn't expecting it. I just want to get there. I am there.

Day Two: Wednesday 30 May 2018
This morning as I wake up, I am both elated and worried. I've got nearly another 20km to go. The Galician countryside is so beautiful, I feel tearful. The mist, the green, the rolling hills. A cockerel crows.

I think of the time I didn't turn up for my dad's birthday supper that I'd agreed to go to. I'm still filled with shame at that. A girl had asked me to go out on a date and I didn't want to say no to her, and I didn't want to disappoint my dad, so I did nothing. But I can look back now and see this crippling anxiety that I would be rejected if I said no… that came from boarding school. I feel more compassion towards my younger self. My mum said that my dad kept looking out of the window waiting for me to turn up. That's kind of symbolic. And the person never comes. Shame keeps me in the past and makes me anxious about the future, that I would be exposed about something that happened in the past. I left my little iPad in the big bag that is being transferred on. I'm now worried I should have carried it in case it gets stolen en route. My mind is like a phone, pinging constantly with alerts from different apps.

Thank You, Lord, no injuries, no diarrhoea. Stretching was good this morning. *I let go of the desire to change anything. I let go of the desire for security and control, for affirmation, for happiness.* I'm filled with peace. I let it go. I have italicised above a prayer from my spiritual scaffolding. It's called the Welcoming prayer and comes out of the Centring Prayer tradition.[121] I have found it very helpful. So much energy is tied up in trying to control our security ('whoever wants to save their life…'), the affirmation we get. I'm back in the present moment looking for the yellow signs. Where does this strange willpower come from, to want to

---

[121] A good description of this prayer can be found in Cynthia Bourgeault, *Centering Prayer and Inner Awakening* (Lanham, Maryland: Cowley Publications, 2004), 135-152.

walk for another 20km?

Public school is presented as a symbol of privilege; it is therefore hard to tell a different narrative. In evangelicalism, meditation and mindfulness are often presented as a symbol of the East, a negative symbol. I wish to represent it as a positive Christian symbol of transformation. Meditation is the wrong word really for mindfulness practices because they are all about cultivating mindful awareness of reality. I pray for my friend's daughter and her diabetes. I just love the space out in nature on my own, the great expanse of sky. I know in my head that sometimes I am in a spacious place; I am there briefly right now. I let go of the desire for power and control. Break shame into bite-sized chunks. There's a good feeling in my lungs as they work. I feel a kind of ecstasy already. Does ecstasy burn up shame? One of the ways to deal with shame is to cultivate something else like joy, like ecstasy, like peace.

I have been walking for an hour and I am feeling good. I feel my body is part of myself and I am in tune with it. How can I paint this mist, and this earth, and these seedlings, and these trees, and these colours? I must email some photos to my mum and dad. I was walking on the flat bit without stones and a big guy was walking towards me on the same path. Who was going to step off first? And he did... I feel childishly elated. I record that because these are things that I would self-censor, not share out of shame. This is freedom.

Anxiety is like walking on a stony road. All these little thoughts stab me. But there is a clearer path. First test of my wet weather gear. There's a strong drizzle. Mindfulness is like wet weather gear that helps protect you in a storm. I feel new shoots popping up in my mind... about mindfulness research, about life, about family, about God. Just praying for my supervisor. There's a circle ahead of me where the trees overhang. I feel I am walking through a portal into a mystical place. It has symbolic significance for me.

May she know happiness, may she know health, may she know peace of being.[122]

I have been walking for two hours. I see the sign for a taxi. I am not tempted. I have lost so much of my life to shame, to anxiety. Trying to save it. I feel a great anger as the birds sing around me. If mindfulness is in part a capacity for self-awareness, and about developing self-awareness, then the fact that I realise I'm a symbolist is mindfulness in action. *Lord Jesus Christ, Son of God, have mercy on me, a sinner.* Shame is like an injury that you nurse but nobody can see. Shame is a feeling I have not learnt to tolerate so I try to avoid it. But if I can learn to tolerate it and allow myself to feel it, I believe it goes. Surf the wave of shame. *May your healing loving presence flow through me.* Taxi is the sign of experiential avoidance.

The cool weather is great, but I crave the experience of sun on my skin. I pray in tongues. My body is remembering things like how to just keep going. I notice the silence, the birds, the wind, the sound of me walking. The silence. I'd like a coffee now. Close to 10 km, halfway through. I wonder if mindfulness can be used to uncover our unconscious symbols, symbols out of our awareness, symbols of conformity to culture. There are crosses along the way. The Jerusalem cross, the St Benedict symbol, the patron saint of traveller's symbol around my neck, they're all symbolic. They speak to me.

Mark talks about having a perceptive faith. 'Whoever has ears to hear, let them hear' (Mark 4:9). Reperceiving is the goal of my mindfulness of God, seeing more clearly. The phrase, another metacognitive proposition from Mark, 'whoever wants to save their life will lose it' (Mark 8:35) is morphing in my consciousness. Weaving itself into my narrative of anxiety and shame. Where does my shame come from? I realise that I was shamed. That it wasn't originally part of me. Shame was a form

---

[122] This is an adaptation of a mindful awareness practice of befriending, 'May I be free from suffering. May I be as happy and healthy as it is possible for me to be. May I have ease of being.' See Mark Williams and Danny Penman, *Mindfulness: A Practical Guide to Finding Peace in a Frantic World* (London: Piatkus, 2011), 195, Kindle.

of control, like a heavy weight they bound us to at boarding school. Shame cannot keep up with my walking body; it is blowing away behind me. Shame is a weed. It can be pulled out. Though it is bindweed. Swallows fly as I crave bacon and egg.

The baker delivers in this village by car and beeps his horn to let everyone know he is here. *Clun* lorries are collecting the milk. Mindfulness pasteurises anxiety and shame. I see a stream. How did a little stream of words, 'Fix your eyes on the depths of your heart with an unceasing mindfulness of God,' how did such a little stream become a major river leading to a sea in my life? How did it become woven into the fabric of my being?

The time is 11.53am, the end of my third hour of walking. Things keep popping up symbolically. 'Are you ready to go home?' the poster says. I have seen it twice. I realise I am not running away from home. My body remembers the willpower I built up last time. It's come back to me. The Welcoming prayer emerges into awareness. *I let go of the desire for power and control, for safety; I let go of the desire for safety.* It is how we lose our life, trying to anxiously stay safe. I see a slug, a spider web, a snail. I feel a little burst of joy. It is now 12.30pm, and I am doing recording number six. I feel good. I have just had a rest and some food. I found a seat at the top of a big hill. Is cultivating pride in an achievement an antidote to shame? We put skin on feelings, like the peel of a fruit, and then we must stay with the feeling for it to be unpeeled and tasted. My mind is slowing down to the pace of walking. My breath feels clear of the asthma of anxiety. I recognise that normally anxiety is there most of the time.

I just got a message from somebody I thought I had offended and was in a pit of shame about. It was a lovely message. My shame was false shame. It is like a cloud has lifted even though the clouds are still there in the sky. I am getting to the bare rock of where the anxiety and shame come from. Shame makes me think everyone is going to point their finger at me.

Nothing but walking is left. Have I emptied my mind? No. It is just turned into still water from fizzy water. I've entered a different state of mind, one that just is. I am entranced by the swallows flying so low all around me. What do they symbolise? They fill me with joy. The time is 2.13pm; it is the end of the fifth hour of walking. I am still entranced by the swallows. I reach the hotel. I have walked 19.6km, 30,753 steps, over five hours and eleven minutes. My body is tired, but my mind is free. The symbolic meaning of the swallows for me still eludes me. Olveiroa and a converted farmhouse awaits.

Pilgrimage – an archetypal journey for all of us
The experience of the second day's walking is completely different from the first. I am largely free of anxiety. I know I need to interrogate and understand this stream of consciousness I have recorded. I need to examine it. Although I have followed research methods to do this there is a simple archetypal practice of self-examination and self-awareness in here.

I want to show you later how I undertook this process of self-awareness and self-examination and offer you a simple but profound way of capturing something of your everyday stream of consciousness and then examining it for what you do automatically and out of awareness. The simple question to ask right now is, 'How much of the present moment is lost to me and why?' Allow yourself to slow down, give yourself time to examine yourself, go on retreat – be intentional, using this book as a guide.

Window two: The lost moments

I pick up this theme of lost moments again. In LIGHT TWO at the cathedral the scene is a representation of when Gurney remembers a beautiful moment, walking among orchards. His reality in Flanders, amid all the chaos and mud of the First World War, is quite different. Denny's window is full of orange, blue and light. As I look at the figure walking in his beautiful scene, he seems grey and hunched. His back is turned away from the colour. It is both the colours and the symbolic nature of this figure that inspires my second Window.[123] My figure is grey, hunched and turned away from the colours my unconscious has chosen – green, blue and orange – and three trees. I cannot see the natural beauty, or the shelter of the three-in-one God. I am aware of my lost moments. This is the association that comes to mind:

> Each present moment
> Full of colour and beauty
> I lose to anxiety.

What are the lost moments in your life? What holds your attention captive?

Window three: The Light was coming

In Denny's LIGHT THREE it is night, and the light is coming from the stars. It is a scene from Gurney's home valley, prior to the pain and darkness of First World War France. It is a window that shows how remembering can bring light into present moments that are lost to pain and anxiety and fear.[124] Later in the research, I find symbolic memories that bring light into my present. In my Window three, although I was not aware of it, the light was coming. And so, I have represented my inner landscape in dark blue, black and red. The dark blue and red bleed through tears, rents in the paper:

> The fabric of being
> Was night, rent and torn inside
> But the light was coming.

The top pane has the light represented as stars, and the light was travelling towards me. If we want to move out of the shallow end of our life and go deeper, then we need to keep revisiting

---

[123] Denny, 4.
[124] Denny, 5.

key themes that emerge for us, in a form of spiral process. This is how mindful formation happens. I revisit here the finding of both secular mindfulness and mindfulness of God, for its symbolic importance to me as a light to my path.

The first light that found me, as if searching for me, was secular mindfulness. It helped me face the feelings of anxiety I was avoiding. Because I had first avoided homesickness, anxiety, grief and the trauma of separation at boarding school as a child, I learned to avoid my body, because that is where feeling is held. If I was to avoid feelings and body, I had to live an unaware life, on automatic boarding school scripts. The light of understanding that came was that I needed to inhabit my awareness, and through awareness inhabit my whole being. As I came back to awareness and my body, I was able to hold and experience my feelings. As I did this, I became more spiritually alive.

The light that also found me, travelling from a more distant star, was the phrase from fifth-century pioneer of the Jesus Prayer, Greek bishop Diadochus of Photike, as translated by Olivier Clement: 'Let us keep our eyes always fixed on the depths of our heart with an unceasing *mindfulness* of God.' In my writing process I consistently revisit, circle round this phrase, and meditate (ruminate) on it. The translation is important because of the word mindfulness. This phrase was like a star that is just emerging in the night sky as our eyes get their night vision. It pulsed at me as it was emerging. It became the star. In my darkest moments I did not realise the light was coming, but this was the moment that held me and turned me towards this luminous body of contemplation. The light got brighter; the star got bigger in my mind's eye. I was aspiring somehow to a greater awareness. This phrase spoke to me like a speech-act, it had power and I felt compelled to let it take me by the hand.[125]

'The fabric of being was night' is a phrase I have written intuitively. This is the fabric of my being and I realise later is a

---

[125] See Louise Lawrence, 'Exploring the Sense-scape of the Gospel of Mark', *Journal for the Study of the New Testament* 33, no. 4 (2011), 391.

weightier phrase than I knew at the time of writing it. This idea is something I return to. You too may know of a dark night of the soul in your experience. In mindful formation we turn and face our shadows and the darkness in our lives.

Window six: The second-person guide

Denny's LIGHT SIX is a rural scene. The autumnal colours of orange, yellow, blue and white are another remembrance of a better day for the poet. Here a couple walk through a gate that Gurney believes his friend and fellow-poet F W Harvey will never walk through again.[126] They walk among grazing sheep and seem turned towards one another.

In my Window the colours of orange, yellow and blue symbolise the fruitfulness that mindfulness of God has brought me:

> The second person
> Walking with me as my guide
> Contemplative books supplied.

At one level it was books that guided me on this contemplative path. At another level, in that place where one knows without thinking, there was another who guided me. The One who walked everywhere in Galilee and Jerusalem.

This was the second time that books had come to my rescue. The first was at boarding school, when reading became the only place of refuge and sanctuary. They are my colourful haven where I gather myself. I have never questioned their role, but I am filled with gratitude that I have them and was taught to read at such a young age.

My own experience of not having a guide has motivated me to create a second-person guide for others to follow – one that they can identify with – especially for those who need to reclaim their present moments because of mental health distress.

---

[126] Denny, 6.

I have placed a gateway in my painting because books were a gateway into new life. I have represented my second-person guide as wisdom personified, leading me by the hand. I ask you to allow this book to take you by the hand (manuductively) and lead you into mindfulness of God and mindful formation.

Window eight: The eighth day

In Denny's LIGHT EIGHT a figure faces the light streaming towards him. He is reaching out to it with hands raised, transfigured and transcending the pain in that moment, symbolised by the deep blue of the window.

Denny's inspiration are these words of Gurney: 'Out of sorrow have I made these songs.'[127] But the poems are also made from memories – memories of more peaceful moments, epiphanies that change things in the present moment of pain. We can allow ourselves to be mindfully formed through the songs of sorrow in our lives and of peace.

My Window is called 'The Eighth Day', to symbolically reflect that there has been a time of transformation and resurrection in my life. It is through mindful awareness that I rediscovered my incarnational being, God-given senses along with self-awareness, and the ability to regulate my emotions and thoughts and to transcend anxiety. Every embodied part of me has learnt to resonate with God's presence; this is a graced response as I collaborate with God. In my Window I am much closer to the light, and the light is streaming towards me. I am in a place of deeper awareness. I am bathing in the light. In the second pane there are three figures who are waiting for me to return to them. They symbolise parts of me and my family.

> Incarnated streams
> Of awareness, eight senses
> Becoming spiritual.

---

[127] Ivor Gurney, *Severn & Somme and War's Embers,* ed. R K R Thornton (Manchester, Carcanet Press, 1997), 32, quoted in Denny, 7. Reprinted by permission of Carcanet Press. Title of poem is 'Song and Pain'.

I recognise, however, the fragility and ongoing pilgrim nature of my journey. Part of our mindful formation is one of recognition – recognising and being real about our own vulnerability. Perhaps my story will enable you to own your own story.

Fragments and mending

Like a broken Japanese pot, I have been broken and glued back together. In kintsugi, 'the breaks are made *more* visible'.[128] In my story of interaction with culture I am not hiding my brokenness, or the fact that I have been glued back together. The word fragment occurs intuitively in writing to refer to the broken part of me. Later, as I work with my symbolic landscape, I pick up the idea of a broken and fragmented mosaic. However, it was not until my research into shame that I came across the idea of working with theological fragments – something Stephen Pattison does explicitly.[129]

This idea of theological fragments is a strand within practical theology which recognises that other forms of theology are needed alongside systematic theology. I have explored this theological strand further and found it resonates with my work.[130] Terry A Veling takes an image from nature to make the point that we can use fragments, 'like a bird bravely building its nest. The sticks and twigs, however, do not serve fragmentation.

---

[128] Mary Elizabeth Podles, 'A Thousand Words: Kintsugi Bowl', *Touchstone: A Journal of Mere Christianity* 34, no. 5 (Sep/Oct 2021): 62-63, for an introduction to kintsugi pottery.
[129] Stephen Pattison, *Shame: Theory, Therapy, Theology* (Cambridge: Cambridge University Press, 2000), 300-301.
[130] See Heather Walton, 'A Theopoetics of Practice: Re-forming in Practical Theology: Presidential Address to the International Academy of Practical Theology, Eastertide 2017', *International Journal of Practical Theology* 23, no. 1 (2019): 3-23, accessed 7th December 2021, dx.doi.org/10.1515/ijpt-2018-0033.

Rather, they create a whole.'[131] I am working with unique fragmented details of my life. With these details I am creating a whole in my self-work; it might be a fragile whole and must be remade constantly, but it still has coherence and structure. This fragmentation and remaking were underlined during the Covid-19 pandemic when old trauma was triggered and the fracture of boarding school separation once again came into my present, as conflict brought those fractures to my front stage.

In this chapter I am asking you to approach yourself obliquely, to allow the margins of your life to be noticed through a more poetic way of representing reality. What associations might have emerged for you? In the next chapter I trace my retrieval of an historic strand of mindfulness of God.

Reflection

Intention
I have intentionally listened to myself by going on a pilgrimage walk. Recognising our own self in self-awareness takes time. Intentionally take time to listen to yourself on a walk without distraction, or another activity that absorbs you.

Attention
Pay attention to the lost and found moments in your life – try to identify some key ones.

Attitude
What difficult experience or shadow aspect of your life have you avoided? Decide to turn and face the difficulty.

Reperceiving
Have you had any insights, epiphanies, moments of meeting, reading this chapter? Are there aspects of your creativity that you have laid aside and feel a heart impulse to pick up again?

---

[131] Terry A Veling, 'Poetic License', *International Journal of Practical Theology* 23, no. 1 (2019): 40, accessed 7th December 2021, dx.doi.org/10.1515/ijpt-2018-0029.

5
Retrieving mindfulness of God

Introduction

In this chapter I outline how I retrieved a historic strand of mindfulness of God which intersected with my discovery of secular mindfulness. Mindfulness of God is an important scriptural and historical strand of contemplative history for Christians. I came across secular mindfulness in 2006 while studying psychotherapy part-time at Roehampton University. I was suffering from stress, anxiety and burnout and found mindfulness transformational.

At the same time, while on sabbatical and doing a placement as a journalist, I met Simon Barrington-Ward, former Bishop of Coventry, who lived in Cambridge. He had written a book on the Jesus Prayer, and I met him a few times to learn about that ancient Christian prayer: 'Lord Jesus Christ, Son of God, have mercy on me, a sinner.'[132] He advised me to read up on the Jesus Prayer, and especially its history. The phrase from Diadochus of Photike that I keep returning to was a moment of meeting with God, and 'mindfuness of God' was the key part that caught my imagination.

I don't know if you have had a moment of meeting with God that has stayed with you? As mentioned earlier, the original Greek word translated as mindfulness can also be translated as remembrance. I have researched mindfulness of God ever since. I knew secular mindfulness and Buddhist mindfulness

---

[132] Barrington-Ward, *The Jesus Prayer*.

dominated the marketplace, but I realised mindfulness of God as a Christian theme was absent. The two main themes of this strand of contemplative history are mindfulness or remembrance, and attention and awareness, which can also be conveyed through the theme of watchfulness. This is how mindful formation occurs in this historic contemplative strand.

I sought to understand what mindfulness of God was and how I might cultivate it, to redeem my present moments from anxiety and the shadow of the past. I also wanted to establish how I could be fully aware of and at home in my whole embodied self (life in all its fullness). It was books, articles and texts that guided me. In this chapter I have gathered the key spiritual texts that have enabled my quest to be mindful of God. I reflect on the secular mindfulness texts in the next chapter.

I outline how these texts have been a second-person guide to me. However, other texts emerged in later chapters that were helpful psychologically, spiritually or theologically – for example, theological texts around the spiritual senses, or embodied trauma theory. For this reason, I do not outline them in this chapter as I have developed and reflected on them in later chapters, within the context of their emergence. I realised that this strand of contemplative theory and practice could lead to mindful formation through a creative synthesis with secular mindfulness.

Some of my wider reading has been particularly pertinent to my manuductive strand of reading (where the book leads you by the hand to participate in the spirituality the text guides you towards), and so I weave that into this chapter where appropriate. For example, in the process of exploring mindfulness of God, questions or problems have emerged, such as, 'How can I be mindful of God if there is an insurmountable gap between myself and God?' I have then paused, stepped back and taken a wider look at what I am doing, and so a further layer of reading has accompanied my manuductive reading. This chapter mirrors that process of pausing and addressing that theological question about the gap between God and myself. In other parts of the journey my wider reading has helped clarify what sort of spirituality I have immersed myself in.

I also take a wider look at the Jesus Prayer and Diadochus of Photike in their historical context, to help me place my use of the Jesus Prayer which I have adapted using secular mindfulness theory. Finally, Mark's Gospel has been both a manuductive text and one that has enabled me to examine my discoveries from a wider angle and informed perspective. I have a chapter on the importance of Mark's Gospel to me in this dual role.

I can observe my lived contemplative experience. I am trying to observe the details of my participation in mindfulness of God. This is called a first-person approach to research or contemplative formation. I would add to this that God is in the details of our senses, our bodies, our breath, our imagination, our unconscious. Part of mindful formation is learning to observe or witness our lived contemplative experience.

Within first-person approaches there is traditionally a second-person guide who helps you practice your contemplation.[133] Early Christian contemplatives acted as second-person guides to others both in person and through their writings.[134] When I started to explore mindfulness of God in 2006, I could not find any second-person guides who might help me to explore this within my own Christian culture. I therefore turned to texts, to books and articles as a second-person guide. However, through this book I myself am now able to offer a second-person guide to mindful formation. Through a sustained immersion in these texts a map of mindfulness emerged in my head and memory.

---

[133] Francisco Varela and Jonathan Shear, 'First-person Methodologies: What, Why, How?' in *The View from Within: First-Person Approaches to the Study of Consciousness,* eds Francisco Varela and Jonathan Shear (Thorverton, UK: Imprint Academic, 1999), 8-9.

[134] A M Casiday, for example, calls Evagrius a guide in A M Casiday, *Evagrius Ponticus* (London, New York: Routledge, 2006), 36-38.

A map of mindfulness

The Scargill community where I lived and am now part of the extended community live on a ninety-acre estate. Maps of the paths on the estate, with other key features, like a labyrinth, have been printed to give to guests. Through mindful repetition and revisiting of the key mindfulness texts, a map of mindfulness has been created in my head following my immersion in those texts.

Another analogy for me is the night sky. Scargill is in a dark sky reserve with very little light pollution, and so when the sky is clear there is an amazing view of the stars. One of the constellations I am fascinated by is Orion, which can be seen from Scargill. The key navigational points of mindfulness exist in my head like a constellation. I see them as stars as they glow in the dark of my mind and enable me to navigate life and orient myself in my own self and in the world. Jonathan Gibson points out that mindfulness is used as an 'umbrella term' which can lead to confusion as to what mindfulness is. I will draw on some of those related definitions to construct my map as they have steered me and to bring some clarity to the term.[135] I begin with a Christian map. This map helps to outline the key aspects of mindful formation.

As I explored this strand of mindfulness of God, there were two main stars to navigate by: remembrance or mindfulness, and attention and awareness (sometimes called watchfulness). These enable what the contemplatives in the early Christian East called *diorasis*, a clear diagnostic seeing.[136] My spiritual reperceiving through mindfulness would be a form of *diorasis* that involves all the senses, with awareness at the heart. I am

---

[135] Jonathan Gibson, 'Mindfulness, Interoception, and the Body: A Contemporary Perspective', *Frontiers in psychology* 10 (September 2019): 1, accessed 2nd November 2021, dx.doi.org/10.3389/fpsyg.2019.02012.
[136] Tomas Spidlik, *The Spirituality of the Christian East*, Collegeville, (Minnesota: Liturgical Press, 1986), 77. See also Irenee Hausherr, *Spiritual Direction in the Early Christian East*, translated by Anthony P Githiel (Cistercian Publications, 1990), 91-2.

aware that the language of biblical studies has been critiqued for its 'eye-centricity' from the perspective of disability studies, and that using the metaphor of seeing clearly or not clearly is problematic.[137] My preferred term is reperceiving, which takes in all the senses, awareness, imagination, body, emotions and thinking.

This map has also enabled me to reflect critically on the cultures I inhabit, to bring them into greater awareness. Another aspect of this attentional training is as an antidote to the shaping of us by culture. I know that my boarding school culture made me unaware through blinkered loyalty, and my church experience was to inhabit activity and service, not awareness. I also know that our attentional capacities are being reshaped by the digital world in which we live.

The mindful turns in my life and spirituality

I was not living an aware, embodied or emotionally full life. Mindfulness enabled some crucial turns: a turn to awareness, a turn to the embodied, a turn to the emotional life and a turn to incarnational spirituality. As I look back now reflectively and critically, I am aware that I experienced these turns in my life as illuminative turns, and they will frame my outline of this immersion in mindfulness. These turns frame our mindful formation. The turns are connected – a turn to awareness out of automaticity enabled a turn to the body and senses; the turn to the body and senses enabled a turn to unpleasant and pleasant emotions, a shift in perspective sometimes called reperceiving, and most unexpectedly a turn to incarnational spirituality. I focus on the spiritual aspects of these turns in this chapter before returning to the impact of secular mindfulness on these turns in the next chapter.

The first mindful turn was to awareness. A spiritual dimension to this turn was that it was an ethical mnemonic

---

[137] Louise J Lawrence, *Sense and Stigma in the Gospels* (Oxford: Oxford University Press, 2013), 25.

awareness as outlined in the introduction. In Mark 8:33 I am invited to remember (be mindful of) the things of God in each present moment. Manuductive reading is historically connected to this idea of 'remembrance of God'; manuductive texts lead us by helping us hold the way to God in our memory.[138] My emphasis on the importance of remembering the things of God in each moment is one reason that I make use of manuductive reading, with its emphasis on helping one remember.

However, it is the turn towards an incarnational spirituality that I want to focus on now. A key season in my life was in 2006, a year of discovery and transformation. As well as finding secular mindfulness I discovered two contemplative practices. The first was the Jesus Prayer and the second was *Lectio Divina*. The Jesus Prayer is implicitly embodied in that you say the first part of the prayer on your inbreath, and the second part on your outbreath. You can also use a prayer rope, where each time you say the prayer, you measure off a knot.[139] This adds to the embodied nature of the prayer. I had some conversations with Simon Barrington-Ward, the former Bishop of Coventry, about the prayer and how to use it, as well as using his book as a guide. Simon was able to be a true second-person guide for the Jesus Prayer.

I intentionally made the Jesus Prayer an embodied, attentional training practice, like the mindful awareness practices of secular mindfulness, using insights about the link between breath and emotion, and intentionally using the muscle of attention. I have also created an attentional training model out of *Lectio Divina*, the traditional meditative reading of Scripture. These attentional training models are key parts of mindful formation, and I come back to this and other models in a later chapter.

---

[138] Candler, 35.
[139] Barrington-Ward (2011), 84.

Secular mindfulness and God

I have used secular mindfulness to direct me towards God and translated my understanding of mindfulness of God into accessible secular language. This is to help those outside the Church to engage with mindfulness from a spiritual perspective in language they understand. It is also because secular mindfulness provides an in-depth anthropological map of our attentional capacities. Much Christian engagement with secular mindfulness has been in the other direction, bringing secular mindfulness into the Christian world for therapeutic reasons.

I argue later that mindfulness opens the door to kataphatic spirituality, which is incarnational and embodied. Kataphatic practices are much more accessible and more formational – anyone can access them, which is an important point for accessible spirituality.

Tracking mindfulness of God

As noted earlier, within this foundational reading and practice to develop mindful awareness there was a key epiphany in my spiritual journey, which was the discovery of Diadochus of Photike, the fifth-century Greek bishop and pioneer of the Jesus Prayer and his concept of mindfulness of God: 'Let us keep our eyes always fixed on the depths of our heart with an unceasing *mindfulness* of God.' I revisit the idea of mindfulness of God here, as I track the historical arc of which it was a part, since its history helped me place my adaptation of the Jesus Prayer within that arc. Tracking this historical strand is not easy – it is fragmented and complex. Don't worry if you find some of it difficult to follow at times; I think that is part of the journey. But stay with the process and allow the understanding to emerge as we spiral back to the key themes again and again.

This historical strand is important in my journey of mindful formation – it enabled me to place the idea of mindfulness within a spiritual and scriptural perspective. Outlining it here in an in-depth way matters. Mindfulness as paying attention and being aware is very significant from a Christian perspective – especially mindfulness of God.

This strand of the remembrance of God can be traced within the history of the Jesus Prayer.[140] Johnsén identifies three main authors in which this theme appears in early monastic sources: John Cassian, Diadochus of Photike and John Climacus.[141] Why Clement translated this phrase of Diadochus as 'mindfulness of God' would require a speculative answer, but when I read it in 2006 it was for me a culturally resonant translation. It may be that Clement was aware of the use of the Hebrew word in Psalm 8 generally translated 'attend to' or 'mindful of', which Megan I J Daffern calls a 'Remember'-related word' in the 'semantic field' of remembering in the Psalms.[142] She argues that 'remembrance and attention are closely and poetically linked'.[143] I have linked attention and awareness to remembering in my model of ethical awareness. To root this in your own life, are there significant texts in Scripture or devotional writing that have stayed in your memory and guided you?

References to the Jesus Prayer in these early sources are fragmented and, as Johnsén points out, 'none of these texts were really a practical handbook on the Jesus Prayer'.[144] As the tradition developed there appeared to be different intentions or aims in addition to the remembrance of God. Ware identifies that for Evagrius the aim is to arrive at 'non-discursive or "apophatic prayer"'.[145] In the sixth century, St Barsanuphius and St John based in Gaza did not use the Jesus Prayer in the

---

[140] Henrik Rydell Johnsén, 'The Early Jesus Prayer and Meditation in Greco-Roman Philosophy', in *Meditation in Judaism, Christianity and Islam*, ed Halvor Eifring (London: Bloomsbury, 2013), 93-106.
[141] Johnsén, 94.
[142] Megan I J Daffern, 'The Semantic Field of 'Remembering' in the Psalms', *Journal for the Study of the Old Testament* 41, no. 1, (2016): 94.
[143] Daffern, 94.
[144] Johnsén, 94.
[145] Kallistos Ware, 'The Origins of the Jesus Prayer: Diadochus, Gaza, Sinai', in *The Study of Spirituality* ed. Cheslyn Jones, Geoffrey Wainwright and Edward Yarnold, SJ (London: SPCK, 1986), 177.

service of apophatic prayer, but to cultivate an ethical awareness based around 'humility, obedience and the excision of self-will'.[146] This is more in the spirit of how I have developed the Jesus Prayer, as a spiritual mindful awareness practice, with an intentional attentional training element – making it a kataphatic practice.

An important element of the Jesus Prayer for my kataphatic spirituality is that the focus is on the incarnate son of God, not the 'unknowable God' of the apophatic tradition.[147] My charismatic focus on the human Jesus of Nazareth, who though divine, performed miracles through His humanity in the power of the Holy Spirit, made the incarnation of Jesus very important to me spiritually. Later I engage with Balthasar's emphasis on incarnational, kataphatic spirituality, which is a helpful theological frame for my mindful spirituality.[148]

St. John Climacus from the seventh century links the Jesus Prayer to stillness (*hesuchia*).[149] His later follower Hesychius emphasises the Jesus Prayer as a way of cultivating watchfulness (*nepsis*).[150] Watchfulness does become a major theme associated with the Jesus Prayer.[151] In a collection of contemplative texts from the early Christian tradition the following comment is made about these spiritual writings: 'They show the way to awaken and develop attention and consciousness, to attain that state of watchfulness which is the hallmark of sanctity.'[152]

I interpret watchfulness as a state of prayerful attentiveness,

---

[146] Ware, 179.
[147] See Edward Howells, 'Apophatic Spirituality', in *The New SCM Dictionary of Christian Spirituality*, ed Philip Sheldrake (London, SCM Press, 2005), 117-119 for a summary of apophatic spirituality.
[148] See Stephen Fields, SJ, 'Balthasar and Rahner on the Spiritual Senses', *Theological Studies* 57 (1996), 224-241 for an introduction to this theme.
[149] Ware, 182.
[150] Ware, 182.
[151] G E H Palmer, P Sherrard and K Ware, eds, *The Philokalia* (London: Faber & Faber, 1979), 164.
[152] Palmer, Sherrard and Ware, 13.

and Ware makes the point that 'Continual prayer does not mean merely the continual saying of prayers; it may also take the form of an implicit state.'[153] A probable source for the idea of watchfulness in Diadochus and the development of the Jesus Prayer was the Gospels, including Mark's Gospel. The Jesus Prayer itself is based in part on the prayer of Bartimaeus in Mark 10:47. The Jesus Prayer's link to watchfulness may well also be inspired by a command of Jesus in Mark's Gospel to be watchful (13:37), a command that is present continuous in the Greek. In other words, we are commanded to 'go on being watchful'.[154]

The idea of mindfulness or remembrance of God also occurs within the Benedictine tradition of monasticism, which has been very important in my spiritual journey and may help in part to explain my intuitive connection with it. A key summary of this strand is given by Michael Casey. Michael Casey says mindfulness of God is at the heart of the monastic tradition and the key to personal and community transformation.[155] He takes the more traditional term, *memoria Dei,* memory (remembrance) of God, and defines it as a form of mindfulness of God.[156] He argues that it is a biblical doctrine and practice, tracing it from Deuteronomy and the Psalms, through the early Desert Fathers and Mothers and into the monastic tradition.[157]

Columba Stewart, another Benedictine scholar, puts 'mindfulness of the divine presence' as central in Benedictine spirituality.[158] Terrence Kardong, in his translation and commentary on Benedict's Rule, highlights that 'mindfulness

---

[153] Ware, 180.
[154] For the influence of the New Testament on the pioneers of the Jesus Prayer see Simon Barrington-Ward, *The Jesus Prayer* revised edition (Oxford: Bible Reading Fellowship, 2007), 29-35.
[155] Michael Casey, 'Mindfulness of God in the Monastic Tradition', *Cistercian Studies Quarterly* XVII, no. 2 (1982): 111-126.
[156] Casey, 111.
[157] Casey, 112.
[158] Columba Stewart OSB, *Prayer and Community: The Benedictine Tradition* (London: Darton, Longman & Todd, 1998), 31.

and remembrance' is a 'favorite theme of Benedict'.[159] I highlight the contribution of Benedictine scholars here, in a selective way, to emphasise that others have worked with the idea of mindfulness of God and seen it as central to the Christian life. Why these important Benedictine scholars all work with the same idea is interesting.

The foundation of Benedictine life through *Lectio Divina* may have highlighted the scriptural strand of remembering God. Benedict's Rule also takes up this idea. It may be that Christian-Buddhist dialogue, for example, what was called 'The Gethsemani Encounter' in July 1996, also contributed to this usage of the term, in which dialogue Benedictines attended and played a key role.[160] In his outline of the contemplative life in the book entitled *The Gethsemani Encounter*, James Wiseman OSB also alludes to the centrality of mindfulness of God. He describes the contemplative life as 'a fully integrated life, in which *all* our activities, whatever they may be, can be the occasion for, or can grow out of, that mindfulness of God which is the heart of contemplation'.[161] Within this broad focus on God he emphasises the centrality of Christ, with the importance of 'holding him in view'.[162]

I am seeking to emulate this holistic approach and central focus on Christ in my life. One section of Wiseman's chapter is 'Being Mindful of God in All Walks of Life'.[163] My attraction to Benedictine spirituality has also been its compatibility with ordinary life. In a beautiful phrase, Wiseman's description of the contemplative life is summarised as 'one of graced attention to

---

[159] Terrence G Kardong, *Benedict's Rule: A Translation and Commentary* (Collegeville, Minnesota: The Liturgical Press, 1981), 140.
[160] Donald Mitchell and James A Wiseman OSB, 'Introduction', in *The Gethsemani Encounter*, eds Donald Mitchell and James A Wiseman OSB (New York: Continuum, 1998), xx.
[161] James A Wiseman OSB, 'The Contemplative Life', a sub-section of 'Prayer and Meditation', in *The Gethsemani Encounter*, eds Donald Mitchell and James A Wiseman OSB (New York: Continuum, 1998), 57.
[162] Wiseman OSB, 'The Contemplative Life', 55.
[163] Wiseman OSB, 'The Contemplative Life', 59.

Christ'.[164] In the Benedictine tradition, grace and awareness go together.

In this chapter I mainly engage with the spiritual texts that focus on mindfulness of God. I argue that the same attentional capacities are at work in both. These capacities are a common factor between secular mindfulness and mindfulness of God. I have also identified distinctives. For example, there is the question of intention. In secular mindfulness for health the intention might be to shift from being a victim of your thoughts to a witness of them, or to hold anxiety rather than be held by it. In mindfulness of God, I am seeking to be continuously aware of the presence of God. Can you identify your intention(s) for engaging with mindfulness of God?

I am also looking to cultivate an ethical awareness so that I can choose the concerns of God in each ethical moment of choice rather than the anxious human 'concerns jostling for my attention. This emphasis on the ground of all mindfulness being our God-given attentional capacities enables me to address the main concern raised by some evangelicals towards mindfulness, that it is solely a Buddhist construct.[165] This is a central question raised by some of those who have attended the many retreats, seminars and lectures I have given on mindfulness.

Evangelical suspicions of mindfulness

I have had many conversations with other Christians who believe that mindfulness is Buddhist and has no other history. They therefore believe that mindfulness is suspect. Through paying careful attention to mindfulness literature, this question about the roots of mindfulness can be addressed. I am looking

---

[164] Ven Dr Dhammarakkhita, 'Prayer and Meditation', in *The Gethsemani Encounter*, eds Donald Mitchell and James A Wiseman OSB (New York: Continuum, 1998), 35.

[165] See Roger Bretherton, 'Mindfulness: What's All the Fuss About?' in *Being Mindful, Being Christian: A Guide to Mindful Discipleship*, eds Roger Bretherton, Joanna Collicutt and Jennifer Brickman (Oxford: Monarch Books, 2016), 18-20, where this question is addressed.

at these definitions from a theological angle, and so the key question to ask in answer to this concern about the Buddhist roots of mindfulness is, what is the origin of mindfulness?

I am using here the main definitions to be found in secular mindfulness. However, there is a consensus that we have mindful capacities of awareness and attention, of self-awareness, self-regulation and self-transcendence. I have already outlined these terms, and from the perspective of theological anthropology these are God-given capacities. God is the origin of mindfulness.

Another common misunderstanding is to narrowly define mindfulness as practices or meditation originating with Buddhism.[166] Mindful awareness practices are only effective because there are mindful capacities that can be enhanced. However, one can be mindful without having a meditative practice.[167] Many new mindful awareness practices have been developed in mainstream mindfulness. I would argue that mindfulness for health in psychology has transcended any earlier influences. That the ground of all mindfulness is the existence of these attentional capacities explains why historically there are different forms of mindfulness, including Buddhist, Christian, Jewish, secular and so on.[168] Secular mindfulness has produced the most researched map of our attentional capacities.

From a theological perspective, however, there is a problem in asking the question, 'How can I be mindful of God?' This question came out of my wider reading. In the process of examining my quest questions I paused, took a deep breath and

---

[166] In many conversations with people talking to me about mindfulness, they define mindfulness as Buddhist meditative practices.

[167] See the work of Ellen Langer, who writes about mindfulness from a psychological perspective, without practices or a religious element; Ellen J Langer, *Mindfulness* (Cambridge, Massachusetts: Merloyd Lawrence, 1989).

[168] I have talked about secular mindfulness, Buddhist mindfulness, Christian mindfulness, but I have also come across Jewish mindfulness in conversation with rabbis.

looked at this question carefully. This was a key moment of stepping back from the manuductive process and taking a wider look at what I was trying to do – discover my part in being mindful of God. This led to some wider reading in spiritual theology. I examine this problem here, as it also helped to direct me in my quest.

A theological problem

Here we touch on a central paradox of the relationship between God and me, the gap between Creator and myself as a created being: 'Yet of *themselves* not even personal beings are capable of entering into a relationship with God.'[169] How can I be mindful of God if there is this insurmountable gap between myself and God? This is a key theological difficulty that needs addressing. The entering into a relationship with God is a graced response through the Holy Spirit. However, another paradox is in play here: 'God's transforming grace is *super*natural; yet it could not transform us unless God has already set in our natures an affinity to himself,' often defined as 'the image of God' within us.[170] Here, spiritual theology provides guard rails for how I am mindful of God. I play my part, but it is a graced response. I cannot be mindful of God unless God is first mindful of me (Psalm 8). The literature has helped me to frame my experience to see that my God-given attentional capacities are part of the image of God in me, and part of my affinity as a created person to relate to God. I might be able to reclaim my present moments through mindfulness, but only God can redeem them.

Reflection

Intention

As Christians, to read devotionally is important, allowing

---

[169] Edward Yarnold, 'The Theology of Christian Spirituality', in *The Study of Spirituality*, eds Cheslyn Jones, Geoffrey Wainwright and Edward Yarnold, SJ (London: SPCK, 1986), 11.
[170] Yarnold, 12.

Scripture or other texts to lead us by the hand into spiritual formation. It is also crucial to have a strand of informed reading: theological books, commentaries and other texts. Make it your intention to build both these strands of reading into your lives.

Attention

Reading is one way you can train your attention to move from hyper-distraction to deep attentiveness. Learning to read slowly, meditatively, staying with a passage longer and using the muscle of attention is also important. Use Matthew 16:13-20 as a starting point. Also have a go at the Jesus Prayer, which can be used as an attentional training tool.

Attitude

You might love reading more complex material or dislike it. Examine your attitude and resolve to stay with concepts that are complex and spiral back to them to grow your understanding.

Reperceiving

Can you recall any epiphanies, or 'aha' moments in your life where you have had a sudden insight or reperceived a situation or a person?

6
The influence of Mark's Gospel

Mark as a manuductive text

Mark's Gospel has shaped my mindful spirituality. It has been a manuductive text for me, a devotional read as the Holy Spirit led me by the hand. I have engaged with it since 2010 when I discovered its emphasis on watchfulness – and have a shelf load of books on it! I have developed an informed level of reading through engagement with commentaries, articles and books. Although there is a great deal to say about Mark's Gospel, I want to just focus on the strand of narrative criticism and how it has helped my devotional reading.

I have found narrative criticism particularly helpful in shaping my reading of the Gospel. Important elements of this include looking at Mark as a whole, rather than just parts of it – an insight gleaned from studies arguing for its oral origins, and its performance from memory to its hearers as a whole.[171] Textual evidence also supports the theory of it being a deliberately constructed narrative that is worth hearing and reading as a whole, because that was what it was designed for.[172]

My devotional application of key verses to my life agrees with Rhoads' narrative criticism reading of what he calls the 'rhetoric of contrast' in Mark's Gospel, which outlines 'two

---

[171] See for example, David M Rhoads, *Reading Mark: Engaging the Gospel* (Minneapolis, Minnesota: Fortress Press, 2004), 3 on treating Mark as a 'whole cloth', and 177 for its oral origins.
[172] Rhoads, *Reading Mark*, 3.

contrasting ways of life'.[173] I wish to be mindful of God and the things of God (the Way of life), and choose the things of God over the human things jostling for my attention (an anxious way of life): two contrasting approaches. In my church culture and in my ministerial training, it is normative to both apply Scripture to my life and draw on new forms of textual analysis as with narrative criticism.

A key transformative verse for me, as previously mentioned, has been Mark 8:33: 'But when Jesus turned and looked at his disciples, he rebuked Peter. "Get behind me, Satan!" he said. "You do not have in mind the concerns of God, but merely human concerns."' As I analyse the impact of this verse on me from a faith perspective, it has become an important theological principle of discipleship. I must have in mind the things of God and choose them over the human things jostling for my attention, in each ethical moment of choice. Here Jesus recognises that Peter does not have 'in mind the concerns of God, but merely human concerns'. I have recognised that I do not have in mind 'the concerns of God', although I believe I should. I want this to emerge from the background of my memory to be an ethical figure that guides me. This is a key part of mindful formation. My reading of it is a devotional one supported by another layer of informed reading.

I have then asked myself, 'How do I have in mind the concerns of God?' I have also asked what are the things of God that are relevant to me, and what human things get in the way for me? One of the human things that gets in the way of my present moment ethical awareness of the things of God is anxiety and its root in boarding school. For example, if something makes me anxious (like travelling somewhere on my own) I might be tempted to avoid the experience rather than doing it (which would be the thing of God). These afflictive thoughts can get in the way of us living by our values.

In terms of how I have in mind the things of God – they are

---

[173] Rhoads, *Reading Mark*, 45.

not in my mind automatically; they have to be placed there. The way I have done that is through a modified *Lectio Divina*, a slow meditative reading of Scripture which creates mnemonic propositions that become part of the ground of my memory, and these become insights that can be recalled, remembered in a graced response as I actively cooperate with the Holy Spirit. It may also be the Holy Spirit who attracts our attention to certain verses.

My reading is that if I take a narrative criticism perspective, then Mark 8:33 is part of a wider pattern where the Markan Jesus models this idea of choosing the thing of God over the human thing, culminating in the Garden of Gethsemane where He chooses to do the will of God over His own desire to let the cup of suffering of the cross pass Him by (Mark 14:32-42). Rhoads argues this in a whole chapter: 'A study in standards of judgement shows that the gospel of Mark is a tightly woven narrative reflecting two contrasting ways of life,' and he sees Mark 8:33 as the summary statement for these two ways of life, '(1) the things of God, that is, what God wills for people and (2) the things of people, that is, what people want for themselves'.[174]

In charismatic relation to the text, I have asked the question, 'How do I have in mind the things of God and choose them over the human (usually anxious) things jostling for my attention in each ethical moment of choice?' In Mark's Gospel, 'remembering' is part of seeing and hearing clearly in a spiritual sense (Mark 8:17-18), and remembering is central to my ethical model. I also see attentiveness to the things of God as an important component and make an associative link with watchfulness in the Gospel.

Watchfulness and living out Mark 8:33 are another way of framing spiritual mindful awareness for me, a form of mindfulness of God. Watchfulness (mindful awareness of the things of God) is how I have become aware in each moment of

---

[174] Rhoads, *Reading Mark*, 45.

choice what is the thing of God and what is the automatic script getting in the way. I wish to be an informed reader and have a sustained engagement with Scripture that fulfils my faith aim for Scripture to guide me in this journey to be mindful of God. This is in the service of lived experience. I have written substantially about watchfulness in Mark's Gospel elsewhere.[175]

I am engaging with the text in an embodied way, and the embodied nature of the culture that Mark wrote in is addressed by Louise Lawrence in her writings. Lawrence takes up this theme in her *Sense and Stigma in the Gospels*. She applies sensory criticism to the Gospels, examining what she calls the 'sense-scape' in Mark's Gospel, and points out that New Testament studies have neglected this area. 'Even a cursory look at New Testament texts reveal "corporeally" inclined cultures, where understanding is formed by sense experience just as much as words.'[176] In a mindful approach, understanding is formed by sense experience as well as words. She informs my reading of Mark in support of an embodied spirituality.

What has emerged from my immersive reading of Mark's Gospel is the importance of watchfulness and having in mind the things of God. To me this is something to do with awareness and attention rather than thinking. The text itself only gives some broad-brush pointers to how I might be watchful, but an examination of some of the history of reception of the idea of watchfulness gives more idea. My own contemporary reception of the idea linking it to insights in secular mindfulness offers further scope for understanding how I might cultivate watchfulness within a biblical spirituality.

Summary

In this journey, my context of being a Baptist minister, psychotherapist, mindfulness researcher and contemplative

---

[175] Shaun Lambert, *Putting On The Wakeful One: Attuning to the Spirit of Jesus through watchfulness* (Watford: Instant Apostle, 2016).
[176] Lawrence, 'Exploring the Sense-scape', 387.

works together intuitively to create a synthesis between secular mindfulness and mindfulness of God. My felt sense was that this was possible because I am using the same attentional capacities in both, but that in mindfulness of God I am cooperating with the Holy Spirit. I have seen a family resemblance between mindful awareness and the watchfulness commanded by Jesus in Mark's Gospel. I have been led to cultivate an ethical mnemonic awareness in the present moment. This creative fusion is the most helpful aid to mindful formation that I have come across.

I began to move in a way that shifted from self-focus to attending to others, and I began to self-transcend my anxious self and wounded self. All of this is a graced response – but within this grace I can play my part. As I free up my attentional capacities from self-focus and automatic cultural scripts, I can move to this place of mindful or watchful awareness and begin to sense the person and presence of Christ. I begin to develop a mindfully aware self in which I cooperate with the new creation enacted within by the Holy Spirit. I create a further strand of mnemonic awareness through intentional meditation on certain Scriptures, which have been 'the things of God' for me to enact in the present moment. This pattern is mindful formation which is accessible to others.

In the process of mindful formation, alongside my manuductive reading I created some intentional pieces of self-work which I talk about in some of the following chapters. Intentional self-work is an integral part of mindful formation. The pieces focus on the iterative insights that emerged out of the journey: the reclaiming of my present moments from anxiety, the reclaiming of my present moments from the shadow of the past, and the more fully inhabiting of my whole self in mindfulness of God. They are a response to my quest questions and are part of the mindful formation I offer in this book. The next chapter takes up the theme of reclaiming our present moments through the creative synthesis with secular mindfulness.

Reflection

Intention
Part of mindful formation is intentionally making the values of God something you are mindful of (Mark 8:33). It is also noticing the human things, such as anxiety, that stop us living out those values. Have you any explicit values you try to live by?

Attention
We pay attention to small passages of Scripture, but it is important to read or listen to whole books. Mark is an excellent Gospel to do this with. I especially commend listening to any performances of Mark that have been done, for example, by Max McLean.

Attitude
Try to become aware of what gets in the way of you living out the values of God in your life. What we pay attention to is normally our own self – and so it is often the preoccupation with our own comfort that is the human thing that gets in the way of having in mind the things of God.

Reperceiving
Mark's Gospel is often perceived as simple and repetitive. Do you need to reperceive it? What are your own views about it?

7
Reclaiming my present moments through a creative fusion with secular mindfulness

Introduction

In this chapter I outline an intentional piece of self-work through a creative fusion of secular mindfulness and mindfulness of God. Self-work is when we apply the wisdom of contemplative history and mindfulness to our own lives. It is here I answer our second quest question: 'How can we reclaim our present moments from anxious rumination to be mindful of God?' Being shaped to be fearfully anxious about our own self is a common trope of being formed by our culture. As my journey unfolded, I became aware of obstacles to my being mindful of God. One of those obstacles was the inability to remain in the present moment because of anxiety. What obstacles do you face? Is it another mental health condition or the distractions of our virtual world?

There are no quick fixes, or 'ten ways to be mindfully formed in less than a month'! Mindful formation into the likeness of Christ is a lifetime of graced self-work. That's why it's helpful to take a longer-term view of our transformation. It's important to look back at the history of your life and look for elements that might already be there in the service of mindful formation. Are there key moments of meeting with God you've forgotten about? What about spiritual practices you have let go of? Or has a historical figure inspired your own spirituality?

In 2017 a key intuitive impulse led me to go on pilgrimage walks for mental wellbeing and spiritual transformation. I had noticed that on long walks it was as if my more difficult feelings flowed out behind me as I journeyed. My narrative on that pilgrimage walk, which appeared earlier, may allow you to identify with that story and seek your own quest. As you read, note any points of identification and follow your intuition as to where they may lead you in your quest.

After that first mindful pilgrimage walk, I decided to set up an intentional pilgrimage walk in 2018 recording all my thoughts and feelings as they occurred in the present moment over a two-day period. This would enable me to track my thoughts and feelings, while engaging in mindful practices, to see what happened to the trajectory of my anxiety and other hindrances. I have analysed in this section the transcripts of the two days walking in Chapter Four to highlight my shift from anxiety to peace as it happened.

The key finding from this intentional piece of self-work was that my present moments were far more overwhelmed by anxious thoughts than I realised. I think this lack of self-awareness about how much time we spend in mental time travel is true of many. However, the mindful practices did reclaim my present moments as the walking unfolded. I realised that to be more mindful of God and others I needed to reclaim my present moments from the afflictive thought of anxiety. I offer an opportunity to do this deeper self-work in a simplified form to help you cultivate a similar self-awareness of your present moments. Going on annual retreats can also be a helpful practice in our mindful formation.

I first went on retreat at Worth Abbey, a Benedictine Roman Catholic monastery famous for a BBC television programme.[177] It was a guided retreat to Benedictine spirituality, and this was where a door opened into contemplative spirituality for me. Times of silence and solitude are helpful on retreat, based on

---

[177] *The Monastery*, BBC Television, 2005.

Jesus' own practice (Mark 1:35). It's important to do something in the silence, and that's where traditional practices like the Jesus Prayer and *Lectio Divina* are helpful. I outline adapted models of these for you in the book. This book can be used on a retreat to guide you into a mindful, contemplative state of mind in the moment where you can listen to God. I outline the significance of the present moment to mindfulness for health and mindfulness of God in the next section.

The problem of the present moment

There is a universal consensus in secular mindfulness that paying attention in the present moment is a central component of mindfulness, to enable mindful awareness of reality.[178] However, staying in the present moment consistently is the problem of the present moment, as the narrative self in our head is often preoccupied with mental time travel and rumination which takes one out of present moment reality. When I am in the present moment, I am better able to regulate my anxiety as I cultivate present moment mindful awareness of it. I am also interested in the present moment from a spiritual perspective. In C S Lewis' *The Screwtape Letters*, the senior devil writes to the junior devil about their enemy, God:

> The humans live in time but our Enemy destines them to eternity. He therefore, I believe, wants them to attend chiefly to two things, to eternity itself, and to that point of time which they call the Present. For the Present is the point at which time touches eternity.[179]

From this spiritual perspective it is important that I live in the present moment, as the point of intersection with the eternal.

---

[178] A summary statement of the centrality of present-moment awareness as part of mindfulness definitions is presented in Vago and Silbersweig, 4.

[179] *The Screwtape Letters* by C.S. Lewis © copyright 1942 CS Lewis Pte Ltd. Extract used with permission.

My experience is that to live in the present moment is crucial in terms of my mental and spiritual wellbeing. This is a general truth for human flourishing. I have also been influenced by the Christian idea of the 'sacrament of the present moment'.[180] Every moment is sacred and pregnant with the possibility of meeting God. As I knew my ability to be in the present moment was limited through anxiety, I needed to cultivate a present moment mindful awareness that was both therapeutic and spiritual, to relativise my anxious thoughts and be more mindful of God's presence. In this sense I am interested in the present moment from my psychological and spiritual experience, while reflecting on it theologically.

I am aware that in secular mindfulness there is an implicit mnemonic element to present moment mindful awareness that is being cultivated – remembering key values and propositions in the present moment is central. Memory, in this sense, helps to reclaim the present moment. In reclaiming my present moments, I am also changing my view of the future, namely a future less overshadowed by anxious thoughts. I recognise that I will also have to reclaim elements of the past mindfully to free my present moments, since the genesis of my anxiety is rooted in the past. The lived experience of the past impacting the present is also true for many others. Part of mindful formation is being able to reclaim our past and future as well as our present.

To help me answer this problem I have taken some theoretical inspiration from secular psychology. The idea of implicit relational knowing developed by the Boston Change Study Process Group argues that as human beings we are in implicit relationship with each other, with much of our relational interaction out of our awareness. However, there can be moments of 'charged meeting'. I have applied this as an

---

[180] The sacrament of the present moment is emphasised in Jean-Pierre de Caussade's *Self-Abandonment to Divine Providence*, translated by Alger Thorold (London: Collins, 1977), 7.

analogy for the human-divine relationship.[181] Besides our conscious experience, this theory argues there is an underground stream of relational knowing that is implicit since it is 'a process that is conducted out of awareness most of the time'.[182] Another way of describing this process could be the 'unthought known'.[183] This hidden stream carries 'hidden or potential now moments'.[184] In mindful formation we need to engage in a graced way with the unthought known. This is a missing dimension.

A 'now' moment is a present moment that 'gets lit up subjectively and affectively, pulling one more into the present moment' and moving the '"shared implicit relationship" into the open'.[185] This unthought known now moves into conscious awareness and there are two possible responses to this now moment. There can be a 'therapeutic reorganisation or derailment' of the relationship, but both parties in the relationship 'recognize' that 'a window of opportunity' has opened to them.[186] It is interesting that the word 'recognition' is used as an important part of this moment, considering recognition theory. This also resonates with mindfulness theory that recognises we are on autopilot much of the time and so need to intentionally step out of automaticity into awareness.

Lying behind the Boston Change Study Group's interest in 'now moments' and 'implicit relational knowing' is an attempt to identify when positive therapeutic change happens.[187] Their argument is that a 'now moment that is therapeutically seized

---

[181] Boston Change Process Study Group, *Change in Psychotherapy:* 5-7, 10-24.
[182] Boston Change Process Study Group, *Change in Psychotherapy:* 14.
[183] Boston Change Process Study Group, *Change in Psychotherapy:* 15, a term developed by C Bollas, *The Shadow of the Object: Psychoanalysis of the unthought known* (New York: Columbia University Press, 1987).
[184] Boston Change Process Study Group, *Change in Psychotherapy:* 17.
[185] Boston Change Process Study Group, *Change in Psychotherapy:* 16.
[186] Boston Change Process Study Group, *Change in Psychotherapy:* 17.
[187] Boston Change Process Study Group, *Change in Psychotherapy:* 1-5.

and mutually realised is a "moment of meeting".[188] This is when therapeutic change happens. Now moments can also be 'missed' or 'failed'.[189]

I am aware that I am in an implicit relationship with God. God's presence is always there, but most of the time it is out of my conscious awareness. However, as I become more present to reality in my own self, through a graced response, it is possible to have some charged 'now' moments, magnetised through the Holy Spirit that become 'moments of meeting' with God. When I first read the phrase 'mindfulness of God' I experienced a charged 'now' moment with God. It is a graced response because I cannot find God unless God first finds me, but I can play my part. These moments can lead to the ideal contemplative state, which is a continuous awareness of God's presence. I later create a model for examining our time in relationship to God and the present moment, adapting this theory of implicit relational knowing.

Introspective phenomenology and mindfulness

I have sought to be continuously aware of the presence of God and have identified obstacles to this and ways to overcome these obstacles. My method of directly contemplating God, while *in obliquo* observing my contemplative participation, follows the historic Christian contemplative path of first-person research for the benefit of others. This is how the early contemplatives developed the contemplative tradition. They observed their own participation in contemplation of God and then wrote about it. Others were then able to develop their own contemplative life using the pioneers as a guide.

Out of this broader strand I am now, in this chapter, looking to focus on reclaiming my present moments from anxious overload through spiritual practices that cultivate my

---

[188] Boston Change Process Study Group, *Change in Psychotherapy:* 18.
[189] Boston Change Process Study Group, *Change in Psychotherapy:* 22-23.

mindfulness of God. The spiritual practices were mindful pilgrimage walking and the turning of a new verse from Mark into a metacognitive proposition ('whoever wants to save their life will lose it' (Mark 8:35)). I outlined this process of working with verses as metacognitive propositions earlier in the book.

I have taken Mark 8:35 as another key verse because my reader-response to this phrase was to hear it in my context of anxiety, that 'if I try to save my life through anxiety, I will lose it through the experiential avoidance that is my anxious reaction'. I have intentionally turned this verse into a metacognitive proposition for my mindfulness of God. I am turning a scriptural verse into wisdom for living. Through intentionally meditating on it as a proposition for my life, the aim is for it to become an insight that enables me to catch anxious experiential avoidance in the moment. I do this by holding in mnemonic awareness the insight that if I try to save my life through anxiety, I will lose it. This enables me to live by my values in the present moment, a key part of mindful formation. This model will work with others reading this book to enable them to live by their values in each ethical moment of choice. Why don't you pause and consider what biblical propositions or values you might like to become insights in your life?

I created a distinctive analytic process to underpin the intentional two-day pilgrimage walk in northern Spain based on adaptations of tried and tested methods, including introspective phenomenology. Introspective phenomenology is simply 'observing and reporting on one's own subjectivity with as much accuracy as possible'.[190] The research was to record via my iPhone whatever thoughts, feelings and bodily sensations came into my awareness over a day's walking, breaking the recording into individual hours but recording in real time. When

---

[190] Tim Lomas, 'A Meditation on Boredom: Re-Appraising Its Value through Introspective Phenomenology', *Qualitative Research in Psychology* 14, no. 1 (2017): 6, accessed 18th March 2018, dx.doi.org/10.1080/14780887.2016.1205695.

we observe our contemplation of God, we are being introspectively phenomenological.

I collected the present moment data by recording on my phone whatever popped into my awareness as I walked. I also set an alarm on my phone every hour to remember to stop and record what I was feeling in that moment, and to start a new recording for the next hour. I collected data for two days of walking. The idea was to record whatever appeared in my awareness, non-judgementally and without self-censorship. I typed up the data on the evening of the day I walked. As well as walking, I followed my normal scaffolding of mindful and spiritual practices in the early morning and added an intentional meditation on Mark 8:35, turning it into a metacognitive proposition. This is a way of observing my present moments.

On the following two days of the walk, I rested and analysed the data recorded. Although that was part of my formal PhD research, in this book I suggest a simpler model for examining our own subjective experience. This is to enable us to become aware of how much mental time travel we are doing in everyday life. Dr Amishi Jha suggests we are missing fifty per cent of our lives in mental time travel when we are not in the present moment reality.[191] It is crucial, therefore, that we identify this black hole in our present moment living for our own lives.

Self-examination

Any period of walking in which you capture your stream of consciousness is helpful. If walking is not a possibility, then another way of capturing your stream of consciousness can be used. One researcher, for example, spent time sitting on a plane to examine his experience of boredom. We can also imagine movements in our mind's eye. There were two main themes for me – a high level of anxiety and shame on day one, and a substantial reduction in those negative feelings on day two – and the emergence of a spiritual theme. I have called the spiritual

---

[191] Dr Amishi P Jha, *Peak Mind* (London: Piatkus, 2021), 1, Kindle.

theme 'the concerns of God' (Mark 8:33). The anxiety and shame I have called the 'human concerns' jostling for my attention.

The key thing is that mindful formation requires us to give it time. We cannot change what we are not aware of, so take a day out of your normal routine. Do something that you find helpful, perhaps a walk as I did. Record your thoughts on your phone as you become aware of them. Stop every hour and record whatever you are aware of in that moment.

Then spend some time writing up a transcript of your thought life. Once you've done that look for themes: are there any afflictive thoughts like anxiety, stories you return to, things you ruminate about? Is there a shift during the day?

Anxiety and shame

I want to pick up on the themes of anxiety and shame, which are very prevalent in our culture and may be themes you identify through self-examination. They are emotions I became aware of. We often avoid these more difficult feelings. Some personal and theoretical reflection here may help you understand how anxiety or shame feature in your life. My own psychotherapy training was integrative and relational, drawing on cognitive-behavioural therapy (CBT), person-centred and psychodynamic theories. I am aware that there are different ways of handling shame and anxiety within these approaches. For example, CBT would seek to change your thoughts. I am using mindful theory which does not try to change your thoughts, but your relationship to your thoughts.[192] It may be that I always have anxious thoughts, but in mindful theory thoughts are not facts; they are just passing mental events. I notice them and let them go, like watching leaves in a stream go by.

---

[192] Kirk Warren Brown, Richard M Ryan and J David Cresswell, 'Mindfulness: Theoretical Foundations and Evidence for its Salutary Effects,' *Psychological Inquiry* 18, no. 4 (2007): 213, accessed 20th March 2022, dx.doi.org/10.1080/10478400701598298.

On the first day of my Camino walk, I became aware how prevalent shame and anxiety were. Most of the first day I was in my head and not in the present moment. I was involved in mental time travel between the past and the future. Right at the beginning of the walk my anxiety was looking forward: 'Shall I carry the water bottle tomorrow?', 'Will I find somewhere to do a wee?', 'Will I find the way or get lost?' I also looked back in time: 'Should I have stretched?' The data on shame illustrates my mental time travel, this time to the past: 'I feel huge shame and anxiety with a micro-offence I've committed or imagine I've committed.' This 'hot spot' of shame keeps dragging me back into rumination and rerunning the offence. On day one I am finding it difficult to be in the present moment, which is my goal.

On the second day there was a shift out of anxiety and shame. I moved more into the present moment, and this brought freedom from my anxious thoughts. In day two the human concerns moved to spiritual concerns, most of which were prayer, which replaced the anxiety. This is a new spiritual narrative that now has space to emerge. Through an immersion in mindful walking and meditative practice, I step not only into my body and senses and breath, which are always in the present moment, but also into a more open inner space which can hold the other aspects of myself and in which self-awareness, awareness of the concerns of God and God's presence can emerge.

As I enter more into my body, senses, awareness and feelings, my spiritual self emerges. I am calling this a mindful spirituality – where the theory, practice and insights of secular mindfulness, with its emphasis on aware and embodied (incarnational) living, opens the door to the spiritual in my life which has been backstage, while anxiety has been frontstage. Part of mindful formation is carrying out habitual spiritual practices daily, whether we feel like it or not.

This self-awareness is a form of meta-awareness in which I was observing my state of being. For example, I said, 'I feel like a bottle of fizzy water, all shook up,' and, 'I want to walk clear not cloudy.' In this theme of meta-awareness, spiritual meta-reflections emerged, such as, 'I think shame and anxiety lead to self-focus. In that way I lose my life if life is with others.' My aim is to live life in relationship with God and with others, and I define this as finding my life. Here the scriptural metacognitive proposition from Mark's Gospel that 'whoever wants to save their life will lose it' becomes a value in my mind. It has become a metacognitive insight. I am aware in the moment that anxiety tries to get me to save my life by avoiding difficulty. However, I end up losing my life through experiential avoidance, not saving it.

The shame data was also significant. Shame seeped into my consciousness like damp. What brought it to the fore on this trip was that I thought I had offended someone and it was causing me deep shame and anxiety. Perhaps the anxiety came from the shame, or fear of being exposed. I realised I was carrying shame around in the basement of my own self. While on the Camino I had an incredibly positive message from the person I thought I had offended. I had a moment of meta-awareness that many of my reasons for feeling shame are not facts.

My sense is that I was shamed at boarding school, which had a shame culture. I remember that if something was stolen from the dormitory, I would be in terror of being accused and shamed, even though I did not steal anything. I am not trying here to change the shame, but as part of mindful theory to change my relationship to shame. As I shift into mindful awareness, I disentangle my sense of self from the shame. I realise that shame, like anxiety, is just a passing event, not reality – I have not shifted it; I have relativised it. As I do this, in the same way my shirt wicks moisture, it seems I can wick this emotion.

As time developed in day one, a mindful awareness began to emerge and I began to engage symbolically with natural objects around me. There was an associative logic at work as I made spiritual connections with streams and fountains on this first day. I was aware that mindfulness is a fountain of wisdom I have been drinking from. I associated the physical walking across a bridge with the embodied way I must access mindfulness. Later in the day I prayed in tongues spontaneously. I seem to have been in my body, senses and the present moment as I did so, not in my head. I felt myself letting go of anxiety and stress in this more spacious symbolic and spiritual space. I prayed prayers of gratitude and asked to be filled with God's presence. This was kataphatic spirituality.

I became aware that shame also kept me out of the present moment. It seems shame could not live with the new embodied ecstasy I felt in the moment. I was aware that as ecstasy expanded, shame decreased. I knew that I walked a stony path of anxious thoughts, but that I was bigger than my anxious thoughts. I felt and feel a great desire not to lose any more of my life to anxiety. Feelings I normally dampened down were emerging uninhibited and freely. I became aware of the expansive space of silence as I walked, inner and outer silence. I slowed down inside. My breath was not anxious; it was slow and calm. The cloud of shame lifted. I detail this observation of my own experience to show you how this can help in your own self-examination.

As my attention shifted away from self, I became more aware of nature around me. My intuitive unconscious made associative links between further natural symbols and my life. There was a circle ahead made by overhanging branches which felt like a portal into the mystical. The signs for taxis popped up, symbolic temptations to take the easy path. I ignored them. They were frequent and became a symbol for the experiential avoidance of pain.

I was aware in my own story that I painted symbolic paintings, and that was an important way I represented my reality, but I had not reflected on it to any degree. It was in this intentional research on the walk that it hit me with real force, that symbolic representation of my reality is a stream of being within me. I realised, as an epiphany, 'I am a symbolist!' I discovered that there was a strong associative logic at work within me, making connections between natural symbols and my life and God. I see this as a sign of mindful self-awareness. This impacts the representation of my work. I try to make theological sense of this within the contemplative process, through my wider reading.

There is a strand of symbolic theology within the contemplative tradition, exemplified by Denys the Areopagite. Symbolic theology is the 'conversion of what is taken from the realm of the senses to the service of the divine'.[193] My pilgrimage experience is embodied, felt through the senses, and yet I experience a conversion of what I sense into a symbolic spiritual experience. At the time of this walk I had a sense that the swallows have an important connection with my life, but I could not place them fully in my personal symbolic landscape. I revisit the importance of swallows symbolically. Many of us have a symbolic awareness but it gets pushed to the margins of our life, with our cultural and church emphasis on rationality, logic and proposition.

I am also aware that there is another layer to the walking that is symbolic and for a different purpose. Mark Cazelat wrote an article on Tom Denny, the stained-glass artist, who walks an area in a contemplative, prayerful manner to fully inhabit it. Out of this immersion Denny then represents the landscape in his artwork. Cazelat argues that this is part of a wider tradition within British art of walking for inspiration.[194] My inkling is that I am walking intuitively to find space for my creative self.

I began to experience self-compassion, compassion for others and God's compassion for me. God's compassion did

---

[193] Quoted in Andrew Louth, 'Denys the Areopagite', in *The Study of Spirituality*, eds Cheslyn Jones, Geoffrey Wainwright and Edward Yarnold, SJ (London: SPCK, 1986), 187.

[194] Mark Cazalet, 'Walking Man: The Art of Thomas Denny', *Image Journal* 86, accessed 18th October 2019, imagejournal.org/article/walking-man-art-thomas-denny.

not contain shame. A key part of my mindful spirituality is to let go of things I cannot control (the Welcoming prayer): 'I let go of the desire for security and control, for affirmation, for happiness.' I became aware of other people's pain and prayed for them. The daily scaffolding of prayers and practices emerged here as graced memory. There was space for others within, as my awareness became frontstage and mirrored the space around me. I was aware that I stepped into silence and solitude which acted as a portal to stillness and to God. I was aware that in the moment I inhabited my body and senses, my awareness, my emotions, my imagination, my symbolic unconscious.

The metaphor that has come to mind out of the symbolism of my walking clothes, which are breathable and wick sweat away, is that I have emotionally and spiritually wicked away much of my anxiety and shame. My interpretation of this is that the mindful walking, and meditation on a scriptural phrase designed to reframe my anxiety, has enabled this. This phrase of Jesus, 'whoever wants to save their life will lose it' (Mark 8:35), which has magnetic appeal for me, emerged in my awareness and then began to morph into what feels like a wise reframing of the anxiety and shame I felt. I do not experience this phrase of Jesus as a shaming statement but as a wise, compassionate proposition spoken in love. This reframing mirrors the way secular metacognitive propositions have wisely reframed my relationship to my automatic reactions (I have realised that I am not an anxious person, but that I do have anxious thoughts – which are not facts).

I now want to look at my experience from the perspective of mindful theory and my analogical use of implicit relational knowing and moments of meeting, which illuminate this shift out of anxiety and shame into freedom – and how it has happened.

Mindful theory and implicit relational knowing theory

I have already outlined my use of mindful theory and implicit relational knowing theory. In this chapter I revisit them in a new application. Although I am examining my mindfulness of God, my felt experience is that as I practised secular mindfulness, I became more mindful of God and others. My secular mindfulness practice and theoretical understanding have been foundational in transforming me spiritually. Although I originally immersed myself in secular mindfulness for therapeutic reasons, I soon became aware that it cultivated good soil for my mindfulness of God practice, and that I could integrate both secular mindfulness and mindfulness of God in a new mindful spirituality.

I have already outlined the theory of narrative, experiential and witnessing selves. I now apply it to my quest to reclaim my present moments in a spiral process. The anxious thoughts and stories come from my narrative self, where I live most of the time. I can track my ruminative narrative self in the self-interviews (listening to the different parts of my self) through tracking anxiety and shame. Through switching to my experiential self (the body, senses and breath) during the pilgrimage walk I was able to come out of my head and into the present moment. I believe this partially explains the journey out of anxiety in day two. This shift to my experiential self enabled me to relativise my anxious thoughts: I was more than my thoughts. Occasionally on the walk I was able to shift into another, rarely inhabited aspect of myself, an open awareness, sometimes called the witnessing self, where I could hold both narrative and experiential selves.

I also applied the previously discussed theory that I have mindful capacities of self-awareness, self-regulation and self-transcendence. This includes the regulation of our emotions and our attentional capacities. One of the unhelpful ways we regulate our emotions (through not paying attention to them) is to avoid them. I was avoiding the embodied feelings of anxiety. As I made the move out of my head into my body, senses and awareness, I was able to hold and then let go of the anxiety and shame. As I become self-aware and regulate my anxiety and shame, I can transcend my self-focus and pay attention to God and others. This is a key process of discipleship and mindful formation.

Mindfulness is also intentional, present moment focused, embodied and inhabiting the senses, non-judgemental as well as cultivating this wider awareness which can hold both experiential and narrative selves. This helped me reperceive my lived experience on the walk, to see more clearly. Brown, Ryan and Creswell state that mindfulness 'permit[s] the individual to "be present" to reality as it is rather than to react to it or habitually process it through conceptual filters'.[195] That is why in mindfulness practice there is a big emphasis on paying attention to things as they are. In this piece of self-work I began to reperceive my anxiety and shame and my relationship with others. I became aware of God as generous, compassionate and mindful of me, and as a presence that does not shame – this is a form of spiritual reperceiving, and another possible example of a natural capacity becoming a spiritual capacity through the indwelling of the Holy Spirit.

My felt sense is that to live in the present moment is crucial in terms of my mental and spiritual wellbeing. As I made this transition, a mindful spirituality emerged into awareness. The intentional use of memory through meditation on a scriptural verse became a metacognitive insight that enabled me to allow the automatic reaction of avoidance to come into the light and be transcended. It gave me a frame to cultivate through biblical insight a life that was not 'lost' through anxiety.

Through mindful awareness, I can become aware of my automatic reactions and hold them. Through the intentional cultivation of scriptural metacognitive propositions, I can

---

[195] Brown, Ryan and Cresswell, 'Mindfulness: Theoretical Foundations', 212.

remember in the moment a wiser Christian response. This recognition in mindfulness research of the automaticity of my reactions, and that these can be de-automatised through mindful awareness, is a key insight that I have applied to my mindfulness of God. Through the cultivation of an open awareness in which these automatic reactions become visible to me, I can also exercise a more focused ethical awareness.

The reduction in anxious moments and the emergence of spiritual moments over the two days can be seen as 'moments of meeting' with God. For these moments of meeting to emerge, I needed to be in the spacious place of awareness, and to be in the process of wicking away my anxious thoughts and feelings, and my shame. This present moment awareness became inhabited by God's Holy Spirit, and moments were 'converted' into moments of meeting with God. These included the prayers in the moment, the interaction with symbols in the moment, like the swallows, thinking of others and ecstatic feelings. Other feelings that were touched by God's presence were self-compassion and the sense that I was feeling God's compassion for me. In awareness I was also able to make meta reflections, and my metacognitive proposition about anxiety morphed in the present moment into a phrase of wise theological creativity: 'in trying to save my life through anxiety, I will lose it'. Or to phrase it from a positive angle, 'I find freedom and space as I wick anxiety away.'

Conclusion

In this piece of intentional self-work, I put into practice a model for creating ethical mindful awareness of the concerns of God in the present moment. This model helped reclaim my present moments from anxious thoughts that, like an overgrown forest, block my ability to see the light of God's presence. I have been able to find an answer to our second quest question, 'How can we reclaim our present moments from anxious rumination to be mindful of God?' In clearing space in my mind, this enabled me to be open to perceive, as a graced response, moments of meeting with God. Through the creation of another model of my lived experience of time as being in an implicit relationship with God, mostly out of my awareness, the more I create ethical mindful awareness the more I am opened to the possibility of moments of meeting with God. This ethical mindful awareness will be essential in the creation of a mindful rule of life.

A primary element of this ethical awareness is remembering; it is mnemonic awareness. The self-help mindfulness texts I have drawn on are very much designed to help us remember their instructions. In this sense, they are manuductive. Manuductive texts are designed to help the memory remember God; that is, we can remember in the end without recourse to the text.[196] My intention is to create an application which can be remembered, in the end, after constant repetition of theory and practice.

The God I experienced was compassionate and did not shame me. I experienced a conversion of natural symbols into a spiritual symbolic experience on the pilgrimage walk. I can also conceptualise my experience of God on the pilgrimage walk as parabolic, with spiritual experiences breaking into my ordinary reality. I do not draw on dualistic mainstream apophatic spirituality, and my integration of mindfulness of God with secular mindfulness is an original pathway into embodied, incarnational, kataphatic spirituality.

Ellen Langer says, 'Living in a mindful state may be likened to living in a transparent house.'[197] The self-work I carried out after the walk enabled me, almost for the first time, to have some transparent awareness of my whole house. When I was fused to anxiety, I was living in one small dark room, often a room from the past or an imagined future room. I could now see that the main obstacle to mindful awareness of God and others in the present moment was anxiety, and I saw this from a place of open witnessing awareness, an awareness of the whole house having become transparent to me. I was aware that I was

---

[196] Candler, 18.
[197] Langer, *Mindfulness*, 201.

not yet able to inhabit the whole house. My anxiety had its roots in the past, through the trauma of boarding school separation. To further reclaim my present moments, I needed to fully inhabit this past experience, to make it transparent to my awareness. I had also learnt on this Camino walk that I needed to explore my symbolic self, that room which I was reinhabiting and making more transparent.

I realised that anxiety was not an uncontrollable monster in my mind (although it appeared that way), but something that could be wicked away. The walking and the practices (including the breathing required in walking) made me permeable. I cultivated a breathable relationship with anxiety, and it began to be wicked away. As I did that, I became more permeable to God's presence implicitly there, I became more breathable to God's compassionate, non-shaming presence. Anxiety itself was vulnerable to mindfulness practices. A mindful spirituality cultivates this inner transparency to become mindfully aware of my own inner life, and the life of God within me in the present moment. This mindful spirituality enables a turn to others. The sense I had that brought freedom and embodied ecstasy was that I had been graciously allowed to mindfully inhabit God's compassion.

In this chapter I make progress with one of our main quest questions, 'What is mindfulness of God, and how do we cultivate it?' My part in mindfulness of God is to cultivate a continuous awareness of God's presence, but to move in that direction by making myself available for moments of meeting with God. How I cultivate these graced possibilities is to reclaim my present moments through two models, the first using metacognitive propositions that become insights to relativise my anxious thoughts, and the second recognising that I am in an implicit relationship with God where there is an underground stream of knowing, and the unthought known, out of which can emerge moments of meeting that are transformational. This is supported by practices like mindful walking and meditative reflection on metacognitive propositions from Scripture that help me to be embodied, to be aware and to inhabit my emotions – this embodied incarnational spirituality keeps me in the present moment, because the body is always in the present.

This chapter has also helped me answer our second quest question, 'How can we reclaim our present moments from anxious rumination to be mindful of God?' Through this work I was made aware of the limitations of just dealing with present moment anxiety. To cultivate mindfulness of God more fully, I needed to deal with the roots of my anxiety in my boarding school past and begin to access the underground stream of symbolic knowing, running through my life; the stream that for me redresses the balance between boarding school pain and sacramental goodness that constituted my childhood. This became the third, deeper quest question: 'How could I be fully aware of and at home in my whole embodied self, to further reclaim my present moments?' Or, in other words, how can we live life in all its fullness?

Within the chronological arc of this journey, I then intentionally set up a piece of self-work to enter the room of the past, my boarding school experience. I looked at how I can reclaim my narrative self, distorted by my experience at boarding school. I also offer a way for you as the reader to discern if there is a shadow from your past hanging over your present and what you want to do about it. In this chapter I have looked at reclaiming my experiential self and have become more fully aware of a symbolic self that is re-emerging. I spiral back to this symbolic self in a later chapter.

What's next? After a reflection on how our natural senses can become spiritual senses, a chapter based on my informed reading, I then summarise the three models of liberation that are crucial for mindful formation and which have been introduced already.

Reflection

Intention
There's a lot in this chapter we could work with. The central thing is to intentionally try to be in the present moment and to notice when we are not. If you are able to walk and record your thought life regularly, as outlined in this chapter, that would be a good place to start.

Attention
Part of being attentive is noticing when we are in mental time travel, our mind wandering with a negative stance to the past or to the future. You can then bring yourself back to the present moment. Sometimes, when the rumination is overwhelming, you need to find an anchor in your body. For many that is the breath, for the breath and body are always in the present moment. For others for whom focusing on the breath is difficult, it might be feeling your feet earthed to the ground, or your hands resting on your legs.

Attitude
Are you stuck in your spiritual habits, perhaps dismissive of trying new things? Perhaps you don't want to change things because that might be costly. Find a verse that can anchor you in breaking automatic habits and which encourages you to try new things, especially spiritually.

Reperceiving
There may be a particular afflictive thought that brings you out of the present moment – as anxiety did with me. It is just a thought and not a fact. As this becomes our insight, we begin to reperceive the thought and become less fused to it. We become a witness of the thought, not a victim of it.

8
A reflection on spiritual senses

Balthasar's doctrine of spiritual senses

In this chapter I offer another strand of informed reading and an insight that has come out of my lived experience: our natural senses can become spiritual senses – streams of awareness for sensing God's presence. I realised as I examined my contemplative experience that I could sense God through my natural senses. I needed a language for this and wanted to find an expression of it in history. That's when I came across the doctrine of spiritual senses, and I engage with a minority theological strand within it here.

I have retrieved the idea of mindfulness of God from Christian contemplative history. I have recontextualised this theme in creative synthesis with secular mindfulness. I am inhabiting a mindful spirituality, which is a turn to incarnational living. In embodied awareness I hold feelings, bodily sensations and thoughts in a witnessing self that, as a graced response through the Holy Spirit, enables me to become aware of God's compassionate presence and to dwell within that compassionate presence. The idea is that this mindful spirituality is accessible to all. One way to conceptualise mindful formation further is to look at the doctrine of spiritual senses – this can help us with intentional incarnational and embodied living.

I would like to suggest that my experience where my senses, body, emotions and awareness become aware of God can be seen as evidence for natural senses becoming spiritual senses. My experience is that God has communed with me through my natural God-given senses, that they are transformed into spiritual senses while remaining natural senses. That is, through them I can, as a graced response, also perceive the presence of God. Hans Urs von Balthasar is one theologian who has returned to the link between natural senses and spiritual senses. This is in reaction to what he calls an 'anti-incarnational' apophatic strand in Christian contemplation, where the Platonic influence encourages an ascent 'from all incarnate forms'.[198] De Maeseneer summarises Balthasar's doctrine of the spiritual senses.[199] Ignatian spirituality is one theological precedent for Balthasar's argument, but according to De Maeseneer, Balthasar also takes up the patristic idea of assumption and exchange of states: 'God participated in our life to let us share in the divine life. In the process of incarnation, cross and resurrection the human senses are assumed, and opened to a redeeming transformation.'[200] Our physical senses are taken up and transformed so that we can share the spiritual awareness that Jesus modelled for us in His body. Balthasar argues for this non-dualistic incarnational spirituality against the dominant paradigm of apophatic spirituality.

Stephen Fields summarises apophatic spirituality as stating 'that pure religion can be experienced only in "naked faith," a knowledge that entails negating both the intuitions of sensation and the formal judgments of the intellect'.[201] Balthasar argues that Platonic influence is responsible 'for the dualism between sensation and spirit that apophaticism presupposes'.[202] The reason for highlighting this dominant apophatic tradition is that Balthasar's incarnational spirituality could be described as

---

[198] Hans Urs von Balthasar, *The Glory of the Lord a Theological Aesthetics: Seeing the Form*, eds Joseph Fessio, SJ and John Riches, trans Erasmo Leiva-Merikakis (San Francisco, California: Ignatius Press, 1982), 307.
[199] See Yves De Maeseneer, 'Retrieving the Spiritual Senses in the Wake of Hans Urs von Balthasar', *Communio Viatorum* 55 (2013): 276-290.
[200] De Maeseneer, 281.
[201] Fields, 225.
[202] Fields, 226.

kataphatic.

Janet K Ruffing, in her exploration of kataphatic experience through qualitative research methods, also highlights that 'a strong bias in favour of apophatic styles in mystical experience has been dominant since the Counter-Reformation'.[203] In an expanded definition she defines kataphatic experience as incarnational and embodied:

> kataphatic refers to experiences of God which are mediated through one of God's creatures, either something external to the person such as nature, art, language, sound, ritual, another person, etc. or through a content of the person's consciousness such as visions, prophetic words or locutions.[204]

She also highlights dreams, bodily experiences and the symbolic as kataphatic in nature.[205] These overlap with the nature of my mindful spirituality, and so I can describe my mindful spirituality as kataphatic. I would argue that kataphatic spirituality supports the idea that natural senses can become spiritual senses, while remaining natural senses.

Why is this significant? Ruffing highlights that Christians presenting with kataphatic religious experiences are often discouraged by spiritual directors from exploring them.[206] She concludes that 'kataphatic experience is relegated to the beginning of the spiritual journey and excluded by definition from mature mystical development'.[207] She argues for kataphatic spirituality to be treated as of equal value to apophatic spirituality.[208] My spiritual experience is that mindfulness opens a window to kataphatic religious experience,

---

[203] Ruffing, 'The World Transfigured', 232.
[204] Ruffing, 'The World Transfigured', 232.
[205] Ruffing, 'The World Transfigured', 238-245.
[206] Ruffing, 'The World Transfigured', 232.
[207] Ruffing, 'The World Transfigured', 232.
[208] Ruffing, 'The World Transfigured', 233.

as evidenced in this chapter, with embodied ecstasy, natural symbols taking on spiritual significance, and mnemonic awareness of God's Word. This integration of secular mindfulness with mindfulness of God is an original pathway into kataphatic spirituality. I see kataphatic spirituality as more accessible than apophatic spirituality and a missional opportunity in our postmodern culture, because of its turn towards embodied mindfulness.

It is also significant that I am seeing my mindful spirituality as kataphatic and that in my spirituality I am seeking to reclaim my present moments. In my mindful spirituality, with its emphasis on the body, senses, breath and natural world, I am taken into the present moment because the body, breath and senses are always in the present moment. I am, therefore, arguing from this evidence that present moment focus, as well as being an important part of my spirituality, should be an important part of kataphatic spirituality more generally, as kataphatic spirituality also has the body and senses at its heart.

Reflection

Intention

Do you have an informed layer of reading that takes you deeper into theology, spirituality or psychology? I invite you to consider this. It may be that you have a different learning style and would rather approach this through podcasts or videos.

Attention

Are you aware of the Holy Spirit inhabiting your body, emotions, senses or imagination in your life? See if you can pay attention to such moments in the past and recall them. Perhaps even write them down. Meditate on Mark 9:15.

Attitude

One of the attitudes we can carry with us is the self-critical one that we are not clever, or not academic or can't study. This can often have been internalised at home or at school, or both. I invite you to notice this attitude and let it go. Consider the possibility that you can learn anything.

Reperceiving

Sometimes we need to reperceive our own self. Humility is knowing our potential, our strengths, as well as our developmental needs.

9
Three models for liberating our present moments

Introduction – towards three models

To help cultivate mindful formation I have created three models that help us conform no longer to the patterns of this world (Romans 12:2). The first model is about living by our values in ethical moments of choice. The second model enables us to navigate our relationship with God in time by cultivating moments of meeting with the divine. The third model is about attentional training using the ancient contemplative practices of the Jesus Prayer and *Lectio Divina*.

Model one: Living by my values

Within this exploration of my spiritual experience through mindful analysis is the shape of a model of how to cultivate ethical mnemonic awareness which enables me to live by my values, through an adaptation of Teasdale's Interacting Cognitive Subsystems theory and model, as outlined in the introduction. I believe living by our values is not just a biblical principle but also good for our spiritual and mental wellbeing. I apply it here with a new metacognitive proposition that if I try to save my life through anxiety, I will lose my life (my adaptation of Mark 8:35). Through meditating on this proposition, I can hold it in mnemonic awareness. As I do so, anxious thoughts come into my mind, triggering an automatic reaction to avoid a difficulty. I catch that thought in mindful awareness and recognise that if I give in to experiential avoidance, I will lose my life. I turn towards the difficulty, which is the wiser spiritual response. This process has enabled me to choose the thing of God (turning towards the difficulty) over the human thing jostling for my attention (avoidance).

Through mindful repetition the proposition becomes a metacognitive insight; through the remembered proposition I can relativise my anxious thoughts in the moment, as just thoughts. It is no longer an idea, a proposition; it has become a lived reality, an insight.

I can use the model with different propositions and teach others to find and adapt scriptural verses as metacognitive propositions; through meditating on them, these can also become insights held in ethical mnemonic awareness. As I use this model, I am further able to reclaim my present moments. This is a crucial model in allowing mindful formation. Take some time to do a value *examen* of your life.[209] What values (things of God) do you wish to live by in each ethical moment of choice? It is something you can do on a mindful walk. It can be helpful to make the values that are implicit more explicit, which needs time and reflection. You can also ask what are your most common automatic reactions? In conflict do you withdraw from others or go on the attack? An important part of mindful spirituality is to catch automatic reactions and replace them with wise responses that are in line with our values. Your values may be encapsulated in a biblical verse that you can meditate on as a metacognitive proposition.

Model two: Living in aware time

I outlined the implicit relational knowing theory I am using as an analogy earlier. This is the second model. Through this

---

[209] In Ignatius of Loyola's Spiritual Examen, I examine my life through the Holy Spirit to sense God at work, to see the light and the shadow in my life. See Mark E Thibodeaux, SJ, *Reimagining the Ignatian Examen* (Chicago, Illinois: Loyola Press, 2015), ix-x.

chapter I can see that I can use my analogy as an analogical conceptual model of the psychological and spiritual time within my lived experience of God's presence. This conceptual model enables me to make sense of my spiritual life. I can call this model 'the analogical implicit relationship with God'. Through conceptualising my relationship with God as one that is implicit, and still a form of knowing, I am able, for example, to trust God when I do not sense the divine presence. I can also learn not to limit what might be a 'moment of meeting'; I can consider every moment a possible moment of meeting. I can find moments of meeting when I inhabit my *spacious*, open and non-judgemental awareness. It is a model that I want to teach in this book on mindful formation. It is also a form of theological wisdom about how the spaciousness of awareness allows moments of meeting, and about how these moments of meeting continue to inhabit awareness. By being aware in the present moment and attentive to how God colours our moments in the here and now, it also means we don't add the weight of time (past and future) to that perceiving.

I have learned to pay attention to the 'markings', 'colour' and 'shape' of the moments of meeting in the same way I have learned to be attentive to butterflies on the Scargill estate. I have helped to record sightings of butterflies and other species there. These are checked by experts against photos we submit as evidence. Initially I misrecognised the butterflies through not paying enough attention to their markings, colour and shape. In the same way I have paid more attention to moments of meeting. I have noticed that while writing I sometimes have a moment of meeting where I notice ecstasy, enhanced creativity and a sense of oneness with the world. This is an awakened moment with words. Other moments have different markings, shape or colour.

When we are in a place of open awareness, then, in the present moment, I would further suggest we are most open to God's presence, promptings and revelation. We can remember the concerns of God. This is a pattern that fits my wider personal journey, recognising God's continuous mindfulness of me, which most of the time I am unaware of, and occasional moments of meeting. As I work with both models, the aim is to move towards a more continuous awareness of God which is a key aim of mindfulness of God. These models can be used by others as a second-person guide in their own journey towards mindfulness of God through this book. Both are central to mindful formation.

This implicit relationship with moments of meeting can also be evidenced at a wider level. The coming together in my life of the emergence of secular mindfulness and the hidden mindfulness of God strand is also, to me, a sign of God's implicit relationship with me, emerging explicitly in a profound moment of meeting. I see that God appears to be at work in my imaginative unconscious using symbols, symbolic language and associative logic. I read these convergences as graced responses. Another way of describing these experiences of hidden grace is to describe my personal narrative as parabolic. Ask God to reveal any experiences of hidden grace in your life. Take a mindful moment now to consider these.

It is my experience that the kingdom of God breaks through from the future into the present, and that secular mindfulness and mindfulness of God came into my ordinary reality as disruptive and healing kingdom gifts. This is looking for the *kairos* or right moment of the kingdom to break through into our present. Have you experienced any of these moments?

I am enabled through God's grace to reperceive the ordinary world and see God's mindfulness of me. There is a different form of knowing unfolding in these moments of reperceiving.

This is a personal God who has awakened me, my body, my awareness, my emotions, my soul, my senses, and has awakened a new language and way of seeing within me that is bigger than me but transforms me. I am also aware that I chose to go on pilgrimage on my own, to embrace silence and solitude. These are two important practices, alongside the pilgrimage walking and meditating on Scripture that seem to awaken the soul in me.

They were modelled for us by Jesus (Mark 1:35). I had forgotten that I had deliberately chosen to go on pilgrimage on my own to experience both silence and solitude. These ancient practices provide a form of further scaffolding that enables the spiritual to emerge – enabling gateways to God's presence to open.

Model three: Attentional training tools

I now come to the third model, which is the use of attentional training tools. I have adapted the Jesus Prayer, 'Lord Jesus Christ, Son of God, have mercy on me, a sinner,' as an attentional training tool. This enables us to reclaim our attentional capacities from their capture by the media sphere. Remember our life is what we pay attention to, and what we pay attention to forms us.

As I breathed the meditation in and out, I sought to be aware of any feelings that came into my awareness. As I pay attention to my breath, research says that I can become aware of feelings that might have been out of my awareness, as each emotion I feel has a different breathing pattern.[210] I did not try to control the breath. I used the muscle of attention: I focused my attention on the breath; my mind wandered; I noticed (through meta-awareness) that my mind had wandered, what it had wandered to and directed it back to the prayer. I adopted the sitting posture recommended by mindfulness teachers, holding my back straight, my feet on the ground, not using the back of the chair for support.[211] I am not sitting to learn how to sit, but as an embodied way of finding stillness. I could find stillness through walking or lying down.

We are trying to find a place of stillness or awareness, where the emphasis is not on thinking – we are watchful but not in an anxious, fearful way. We are hopefully watching for the

---

[210] Paul Grossman, 'Mindfulness for Psychologists: Paying Kind Attention to the Perceptible', *Mindfulness* 1, (2010): 92.
[211] See Danny Penman, *Mindfulness for Creativity: Adapt, Create and Thrive in a Frantic World* (London: Piatkus, 2015), 49.

kingdom that surrounds us, that is at hand. The Jesus Prayer is very helpful for simplifying the task of the mind. As I've mentioned, we often multitask, try to hold many things in our mind. We often don't put things down but leave them as open windows floating in our mind.

I did not use the prayer as a distraction to keep anxiety at bay, but to face the reality of it. I am using the language of secular mindfulness in all this description. In this spiritual practice I am switching from my narrative self to my experiential self and then to my witnessing self which held my thoughts, my feelings, my bodily sensations and my sense of God's presence in an open awareness. I realised that this was not about emptying my mind, which is not possible, but about stilling it and shifting into the place of open witnessing.[212] All this is in the service of being in the present moment and not being a victim of automatic mind wandering. My experience is that in both the awareness of my thoughts, feelings and bodily sensations, and my awareness of God, I am using the same incarnational capacities.

I followed a similar pattern with *Lectio Divina*. This slow meditative reading of Scripture has a long history but the teaching of it does not usually emphasise how it can be an embodied practice. I first came across this meditative reading of Scripture in a book on preaching, but really developed a practice through going to Worth Abbey, the Roman Catholic Benedictine monastery. I found a book called *Finding Sanctuary* by the then Abbot, Christopher Jamison, a particular doorway into the contemplative.[213] When I practise it daily, I adopt the same embodied posture as with the Jesus Prayer. I notice my breathing.

I use a physical Bible that I can hold in my hands, turning physical pages. I also use the muscle of attention – focusing on

---

[212] Ruby Wax, *Sane New World: Taming the Mind* (London: Hodder & Stoughton, 2013), 136.
[213] Christopher Jamison, *Finding Sanctuary: Monastic Steps for Everyday Life* (London: Phoenix, 2006), 60-66.

Scripture, my mind wanders, I notice through meta-awareness that my mind has wandered, I direct it back to Scripture. The focus is usually on a short passage. Implicit in the instructions to read, meditate, pray and find a place of contemplation is the idea that this practice also arrives at an open, receptive space to simply contemplate God – which I hypothesise is the same space I find in secular meditative practices. I am using the Christian practices for a different intention – a spiritual one not a therapeutic one. However, this is built on the realisation that I could use secular mindfulness practices for spiritual intention, as they had implicitly led me into a spiritual place incarnationally.

The intention would be to reperceive myself, others, God, the world, to perceive as God intends me to perceive. I intentionally made my version of *Lectio Divina* an embodied, attentional training practice, like the mindful awareness practices of secular mindfulness, using insights about the link between breath and emotion and intentionally using the muscle of attention. This reshaping of the *Lectio Divina* is a novel application of it, using secular mindfulness theory. The adaptation of the Jesus Prayer and *Lectio Divina* as attentional training tools is part of the third model of attentional training that enables mindful formation. An adapted *Lectio Divina* is also used to memorise scriptural values which can then emerge into awareness in ethical moments of choice, as 'things of God' as part of my ethical mnemonic awareness model.

Conclusion

These models answer the question, 'Yes, but how am I mindful of God?' and play a key part in mindful formation. The good news is that as we pay attention to our present moments, cultivate intentional ethical values, practise the Jesus Prayer and meditate on Scripture, our attention becomes graced attention.

In the next chapter I answer the question, 'Who am I in the present moment?' Who I am in the present moment is different from who I am in mental time travel, and in the present moment

I am more open to the graced workings of the Holy Spirit. These models are also a form of meta-cognition, helping us to know why we are doing what we are doing.

Reflection

Intention
To be able to focus our attention on God without being held captive by internal or external distractions is a central intention in mindfulness of God. Can you intentionally set aside time each day (I invite you to do this first thing in the morning) to train your attention, using the models above? Start with a *Lectio Divina* on Mark 4:1-9.

Attention
I am arguing that our God-given capacities for attention and awareness are central for living the good life. This is a metacognitive proposition! Work with the proposition, wrestle with it and meditate on it. When it becomes an insight, it moves from your head to your heart, and you will find it much easier to be intentional about training your attention.

Attitude
One of the key attitudes to note as you try to cultivate your attention is restlessness, boredom or irritation. Try to surf the wave of restlessness and don't allow it to distract you into distractions.

Reperceiving
Becoming aware of our implicit relationship with God where the divine presence is always there but often out of our awareness can help us reperceive our relationship with God. Have there been moments of meeting with God where, after a period of apparent absence, you have realised that God had been there?

10
Who am I in the present moment?

Introduction

Who am I in the present moment? This question has a theological perspective. It also has a basis in recognition theory: it is about being recognised as who we really are. It is very important to be recognised by God and others in a mutual way. However, who I am is more often not recognised in the present moment by others. Sometimes I do not recognise myself. But it is in the present moment that I have the potential to be most fully my own self. Here I take up some of the insights of recognition theory, along with a theological perspective on what needs to be recognised. To know who I am I need to know my God-given creative form within. This echoes an Eastern Orthodox idea developed particularly by Maximus the Confessor, that each of us is a word, 'its own "logos"', spoken by God.[214] In that speaking I have been recognised with God and given the clearest sense of who I am in the present moment.

Logos theology

Rowan Williams takes up this idea of the little *logos* within, not only for our own life but also for the life of others, 'finding a way to speak to them that resonates with the creative word

---

[214] Rowan Williams, *Silence and Honey Cakes* (Oxford: Lion, 2003), 72. See also his footnote on page 121 referencing Maximus the Confessor as the main source of this idea.

working in their depths'.[215] This is an example of awakened language awakening language in another, which is an aspect of the mindful spirituality I wish to embody. This calling out the God-given word in each other is a type of kingdom language. I say more about awakened kingdom language in Chapters Fifteen to Seventeen on the mindful rule. This idea resonates with me because I think the making of me at boarding school was a reducing of me. As a minister I have often had people see me in a distorted way, and in doing so they disengaged from my humanity, believing they could say whatever they liked to me – often something intended to reduce me further.[216]

I am aware that with the idea of the creative God-given word in each person, I am working with another theological fragment. Sylvie Avakian develops this idea in dialogue with her context, drawing on the theology of Maximus the Confessor. At the centre of what she calls *Logos* (the Word) theology is 'the divine *Logos*, or Word, the ontological reality of every created existence, since it is through the *Logos* that everything has been made'.[217] This *Logos* theology is drawn from John's Gospel: 'In the beginning was the Word, and the Word was with God, and the Word was God. He was with God in the beginning. Through him all things were made ...' (John 1:1-3). I am 'spoken' into being by the Word. This also means that everyone else is spoken into being by the Word, and this is another reason to recognise them as persons.

As the theology is developed, it is recognised that 'every human being has his/her "purpose" or "meaning" in God,

---

[215] Rowan Williams, *Silence*, 73.
[216] Carrie Doehring, *Taking Care: Monitoring Power Dynamics and Relational Boundaries in Pastoral Care and Counselling* (Nashville, Tennessee: Abingdon Press, 1995), 13-19. In this book, drawing on psychodynamic theory, Doehring has this theme of disengagement from the humanity of another as a running theme.
[217] Sylvie Avakian, 'Christian Spirituality: Maximus the Confessor A Challenge to the 21st Century', *International Congregational Journal*, 14, no.2 (winter 2015): 72.

namely every human being has (or is) a word or a *logos*'; however, it is only together as the '*logoi*' or 'the words' that we 'form the one *Logos*, the Christ'.[218] In the mindful rule at the end of this book we need each other; we are incomplete without each other. To see this completeness, we need to keep helping others find their purpose or meaning in God. I am also arguing that the creative word in each of us is awakened through gracious kingdom language. This includes, in mindfulness terms, our self-language – how we talk to our own being.

The *Logos* theology can also be illustrated with a story. In Matthew 16:13-20, Jesus asks His disciples, 'Who do people say the Son of Man is?' The disciples name different prophets: John the Baptist, Elijah, Jeremiah. He then asks them, 'But what about you? ... Who do you say I am?'

Simon Peter answers, 'You are the Messiah, the Son of the living God.' Jesus replies by calling him 'Simon son of Jonah', and commends him for his insight which He says was revealed to Simon by 'my Father in heaven'. Jesus then says quite deliberately, 'And I tell you that you are Peter, and on this rock I will build my church.' Here Simon is given a new name, Peter, 'the rock', which can be reframed as the *logos* inside him. In this way Simon, now Peter, can be an archetypal disciple for all of us in having the God-given creative word inside him revealed by Christ.

Balthasar seems to say something like *Logos* theology in relation to this story of Simon Peter. Each of us is given a mission and 'the mission itself is christoform, exhibiting the character of the Word, the Logos'.[219] Balthasar develops this idea to say, 'In obeying his calling a person fulfils his essence, although he would never have been able to discover this, his own archetype and ideal within himself' through 'studying his predispositions, yearnings, talents, his potential'.[220] This 'archetype' could be seen as his own God-given creative *logos*.

---

[218] Avakian, 72.
[219] Balthasar, *Prayer*, 60.
[220] Balthasar, *Prayer*, 60.

What is important as well is the point Balthasar goes on to make of our dependency on God, not only for that inner archetype or *logos* but also for His help in finding it. 'Simon the fisherman could have explored every region of his ego prior to his encounter with Christ, but he would not have found "Peter" there.'[221] The reason for this is that 'the "form" summed up in the name "Peter", the particular mission reserved for him alone, is hidden in the mystery of Christ's soul'.[222] I can play my part in preparing good soil for the creative word inside me, but I still need Christ's prior grace to reveal my inner *logos*, my archetype, or as Balthasar also calls it, my 'authentic reality'.[223] In this story I see that the as yet undeveloped *logos* inside Simon has become an actualised event in his life, when he becomes Peter. This gives me hope.

I draw on early contemplative history, which is anthropological in insight, through the idea of *Logos* theology developed by Maximus the Confessor and others. I am attracted to the idea that I am a little *logos* spoken into being by the *Logos*, Christ. I am a word spoken by the Light to be light, and I recognise that every person is a *logos*. This little *logos* has a capacity that can expand and stretch; it is not limited in nature. It can become a cathedral, a world within me. It has space for others, God and creation.

The existential task is to recognise the creative word within. Recognition theory is needed here. What started as a personal journey found its way to the theory of recognition, which helped shape my ethical view on life. In recognition theory I treat people with respect because they are persons, not just individuals.

As a minister I have often been misrecognised. Psychodynamic theory, with its recognition of the distorted dimension of relationships through transference and projection, was very helpful in understanding this experience. I expand on

---

[221] Balthasar, *Prayer*, 60.
[222] Balthasar, *Prayer*, 60.
[223] Balthasar, *Prayer*, 59.

this theory later. The reaction to me as a minister at a time of crisis during lockdown from some, drawing on psychodynamic theory and the ethics of recognition, can also be seen as those people disengaging from my humanity, as misrecognising me as a threat, someone to be feared, and the projected fantasy image of me to be destroyed.[224] The mindful rule and recognition theory as I apply them are the subversive resistance to all such distortions in relationship.

Recognition theory

Recognition theory works from the premise that freedom 'in the sense of independence from others' is illusory.[225] One part of recognition theory that I am trying to walk is the idea that freedom comes from 'knowing oneself in otherness'.[226] It is in community with others that I find true freedom. I must also cultivate self-awareness, an ability to regulate my emotions and my words, and transcend my automatic self-focus. Part of mindful formation is to recognise and inhabit our relational connectedness.

This awakening requires the recognition of the creative word in one's own self and in others, and the recognition of God as the one who interlaces and transforms us. Recognition is not just a theory but an intuitively recurring word in my writing. I recognise my context. I recognise the unconscious elements of my story, I recognise I have mindful states of mind, I recognise I need to own my trauma, I recognise I was shaped to be loyal, that I had an inner critic. I recognise the importance of my early idyllic life in Kenya that acts as a counterbalance to the trauma of boarding school. I recognise shame as a recurring theme alongside anxiety.

---

[224] See Doehring, *Taking Care*, 13-19.
[225] Heikki Ikaheimo, 'Causes for Lack of Recognition: From the Secular to the Non-Secular', 59, in Kahlos, Koskinen & Palmen, *Recognition and Religion: Contemporary and Historical Perspectives*.
[226] Ikaheimo, 59.

I first came across the ethics of recognition as a 'theological fragment' in a partly autoethnographic book on shame by Stephen Pattison. His argument is that those who have been shamed need to go on a journey of recognition about their own part in sustaining submission and oppression. Once this is recognised, the shamed person can resist this aspect of culture.[227] This idea that as a shamed person I have agency resonated with me. In my spiritual journey, I am trying to relativise anxiety, shame and shame-anxiety, and so need to go on a journey of recognition about my agency and the part culture has played in shaming me.

Recognition as a theory is simply and profoundly relational, 'to recognize someone is to grant another human being a positive normative status based on her personhood'.[228] That this theory recognises the centrality of relationship in our shaping as human beings resonates with me as a Christian. This summary statement can be broken down into further dimensions. This granting of the status of personhood also has an active element in that 'an act of recognition means taking and *treating* the other as a person'.[229]

What does it mean to treat another as a person? The first dimension is that the other person is treated with 'respect', recognising others as 'rational autonomous beings', which is 'based on the equal dignity of all peoples'.[230] In recognition theory, respect is not earned but given.[231] As a Christian I believe all people are made in the image of God and are persons who should be recognised as such (Genesis 1:26).

The second dimension is 'esteem', where one's unique context is recognised, including 'personal, cultural, ethnic, or

---

[227] Pattison, *Shame*, 178.
[228] Kahlos, Koskinen and Palmen, 1.
[229] Kahlos, Koskinen and Palmen, 1, treating is in my italics.
[230] Kahlos, Koskinen and Palmen, 1.
[231] See Richard Sennett, *Respect: The Formation of Character in an Age of Inequality* (London: Penguin Books, 2003), 63-64, where he points out the major thrust of our culture on having to 'earn' respect.

religious identities'.[232] I worked in one of the most religiously and ethnically diverse boroughs in London for twenty-three years and recognised that the context of each person was central to my approach.

Finally, recognition theory appreciates that the 'unique individual personhood' in another can elicit '*love* and friendship' from another.[233] The more general respect and esteem to all is balanced by a more focused love and friendship for some. As a Christian I am called to go beyond respect and esteem for all others and recognise that I am to love even my enemies (Matthew 5:44).

I made an associative link between recognition theory and mindfulness, whose change of perspective of reperceiving can be conceptualised as a form of recognition. Through mindful awareness, I recognise reality more clearly. Through self-awareness, I recognise myself more clearly. Through a mindful gaze directed towards others, I recognise others more clearly. In mindfulness of God, I am looking to recognise God more clearly (through God's own self-revelation to me). As I recognise God, God helps me to recognise myself. As I do this, I can change the way I perceive myself, and this may help address the way shame distorts this view. This is where recognition theory put into practice can be transformative for myself and others. Through a God-given recognition of the other as a person, someone to be esteemed and honoured, as someone who could be a friend, I can speak in a way that builds them up and does not pull them down. I place this mindful recognition at the centre of my mindful rule in the process of formation. Attention and awareness bring recognition, and recognition brings freedom.

One of the questions contemporary recognition theory asks is why is recognition so difficult for us when it is 'ontologically foundational' to our flourishing?[234] Recognition appears not to

---

[232] Kahlos, Koskinen and Palmen,1.
[233] Kahlos, Koskinen and Palmen, 2.
[234] Ikaheimo, 51.

be automatic but requires 'capacities or skills' that may not have been cultivated.[235] It may also be that an individual realises that there are 'costs' to recognition, which 'leads to reluctance to grant it'.[236] In recognition theory there is then both a conscious awareness of recognition and a choosing not to do it because as an individual one might have to give something up in recognising the other, and for some an inability to recognise through lack of capacity. This is a brief summary; however, I would also argue that mindful theory with its emphasis on our inability to see clearly, its recognition of our distorted perceptive capacities, also helps explain why recognising each other as persons is difficult.[237] It is also a possibility that mindfulness, with its capacity to help us to perceive ourselves, God and others more clearly, can help us recognise the other as a person worthy of respect and esteem.

Conclusion

Who am I in the present moment? To be mindfully formed I need to recognise, with the help of the Holy Spirit, my God-given creative form within (little *logos*). The more I inhabit this identity the more I am living in the fullness of life. Another key aspect of mindful formation is to move from being an individual to being a person – recognising I am in connected relationship with others, God and creation. Paradoxically, it is self-examination and openness to the gaze of God that enables this transition – I cannot change without self-awareness. That joint attention between our self-awareness and God also needs to examine our past. We look at this in the next chapter.

---

[235] Ikaheimo, 51.
[236] Ikaheimo, 51.
[237] See Vago and Silbersweig, 2, for our distorted perceiving, and how mindfulness reduces such bias.

Reflection

Intention

The question, 'Who am I in the present moment?' is an important one. I am more fully alive in the present moment, less restricted than when I am in mental time travel. Make it an intention of your self-work to ask yourself: who might I be in the present moment? You might have an inkling – you might not – but use *Logos* theology and recognition theory to create an idea.

Attention

Pay attention to when you've been recognised in a valuing way, and when you have been misrecognised. Perhaps unhappiness and sadness in your life have come from times when you have been misrecognised. Resolve to go on a journey of recognition. Use Peter's story in Matthew 16:13-20 as a meditation.

Attitude

It may be that you have misrecognised your own self. Perhaps you have internalised negative judgements about yourself from family, school or work (or other loved ones). Resolve to let go of these negative scripts.

Reperceiving

Recognition theory says we cannot fully be a person unless we are in relationship with others. If your trust in others has been damaged, this can be difficult to repair. Ask the Holy Spirit to help you reperceive this paradox: needing community and relationship and yet fearing it. Ask for courage to go forward in seeking community.

11
Liberating the past through mindfulness of God

Introduction – an encounter with trauma

We have been looking at reclaiming our present moments to find our home with God. I am aware from my own experience of trauma that the past can overwhelm our ability to be in the present. My own integrative and relational training as a therapist, which included psychodynamic theory and the realisation of how the past impacts the present, has also influenced me theoretically.

As part of the central theme of reclaiming the present moment, I also need to reclaim my here and now from the shadow of the past, especially the trauma of being sent to boarding school. Mindfulness theory argues that reality and wellbeing are found by being in the present moment. My sense is that my anxious thoughts are a symptom of distorted narratives, some out of my awareness, from my traumatic boarding school past. In these next chapters I try to answer our third and deeper quest question: 'How can we be fully aware of and at home in our whole embodied self, to further reclaim our present moments?' Or in other words, how can we live life in all its fullness? To do this, we need in part to inhabit with awareness the rooms of our past. This brings freedom. This is incarnational mindful spirituality and the heart of mindful formation. What is true for me is also true for many others: the past, and especially trauma, can overshadow our present life and take us out of the present moment.

You might be sceptical about the use of the word trauma, but there have been helpful changes in the way it is defined. Grosch-Miller defines trauma as 'the response generated when our capacity to adapt is overwhelmed'.[238] In addition, and this is an important aspect of embodied trauma theory:

> It is now clear that trauma is not an external event. Rather it is a specific and automatic collection of physiological responses to an event, which are triggered when an individual's or community's adaptive capacity is overwhelmed.[239]

The clear reality, as Grosch-Miller puts it, is that 'We have no choice about whether to be traumatised or what specific trauma response happens.' This has enabled me to examine myself compassionately and begin to trust myself again.[240] Pastorally, this is a very helpful insight, enabling us to free ourselves of negative self-judgements as if being traumatised was our fault.

I became aware of how the past was impacting my present when a counsellor pointed out my present anxiety was a result of going to boarding school as a young child. Have any remarks from wise people enabled you to have insights about your past?

I then explored what psychotherapy said, through books and articles, about the impact of boarding school. I outline this in this chapter. The most surprising (but accurate) finding was that boarding school can be traumatic. The meaning of the word trauma has shifted as theory has developed. My reading of Schaverien's use of the word 'trauma' for boarding school is that it is based on the evidence presented by her clients – that for many it is an unbearable experience that is dissociated from and

---

[238] Carla A Grosch-Miller, *Trauma and Pastoral Care* (Norwich: Canterbury Press, 2021), 4.

[239] Megan Warner, et al, 'Introduction', in *Tragedies and Christian Congregations: The Practical Theology of Trauma*, eds Megan Warner, et al (London, New York: Routledge, 2020), 1.

[240] Grosch-Miller, *Trauma*, 8.

buried in the unconscious.

In this chapter I tell the story of the development of my understanding of my boarding school experience chronologically. In the next chapter I then spiral back to it (using spiral learning theory which is helpful for complex concepts), each time picking up more insights from trauma theory. I present those insights that helped me understand my trauma and hope that they will help you.

What I outline in the chapter on trauma will help you make an informed decision about how you want to reclaim your present from your past. That doesn't have to mean retelling your story – it could be looking at the impact of trauma on your present, or simply reclaiming your present moments.

I then listened to the different parts of my self in relation to my boarding school experience. This forms another chapter in which I will invite you to listen to your own self.

Being sent to boarding school at an early age is only more recently being recognised as trauma. My experience is a helpful case study as trauma theory has changed and now recognises that many more aspects of life can be experienced as traumatic than just major disasters. It may be as you read this you are able to recognise symptoms in your life as traumatic symptoms.

The impact of boarding school

In 2006 a counsellor highlighted how my boarding school experience may have contributed to my mental health distress. After this insight I began reading about therapeutic work with boarding school survivors in Nick Duffell's psychological book. In this chapter I pick up on the insights from my initial reading of this book. I realised, as part of this journey, that the distorted narrative self I became aware of was also a spiritual issue. If I was to be more mindful of God, I needed to transform the boarding school past that was impacting my present.

I had ordered another book on boarding school experience, which became particularly evocative for me. This was Joy Schaverien's book about boarding school syndrome (BSS). I had been avoiding it and circling around it for some years since buying it in May 2016. Mindful theory argues that therapeutically it is important to turn and face reality, and I argue this is a mindfulness of God principle as well.[241] I therefore finally turned towards the book and revisited the experience of boarding school from her perspective. As I read Schaverien's first chapter it told my story in words that were empirical, psychological and exact, but evocative beyond words for me. It was only after I had read the book that I realised up to that moment I had no words of my own for my experience or the depth of my trauma, but Schaverien gave me the exact words as if she had been there with me.

I also returned to Duffell's book for some theoretical insight. My recognition of needing to own the trauma resonated with his 'five stages of healing' for a boarding school survivor, which includes 'acknowledging being wounded' and accepting our own survival instincts.[242] The key question is: how can I access and heal this dissociated part of myself? I can do it in an integrative way, drawing on therapeutic, contemplative and theological insights – to become self-aware. This is part of my mindful stance, but Duffell also argues that self-awareness is the way out of the survival personality boarding school survivors create.[243]

I wish to cultivate this self-awareness in the service of reclaiming my present moments to be mindful of God, so that I am not overwhelmed with anxious thoughts whose origin lie in this childhood trauma. I am aware that as I am more mindful of God, I may become less anxious; however, my intention here is a spiritual one, not a therapeutic one. I am entering the realm

---

[241] Brown, Ryan and Cresswell, 'Mindfulness: Theoretical Foundations', 213, discuss facing reality in mindfulness and the facing of difficulties through acceptance and non-judgement. They also talk about exposure as part of mindfulness practice which helps us deal with difficult reality, see page 226.
[242] Duffell, 220-221.
[243] Duffell, xii.

of the psychodynamic, the contemplative and the symbolic as I explore this wordless experience I have dissociated from. As outlined earlier, I require a different form of representation, which is more poetic, symbolic and expressive, as such trauma is harder to access through logical, propositional language.

Emergence of trauma

It was important that I became aware and able to name my boarding school experience as traumatic and not minimise it. I sensed that it could be analysed symbolically for the unconscious material I had repressed which was literally unspeakable:

> The Boarding School Syndrome is created as a necessary defence against unbearable experiences. The dismantling of such defences is not a process lightly undertaken.[244]

A key word for this depth work is that it is crystallising, and crystallising slowly. I have placed a line of awareness into my unconscious, and the quest pilgrimage has crystallised around that line. However, it is a slow process, and some elements can only crystallise at the right moment. Only now does it seem the right moment to listen to the unspoken voice of my boarding school childhood.

A response to Schaverien's narrative

I have been implicitly working on the past since 1997 when I started my counselling and psychotherapy training. I journalled the impact of reading the first few chapters of Schaverien's book on Wednesday 25th October 2018:

> I had a disturbed night and Clare told me I was shouting in my sleep. I woke up early with a splitting headache, feeling sick and as if I had a temperature. My neck,

---

[244] Schaverien, 61.

shoulders and lower back were tight like armour, and this tension had brought on the headache. It was as if I had re-experienced the trauma as I slept. I was able to use a mindfulness practice called the body scan to relax my body in the moment. What I wanted to do was to use mindfulness to find a place of open awareness where I could allow the past to emerge in safety.

This was the emergence of long-buried traumatic reactions. We don't always know what will trigger them, but it is important to seek help from a trauma professional if this ever happens to you. Although it is difficult to tell a coherent story of our trauma, I have found my engagement with narrative helpful. For example, listening to the stories in Schaverien's book helped me recognise my own.

Conclusion

I am aware that this story of my boarding school experience has been the most difficult to write. Trauma theory, which I return to, helps explain this, but Schaverien also makes a crucial point. This insight has been working its way out of my unconscious into my awareness like a splinter. She recognises that 'what is lost in boarding school is the narrative function for emotional experience'.[245] She adds that the 'unspeakable loss causes a psychological freezing: the child is literally "lost for words"'.[246] It is through this piecing together of my narrative that I have been able to experience my unfreezing. Listening to one's own self can be the beginning of a narrative.

Trauma is more prevalent than people often realise in their lives. I want to spiral back to trauma theory in the next chapter to expand on how it has helped me, in the hope that my insights might help others find a pathway to freedom.

Some reflection on how we have been shaped or formed in

---

[245] Schaverien, 117.
[246] Schaverien, 141.

our childhood or as a young adult can be a helpful intention. In Hampstead there are a number of ponds on the Heath. Some are suitable for swimming in; others have warning signs about not swimming because of underwater obstacles. You would only see these obstacles if the pond were drained because the water is clean but not clear, and the ponds are very deep. Sometimes we know that there are underwater obstacles in our past that make venturing there more difficult. Sometimes we don't. Others know that their childhood was mostly healthy and nourishing. That makes a decision about the intention to swim or explore the pond of our past more complex. It may be something you can do in discussion with a wise person. For me, visiting my past was one of the most difficult yet transformative things I have done.

Reflection

Intention
What is your intention when it comes to visiting your past in a reflective way or with a wise person?

Attention
What you can do is notice if it is obvious some elements of your past are impacting your present moments. You might be aware that you are defensive, fearful of rejection or don't trust easily. These are helpful clues about the need for any self-work around our past. Perhaps read the story of Joseph and his brothers again, how God redeemed his present in spite of his past trauma (Genesis 37-50).

Attitude
One thing we can also notice is our self-critical voice which originates in our past. You might have judgemental attitudes towards your own self (or others). Try to cultivate an attitude of self-compassion and compassion for others. You might use the Ananias Prayer mentioned earlier:

May the love of Christ take hold of me,
May the light of Christ shine in my heart,
May the love of Christ flow through me like a river.

You can extend this out to friends and family, strangers, enemies, other groups in the world.

Reperceiving

We can have fixed views on our past that are not realistic. We can be in denial about some of the difficulties or see them in more black-and-white terms. Try to cultivate a more open perceiving of your past.

12
A spiral learning approach to trauma

Embodied trauma theory and me

Following the emergence of old trauma in July 2020 I began to read embodied trauma theory in more depth. I revisited my boarding school experience in the light of a further consideration of embodied trauma theory as developed by pioneers such as Bessel van der Kolk and Peter Levine.[247] This is part of the spiralling back to key concepts to engage with them in more depth – allowing understanding to emerge without expecting to understand it all the first time around. The self-interviews I did where I listened to different parts of my self (see the next chapter) could in my experience be a way of getting in touch with the 'felt sense', which 'is our capacity to tune into what our bodies know'.[248] This works because trauma is stored in the body.[249] The self-interviews also enabled me to name aspects of the trauma which is a key aspect in the resolution of trauma.[250]

Let me briefly outline some of the key aspects of trauma

---

[247] Bessel van der Kolk, *The Body Keeps the Score: Mind, Brain and Body in the Transformation of Trauma* (London: Penguin Books, 2014), and Peter A Levine, *Healing Trauma* (Boulder, Colorado: Sounds True, 2008).
[248] Grosch-Miller, *Trauma*, 19.
[249] Hilary Ison, 'Working with an embodied and systemic approach to trauma and tragedy', in *Tragedies and Christian Congregations: The Practical Theology of Trauma*, ed Megan Warner, et al (London, New York: Routledge, 2020), 47-63. See also Grosch-Miller, *Trauma*, 20.
[250] Ison, 59.

theory, as summarised by Ison and by Grosch-Miller, and drawing on Bessel van der Kolk and Peter Levine, that helped me. This strand of embodied trauma theory suggests that my training in talking therapy is unable to help me with my trauma because trauma is not stored in narrative form.[251] This resonates with my experience that I had no words for my boarding school trauma. The trauma is stored in my emotional brain, and the energy of 'rage and terror' associated with trauma is frozen and trapped there.[252] This resonated with me because I had felt rage and terror, frozen and trapped, in a traumatic incident during lockdown.

I went back to read Schaverien and found that rage and terror emerged in her work with a boarding school survivor.[253] Through rereading Schaverien I can now own and name that rage and terror, and the sense of being frozen. In another element of overlap, it is practices such as mindfulness that enable the frozen emotions to be 'titrated' safely and unfrozen because mindfulness enhances our capacity for self-regulation of difficult thoughts, feelings and sensations.[254]

My interpretation is that when I first read Schaverien I unconsciously blanked these two words: terror and rage. My sense is that I needed to unfreeze them in a safe way. Another piece of evidence that supports this felt sense is that Schaverien notes the survivor's 'extreme self-control' to contain the rage and terror.[255] My self-control, especially at times of conflict, is very strong. I remain calm and do not express anger, even though sometimes I should. This has been both helpful and unhelpful, leading to times when I have not defended myself when it was appropriate to do so.

---

[251] van der Kolk, 47.

[252] Levine, *Healing Trauma*, 29.

[253] Schaverien, 49-53.

[254] Ison summarises why mindfulness is helpful in enhancing self-regulation of difficult thoughts, feelings and sensations, 57. She talks about titration on page 58.

[255] Schaverien, 86.

As Levine points out, because there is no coherent narrative to work with, 'you don't have to consciously remember an event to heal from it'.[256] As I read Levine's theory, I could feel the edges of the rage and terror shifting and had a sense of how I have held myself stiffly ever since – and that I could move into a free running state full of fluid energy. This includes the awareness of how my body has been set like concrete and needs loosening up, with back pain, stiff neck and tight shoulders. This profound model of trauma theory can work alongside my uncovering of the schemas and distorted narrative self. Do you have issues with your neck or lower back which could be about storing unresolved emotions?

Trauma past and present

I am drawn back to the trauma theory I have accessed so far, as I focus again on my own story of childhood and present-day trauma during the Covid-19 pandemic, in this spiral process of revisiting key aspects of my journey. I believe these past and present experiences to be connected. It may also help me reclaim my present moments to some extent from the past. There appears to be a growing consensus in embodied trauma theory about the origin of trauma and how to deal with it. I have briefly outlined some key elements already that relate to my research. Here I present a short summary of further salient points for understanding trauma that have helped me.

When the focus is on an event assumed not to have traumatic capability – for example, boarding school – then the traumatic responses of children can be overlooked. Trauma, when it invades the present, can overwhelm us, and I have experienced that, when something reminds in the present of the experience of the past. This is especially possible when the trauma is unrecognised and unresolved, as was the case for me.

One of the key insights from trauma theory is that for trauma, 'the rational brain is basically impotent to talk the

---

[256] Levine, *Healing Trauma*, 31.

emotional brain out of its own reality'.[257] This is because, according to a growing consensus, the trauma is stored in the body and emotional brain, but not as a coherent accessible story.[258] Because in trauma we often dissociate from it, as in my experience, the trauma remains unresolved and can overwhelm the present. I believe this happened in 2006 when I was very anxious, stressed and close to breakdown.

I also believe the trauma for me was re-triggered, in a new way, during the Covid-19 pandemic and lockdown, where shaming and scapegoating language was aimed at me and others, and I felt overwhelmed and powerless to do anything about it. I experienced it as a severe traumatic blow. I saw the negative impact on my mental health and the mental health of others, ending up in A&E and requiring six weeks off work for possible angina and stress. I foreshadow this here because sometimes out of the blue, 'Bad things happen – things that knock the wind out of us, that bring us to our knees, that shatter the world as we know it.'[259] It was as if I was back at boarding school, feeling helpless and powerless. This shattering of the world I knew had a profound impact on the immediate direction of my life.

One of the strongest non-negotiable values that came out of my boarding school experience is to be very careful what I say to people, having seen the destructive impact of critical language on children and young people away from home. I realised as well how easily community fragments under pressure – and the lack of a 'rule of life' in a local church means anything goes in terms of covert and overt exercise of power.

So, if we do not talk through the trauma, what do we do? This is where the trauma theory overlaps very much with mindfulness theory. We work with what has been called our 'felt sense', listening to what our body and gut tells us – for this we need mindful self-awareness.[260] A key element of this is allowing

---

[257] van der Kolk, 47.
[258] Ison, 49.
[259] Warner, et al, 'Introduction', 1.
[260] Ison, 58.

ourselves to experience what we are feeling and to 'name' it.[261] This brings a resolution to the trauma that enables better regulation of our emotions in the present.[262]

Trauma and trust

Trauma and our sense of trust in the world are also connected. I feel the weight of two statements about trust in my self-interviews that I haven't explored: 'so you can never quite trust those times, moments of happiness with your family because it's just going to be taken away again'. It is not just about moments of happiness but also about people: 'I think as an adult there has been a fear that I can't quite trust people, they will (*swallows*) abandon me.' I know this goes back to my childhood experience of separation at boarding school, where I was left watchful in a 'keep me safe' way. I first came across Kai Erikson's sociological theory of trauma in Kate Wiebe's reflections on collective trauma.[263] In a more allusive style of writing, Erikson highlights that a central traumatic response for individuals and communities is the fracturing of trust:

> The mortar bonding human communities together is made up at least in part of trust and respect and decency and, in moments of crisis, of charity and concern. It is profoundly disturbing to people when these expectations are not met ... They have already been made vulnerable by a sharp trick of fate, and now they must face the future without those layers of emotional insulation that only a trusted communal surround can provide.[264]

---

[261] Ison, 59.
[262] Ison, 57-58.
[263] Kate Wiebe, 'Toward a Faith-Based Approach to Healing after Collective Trauma', in *Tragedies and Christian Congregations: The Practical Theology of Trauma,* eds Megan Warner, et al (London: Routledge, 2020), 64-78. Kai Erikson, *A New Species of Trouble: The Human Experience of Modern Disasters* (New York, London: W W Norton & Company, 1994).
[264] Erikson, 239.

Wiebe puts it more starkly: 'trauma breaks your sense of trust in yourself, your relationships, and the world'.[265] This was another sharp fragment of truth that pierced my consciousness. Following the event that I experienced as a traumatic blow during lockdown, my ability to trust myself, some others and even the local church was broken.

My subsequent experience of intentional community life has begun to restore my sense of trust. I revisit my analogical conceptual model of being in an implicit relationship with God considering this insight about trust and realise it has enabled me to continue to trust in God in difficult times when I cannot perceive God's providential care or presence. In this it can function as a model to help cultivate and sustain trust.

As you read this story of my past and my psychological, spiritual and theological reflection on it, you may have become aware of the shadow of your own past. You don't need to retraumatise yourself by going back there. You might need help from a trauma specialist. You can do a simple self-interview and listen to yourself. Try to create some intuitive questions about the impact of your past on your present. Even just naming something in your past as traumatic can begin to bring healing.

I have outlined how the past can impact our present, and few of us escape from its shadow. I have also drawn on trauma theory to show how we can experience many things as traumatic that haven't necessarily filtered into the public consciousness. I have talked about how I learned to listen to myself, and I pick up on that in the next chapter to help you consider that self-work for yourself. One aspect of a wider stance on this is stories that haven't been told.

Trauma and poetics

I have recognised that my story of trauma and accessing it required poetic representation, what Walton calls 'poetics'. I've spoken about representation and poetics in an earlier chapter

---

[265] Wiebe, 68.

and spiral back to it here as another aspect of it is uncovered with trauma. I am asking the question, does what I am doing here with boarding school trauma resonate with any of the wider cultural and theological strands Walton outlines in her work on poetics? One of the meeting points between poetics and practical theology is the work of Rebecca Chopp on 'metaphor, trauma and testimony'.[266] Chopp brings together poetics and testimony: 'The poetics of testimony is my way of naming the discursive practices and various voices that seek to describe or name that which rational discourse will not or cannot reveal.'[267] This is especially true of writings that 'speak of the unspeakable and tell of the suffering and hope of particular communities who have not been authorized to speak'.[268]

My story of boarding school trauma which was literally unspeakable is a form of testimony and sits within the poetics of testimony as outlined by Chopp. As Schaverien underlines, 'I came to realise that there is a cultural taboo on noticing that there is a problem with this socially condoned abandonment of the very young.'[269] She adds that her book 'breaks a cultural taboo and tells stories that many of my clients have feared that, if voiced, would not be believed'.[270] I am aware of the power of that taboo, and in telling my story also break that taboo, and yet I still fear that the pain of the trauma of abandonment and separation will not be believed. I will return to the wider perspective Walton outlines for poetics when I consider the ethical model of awareness in my mindful rule of life from

---

[266] Walton, Writing Methods, 145.
[267] Rebecca S Chopp, 'Theology and the Poetics of Testimony', in *Converging on Culture: Theologians in Dialogues with Cultural Analysis and Criticism*, eds D Brown, S G Davaney and K Tanner (Oxford: Oxford University Press, 2001), 56.
[268] Chopp, 61.
[269] Schaverien, xi.
[270] Schaverien, xi.

another angle. Perhaps you have an untold story that you need help with – to decide whether to voice or not?

Reflection

Intention

My sense is that having some understanding of how trauma theory has developed is important, whether we have experienced trauma or not. I think one aspect of experiencing trauma that is very difficult is not being believed. Perhaps someone thinks an event is not traumatic because it doesn't fit the traditional ideas of what is or is not traumatic. Perhaps you could make an intention to understand some of the theory of trauma. Or consider doing a mental health first aid course.

Attention

One of the most impressive elements of the mainstream mindfulness training I have done is the deeply attentive listening modelled by the teachers. One of the most important aspects of our mindful formation is to be attentive listeners to the Word of God and to other people. This listening is not automatic; it has to be cultivated and is not a strength in Western culture. So, work on your capacity to listen attentively.

Attitude

We live in a culture that can be dismissive of emotion and mental health struggles. Cultivate a different attitude. Catch any attitudes that might be dismissive of others who have a mental health condition. Also consider the context in which they live – is it the context that needs to change?

Reperceiving

Many of our attitudes operate on autopilot, and we make snap judgements without any reflection. Take time to be with people, suspending those judgements and in a slower process try to reperceive them and transcend your first judgement of them.

13
Listening to your own self

Introduction

The mindfulness theory we have engaged with so far has another application – enabling us to listen to the different parts of our self. Mainstream mindfulness theory as I've already outlined talks about an observing self. This has been critiqued by disability studies for centring on sight, and I've used the term 'witnessing' or 'perceiving self' instead. Part of this witnessing of our inner life is listening to the different parts within. I have outlined different ways of conceptualising these parts. We can witness or listen to our storytelling self or narrative self. Often the stories we tell ourselves (influenced by the past) are distorted and negative. These need to be rewritten. We can also listen to our senses and body (our experiential self). Through this listening we cultivate self-awareness. We can also listen to our emotional self to regulate our feelings in a healthy way. We can listen to what our automatic self-focus is so that we can learn to transcend that self-focus. This listening is ongoing self-work daily. We can listen to ourselves more intentionally through spiritual exercises.

One method I have used as a spiritual exercise is the idea of interviewing my self. I first came across the idea of self-interviews in my counselling training. In my PhD I adapted a method in qualitative research, Carol Gilligan's *Listening Guide*, which normally enables listening to others, to listen to my own self. It is a method that draws on psychodynamic theory and the use of poetic and creative language to access the unconscious and dissociated self.[271]

Here I just focus on the simple biblical and psychological idea of listening to our own inner life, which enables us to listen to the different parts of our self. This is important because we sometimes don't listen to our inner complexity. Or this may seem obvious, because we sometimes say, don't we, 'I'm in two minds about this.' I've introduced the mindful take on this – our narrative, experiential and witnessing selves. If this is new for you, another helpful model comes from the Transactional Analysis (TA) model of counselling which says we need to listen to our inner child, inner parent and inner adult. We need to especially become aware of the critical parent we have internalised. This model is called the ego-state model, and an ego-state 'is a way in which we manifest a part of our personality at a given time'.[272] There are helpful variations in which these ego-states can manifest. Dialectical Behaviour Therapy (DBT) talks about listening to our wise mind, emotion mind and reasonable mind, with wise mind being 'the integration of emotion mind and reasonable mind'.[273] Within this listening is a listening for a mindfulness of God awareness. Where is God and what might God be communicating? God can communicate through any part of our being.

Self-interviews in any form, but also the simplified form I offer here, can help us discover aspects of our self that are out of awareness, or an aspect of God that is currently out of our awareness. My earlier work has shown that my mind is strongly associative and symbolic in its workings. This also led me to resonate with Gilligan's work as she has made the logic of

---

[271] Gilligan and Eddy, 'Listening as a Path', 76-81.

[272] See Thomas A Harris, *I'm OK – You're OK* (London: Arrow, 2012) for an introduction to TA. Ian Stewart & Vann Joines, *TA Today: A New Introduction to Transactional Analysis* (Nottingham & Chapel Hill: Lifespace Publishing, 1987), 4.

[273] Michaela A Swales and Heidi L Heard, *Dialectical Behaviour Therapy: The CBT Distinctive Features Series*, series editor Windy Dryden (London, New York: Routledge, 2009), 113.

association a key part of her research. A section of an interview she did on the *Listening Guide* is worth quoting in full:

> The radical potential that inheres in psychological research lies in this recognition: that the logic of the psyche is an associative logic, the logic of dreams and poetry and memory ... Instead of following a deductive logic (how one thought implies another) you follow the stream of associations ... When I ask myself, why artists are often the best psychologists – why, as Freud noted, poets are often light years ahead – it's because of their use of associative methods. This allows them to break through dissociation, to see the cultural framework, which is why artists often are the ones who speak the unspoken and reveal what is hidden.[274]

I am listening to my own self to break free from the dissociated and false narratives of boarding school experience to transform the distorted narrative self. I want to bring into the light of awareness what I had dissociated from using the logic of association. As we talk, we often make unconscious associations, and as we listen to our own physical voice, we can make further associations.

It may be for you, though, that free association understood in psychodynamic terms may not be helpful – it can be contraindicated for some traumatic experiences. In psychoanalysis Rothschild points out, 'The core method of free association will be contraindicated for clients who are unable to contain their trauma memories or suffer from easily triggered flashbacks.'[275] However, that doesn't mean you cannot listen to the associations your mind makes. I will offer you a different way of thinking symbolically.

In interviewing yourself it is important to have some

---

[274] Kiegelmann, 13.
[275] Babette Rothschild, *Trauma Essentials: The Go-To Guide* (New York, London: W W Norton & Company, 2011), 80.

questions to ask yourself. My questions were around my struggles with anxiety, what caused that and what helped. These were the questions I put to myself in the first self-interview:

- What is my story of immersion in mindfulness?
- Why did I have a breakdown?
- What helped?
- Why did my existing Christian ecosphere not help?
- Why did I have to go out of this ecosphere to mindfulness to get help?

Within my journey of discovery, I had identified my immersion in mindfulness, my breakdown, what helped, and having to go outside my existing Christian world as some of the key nexus points in my story. At the end of this chapter I'm going to suggest some questions for you to consider asking yourself.

This chapter picks up on our second quest question: 'How can we reclaim our present moments from anxious rumination to be mindful of God?' I am aware that my anxious thought patterns overwhelm and block my sense(s) of my own self. Boarding school was instrumental in blocking key aspects of my self-expression. I was not in touch with my feelings; I did not express them. I avoided my experiential self. I did not cultivate self-awareness. My experience is that when I inhabit my senses of my own self, I am more able to sense the presence of God, because the presence of God is within me. I am also aware from my earlier work that my mind has a strong associative logic, and this method of self-listening enables me to utilise this to uncover the hidden self that boarding school shaped. This is an important aspect of our attentiveness.

What do my self-interviews look like? I provide them below and present them as an encouragement to consider doing your own self-interviews (the dots represent pauses not missing text).

Reclaiming the past to reclaim the present
18th February 2019

What is your story of immersion in mindfulness?
'And so, the story I want to tell is a story that hasn't been told before. *Aah...* and it is how my *ah* distress and lack of wellbeing brought me into this research. It all began back in 2006 when I was incredibly stressed, very anxious, awfully close to breakdown, to burnout. And to help with this distress we were having some couple counselling... and it is the only counsellor who's made this point *er* in all the counselling I've had in my counselling training *er* she said no wonder you are feeling like you are feeling because you went to boarding school... And that was an "aha" moment, a moment of meeting where I realised something that maybe this wasn't all my fault, maybe I'd been shaped *er* in a particular way.

'So I read a book called *The Making of Them* by Nick Duffell all about boarding school experience and I'm going back now... I picked up three insights. Which are, I would say, these are cold insights now, the initial feeling I had realising these things has gone but... Three things that I realised that I was, I had been shaped, I'd been shaped, I'd been made *Aah* to be self-sufficient, to not ask for help... Because as a child there wasn't anybody who could help, there was nobody you could say, "Help me...!"'

Why did I have a breakdown?
'So, I'd been made... self-sufficient, fashioned in that way (*sniffs*)... also I was taught, learned, I learned that there was no point in expressing (*sighs*) my emotions of homesickness, sadness or anything else, because again there was nobody to talk to, (*inbreath*) nobody who could help with that...

'And *um*... (*laughs, swallows*), that's what got me into trouble... that I thought I had to solve everything myself, that I couldn't express these more difficult emotions because I thought that I mustn't, that I shouldn't... it wasn't allowed. It wasn't right...

'It wasn't what a man did (*sucks in a breath*), and I think the third thing I learnt was to be loyal... I was loyal (*sucks in a breath*).

'And perhaps overly loyal, so (*sucks in breath*) I couldn't up to this point say anything about boarding school and that would have been disloyal, and I wasn't even aware that that's what I was thinking, and that's why I've never looked at this or addressed this... (*swallows*).'

What helped?

'And then at the same time in my psychotherapy training at Roehampton in 2006 I came across secular mindfulness and its practices (*breathes in*), which I found really helpful (*breathes, sucks teeth*). These practices and the mindful theory began to glue me back together (*swallows*). Especially realising that I was not an anxious person... I did have anxious thoughts, but these were not facts (*sniffs*). These were just passing mental events. Difficult ones *ahh um*.

'But at the same time I came across a book called *The Jesus Prayer* by somebody called Simon Barrington-Ward, former Bishop of Coventry... and I met him... and he helped teach me about the Jesus Prayer.

'Which I also found really helpful. And sort of you took the gold and silver of God's kingdom and helped glue me back *aah* together.

'And as I was researching the Jesus Prayer, I came across the fifth-century Greek Bishop Diadochus of Photike and a phrase of his translated by Olivier Clement (*swallows*) *ah*: "Fix your eyes on the depths of your heart with an unceasing mindfulness of God" (*sniffs*). And this phrase, this idea of mindfulness of God, rang me like a bell (*breathes through nose*). And I knew it wasn't part of secular psychology, you wouldn't have this idea of mindfulness of God... I knew from my research Buddhists wouldn't generally talk about mindfulness of God but here was a Christian Bishop talking about mindfulness of God *um*...'

Why did my existing Christian ecosphere not help?
'But I also knew that in my Christian culture, modern day culture, evangelical, charismatic, the idea of meditations or mindfulness was something you weren't supposed to talk about (*pause*). It was taboo almost, *ah*, to be considered suspicious, and *um*... I've been looking back, as part of *um* the data I've collected for this research, to an article I wrote for the *Baptist Times* on Thursday 24th July 2008 (*rustle of paper*)... it was called 'Mindful of Our Lives', and I was talking about mindfulness and *er* talking about its links *er* within the Christian traditions... And I say, "Instead of doing the evangelical swoon the minute words like meditation and mindfulness are used we need to start exploring and practising contemplative prayer in all its rich variety." That's the first time I (*breathes through nose*) WROTE about it publicly.

'And then *um* I did a dissertation called *Why Now for Mindfulness?* as part of my MA in psychotherapy, and it was published in 2010. And I'm very careful there *ah* in the way I talk about mindfulness, and I say, "There is some evidence that mindfulness is a universal human capacity," and that was really *ah* and so as to not rock the boat, to not attract criticism, to be tentative *ah* in what I thought and felt. And looking back now I would be a lot more confident in what I say that mindfulness is our universal human capacity for attention and awareness... and I would say much more than that.'

Why did I have to go out of this ecosphere to mindfulness to get help?
'Um and at the same time I started writing about contemplative prayer, like the Jesus Prayer, like slow meditative reading of Scripture, *Lectio Divina*... and these two things were not part of my Christian culture, nor was secular mindfulness and so I had to go outside my own culture, my Christian ecosphere... to find something that helped... *um*... and I hadn't found the answers, or the insights I needed, up to that point within this expression of my Christian faith... and that's something I will come back to when I'm interviewed again (*door opens*)...'

A second self-interview

I interview myself a second time. I'm reading Joy Schaverien's book on BSS. In this second interview, as I am much more aware of the trauma and feelings, having read Schaverien's book, I ask myself questions that reflect the emergence of related but deeper themes. The question about writing a letter to myself is to let my younger self know I believe the story of trauma. The questions I asked myself were:

- What has emerged from the reading?

- If I wanted to write a letter to someone about my experience, who would I write it to?

- What has the impact been on me in the present moment, in the right here, in the right now?

- How do I feel right now?

Tuesday 30 April 2019

What has emerged from the reading?
'Having read the introduction and the case study of the man whose story sounds very like mine, I am aware that this has given me words for my story... so I didn't have the words to describe it. It has also shown me how deep the trauma (*breathes*) was... strong words... abandoned, without love, without family... or even worse intermittently. Ten weeks without, four weeks with, ten weeks without, four weeks with... so you can never quite trust those times, moments of happiness with your family, because it's just going to be taken away again. And there was nobody (*ironic chuckle*) you could ask for help in the sense of how you were feeling. So, I remember *aah* being sent to boarding school at six and three-quarters to Manor House in Kenya for a term. I had my brother... but I just remember how lonely I felt, how I did not understand why I was there, what I had done, why I had to go for a term... and prior to that it had

been idyllic in the Kenyan highlands, running around, freedom... and here suddenly who could you speak to, I did not know who to ask what to do (*um*)...

'I literally felt like I had been silenced. My memory is being a very chatty child up to that point and after that being much quieter, finding it much more difficult to speak, say what I thought or felt (*breathes in*...). I think I have always been hard on myself and dismissed, had no understanding of how traumatic boarding school was. But now I can see that the person I became was understandable. So, this self-sufficiency, no point asking for help, not expressing emotions, there was no point.

'I remember one evening at the prep school I went to later in England, someone being homesick. And triggering an asthma attack and how it was dismissed and how they'd also tried to run away and they were brought back by the police, and I just realised how pointless it was to try and escape because there was no escape, you were a prisoner, a captive, I was a prisoner, I was captive.

'(*swallows*) And there wasn't intimacy... it was an all-male environment apart from the matron and at the prep school we had a matron who was very tough (*sniffs*), and we had a younger matron who was eighteen and was very kind... and at half term, because I was in England and my family lived in Kenya and there was nowhere to go (*sigh*) home, so often you had to stay at school (*sigh*), you might get invited home to another boy's family... but she invited me and another boy to her family farm, and we stayed there for a week. I remember that kindness...

'I'm sitting here at Scargill House in a walled garden, because it feels safe here... and that's what I did, I walled myself in, built a wall of protection around myself, with gates, doors but difficult to let people in... And in the walled garden I would bring books where I could (*breathes*) escape...'

If I wanted to write a letter to someone about my experience, who would I write it to?
'And in Joy Schaverien's book the client thinks about writing to his mother, and actually that's not what I feel, what I feel is I want to write to my younger self... and that having read these books I feel much more compassion, much more understanding (*aah*) to that part of me... and so that's something I may do as well as part of this research.'

What has the impact been on me in the present moment, in the right here, in the right now?
'And I think one of the reasons I'm drawn to watchfulness and mindfulness (*sighs*) is that I am extremely vigilant and anxiously watching all the time to keep myself safe which is a product of the boarding school experience... What I am intuitively looking for is a kind of more gracious, more spacious watchfulness (*sucks his teeth*) that is different to what I've lived with for so long... (*swallows*)... with this idea that I'm always on the edge of (*breathes*) happiness, I can't quite fully allow myself to experience it, to enter into it (*sniffs*), just in case it is taken away again (*swallows*). And I think as an adult there has been a fear that I can't quite trust people, they will (*swallows*) abandon me, and I think in the past I have withdrawn from people when I've not felt safe... and that again intuitively (*swallows*) through Benedictine spirituality, being in the same church for over twenty years I am trying to live in a place of stability and not withdraw (*swallows*) so, although I am aware that is what I've done to the people I love and have loved at times.'

(*silent pause*)

How do I feel right now?
'And I feel very emotional... I feel it in my body welling up, within my heart, I feel the closeness of tears... it is less intense than the first time I read it... I captured that elsewhere and will use that as part of this research. And I guess what I'm trying to do is bring into awareness what has been dissociated, what I am trying to do is get to the primary wound. And that is not just

about the anxiety but also about the shame... that this was a shaming culture... You had to be constantly vigilant to obey the rules in order not to be shamed... And still now today I want to obey the rules so I am not shamed. I want to be free from this, free from the gravitational pull of this. I've just had an operation for quinsy where they lanced, drew out pus from a very swollen throat wall and tonsil (*aah*). And just the sense that deep down, somewhere deep inside, there's still this pus (*swallows*) of trauma that still infects me, and I'm trying to draw this pus out of this abscess within me. Constantly leaking anxiety and shame, and in this process, I want to draw it out, to lance it. To be healed completely.'

Further theological reflections

I add some further theological reflections around shame, which is a theme that has emerged from my self-listening. A resonant conversation partner has been Stephen Pattison's autoethnographic and practical theological book, *Shame: Theory, Therapy, Theology* (as referenced earlier). Written some twenty years ago, it shows the power and importance of AE and is an early use of this methodology in practical theology. Pattison holds a pessimistic view about whether any of the theory and therapy he summarises helps to lift people out of shame.[276] The book is written before the mindfulness and compassion-based therapies expanded in relation to shame. The aim in my work in terms of dealing with my shame is not therapeutic but spiritual; how can I stop shame taking me out of the present moment into mental time travel so that I can be more mindful of God? The approach I am taking, as with anxiety, which also takes me out of the present moment, is not to try to eradicate shame but to change my relationship to shame. This is the approach of mindfulness. I relativise shame by recognising it is just thoughts, just feelings, not facts. There are reasons posited why mindfulness and compassion-based therapies work with

---

[276] Pattison, *Shame*, 166.

mindfulness.[277]

Written in 2019, an article exploring the relationship between mindfulness, self-compassion and shame supports Pattison's assertion that psychology has made little progress in helping those with chronic shame: 'Although researchers have been exploring shame, the methods by which it could be managed or lessened have received little consideration.'[278] However, there are promising signs that mindfulness and compassion-based therapies can enable those experiencing shame to hold it rather than be held by it.[279] The physical experience of having had an abscess lanced in my throat wall reflects the emotional experience of lancing the trauma. I feel my new self, my mindful spirituality, is coming out of the gravitational pull of the old self, with its hold on my present.

Our third quest question, 'How can we be fully aware of and at home in our whole embodied self to further reclaim our present moments?' I now return to, considering this chapter. My main strand of theoretical and practical help in this quest has been mindfulness. The development of my self-awareness has brought what was hidden, the trauma of my boarding school past, into the light. Mindfulness has been able to help relativise the distorted scripts from boarding school, just as it has helped to relativise the anxious thoughts that overwhelmed my present moments. However, in terms of a more critical reflection on mindfulness, I have realised I need something more than mindfulness to reclaim my past. It is embodied and sociological trauma theory that has enabled me to inhabit and make transparent the room of my past – and live in it with some measure of peace. In fairness to mindfulness, however, embodied trauma theory acknowledges that mindfulness can be

---

[277] Neda Sedighimornani, Katherine A Rimes and Bas Verplanken, 'Exploring the Relationships Between Mindfulness, Self-Compassion, and Shame', *Sage Open* (July-September 2019): 1-9, accessed 7th December 2021, dx.doi.org/10.1177/2158244019866294.
[278] Sedighimornani, Rimes and Verplanken, 1.
[279] Sedighimornani, Rimes and Verplanken, 1-9.

incorporated into the treatment of trauma to enable healing.[280]

My listening to my self revolved around my internal dialogue with two books written about the impact of boarding school on children from a psychotherapeutic perspective. I have then used the idea of a narrative self from mindfulness theory. I am aware that I have been living with a distorted narrative self, a distortion that originated in the past. This is a part of our self it is important to identify. The aim is to be able to recognise the distorted narrative and scripts and rewrite them, so that we can further reclaim our present moments.

I also want to use this chapter to hold my younger self in a mindful and self-compassionate awareness. It is a helpful thing for all of us to do. I then examine these interviews in the light of embodied and sociological trauma theory. These insights of trauma theory may help you. In the next chapter we look at our future and how to liberate it.

Reflection

Intention

If your intention is to listen to the different parts of your self, here is a simple process to follow.

As you listen to your self through a simple self-interview, here are some questions you could use to structure the interview. Record yourself and speak out the answers without trying to curate what you say.

- What are the distorted narratives you tell yourself?

- What are your body and senses trying to tell you right now (are you tired and burnt out, running on empty)?

- Has anyone given you a piece of wisdom (such as that boarding school can be traumatic) that you can reflect on?

---

[280] van der Kolk, 208-210.

Self-interviews have also been done using photos or pieces of music to bring back memories. Is this something that might help you?[281]

Attention

Pay attention to the different parts of your self and name them, either with your own words or using some of the aspects of self I've mentioned so far, such as narrative, experiential and witnessing selves.

Attitude

Can you identify the wise aspect of your self and witness the other parts of your personality through it?

Reperceiving

Can you develop a clear understanding of your strengths and where you need to develop?

---

[281] See the work done at the University of Manchester: hummedia.manchester.ac.uk/schools/soss/morgancentre/toolkits/16-toolkit-using-self-interviews.pdf (accessed 4th March 2024).

14
Liberating the future through mindfulness of God

Introduction

A growing realisation during my journey, which I have described in previous chapters, is the sense that I am a symbolist, that God speaks to me through natural symbols. I think we are all symbolists, and liberation psychology says this different way of knowing is pushed to the margins of our lives. If we want to know ourselves in a deeper way, we need to examine our margins.

I now want to examine and describe this symbolic interaction in more detail. I have a sense that through these symbols I can reclaim my past to some degree. In redressing the balance of my past between negative memories and positive memories, I can further reclaim my present moments through the magnetic pull of these symbols. In this way I can create hope for the future. Mindfulness is not just about the present moment, but about considering the past and the future more mindfully and clearly. I am aware that you may not have any positive memories from your childhood. Perhaps, then, reclaiming the past is in part realising this. Part of that reclaiming is also asking, where is God in all this? For some, that too might be hard to establish.

Our symbolic self is part of the 'house of our being' that we need to make more transparent and inhabit more clearly – also enabling us to answer our third quest question: 'How can we be fully aware of and at home in our whole embodied self, to further reclaim our present moments?' On my journey I am looking to reclaim from the past the natural symbols that fed me with sacramental goodness as well as to represent the trauma symbolically.

In this chapter I wish to revisit the enigmatic lure of swallows as a symbol for me, which emerged in Chapter Four. I do this by an act of retrieval – going back in my timeline when between 1986 and 1987, and in 2009, I had an outpouring of symbolic imagining, writing and painting. I go back to these poems, lyrical stories and paintings as a source of what was happening at the margins. Many of us have journals, poems or reflections we have written in the past and perhaps put aside – they are worth returning to.

After this retrieval from the past, I then outline and examine how we can benefit from the natural symbolic interaction between our environment and our own life. We live in a world where symbols 'beckon us to perceive them'.[282] As they call out our symbolic self, we then need to listen to that creative part of us, and as we do so we can create a hopeful landscape of our being in the world. It may be that these symbols capture the 'attention of the heart' before the attention of the mind, and this is part of God's secret work in us.

Fragments and bricolage

Much of our life is remembered as fragments, like a broken mosaic. How can we work with fragments? I first came across the idea of bricolage or being a bricoleur in counselling research. According to McLeod, bricolage is about improvisation, drawing from different methods flexibly as 'need emerges in

---

[282] The quote is an adaptation of some lines from the poet Rainer Maria Rilke quoted in Julian Hoffman's *The Small Heart of Things: Being at Home in a Beckoning World* (Athens, Georgia: The University of Georgia Press, 2014), 41. The exact quote is, 'Everything beckons us to perceive it,/murmurs at every turn.'

response to the task of conducting a study'.[283] I later came across the idea of the researcher as bricoleur from a theological perspective through the work of Heather Walton. She reviews the emergence of bricolage and argues for the use of theopoetic writing and for practical theologians to be 'bricoleurs, makers and remakers' rather than those embracing 'an encompassing theory of everything'. It is bricolage because we draw on traditions 'that are fragmented and yet re-forming'.[284] I am aware of my own fragmentation and re-forming. These are words that describe my journey. It can also be your journey, and bricolage, working with fragments to create a whole, can give you hope as well.

An act of retrieval – earlier writings

One of the symbols from the Camino walk in Chapter Four that I engaged with was the swallows flying along the Camino way as I walked. They were writing a message in the sky that I have not fully interpreted so far. I decided to go back to even earlier writings when my creative symbolic self (another part of our self we need to listen to) also surfaced to see if swallows appeared in those writings. This was the period 1986-87 when I was working in the desert of a high street bank but experiencing a spiritual awakening that triggered a release of creative language and symbolic painting. This is a poem I found.

> And where I meet with you
> You take away the chains
> The world appears in bright garment
> I walk through the rains
>   the swallows
> And what is sent
> Flight of swallows

---

[283] John McLeod, *Qualitative Research in Counselling and Psychotherapy* (London: Sage, 2001), 119.
[284] Walton, 'A Theopoetics of Practice', 3-23. See page 22 for specific quote.

> Messengers
> >of a holy place
> We shall meet like children there
> In bright garments of love
> >>There.

In the present moment of reading that poem I have an epiphany. Where I will meet my friend is Africa, which was a shared childhood connection. I suddenly realise why the swallows are symbolically important to me. They symbolise Africa, Kenya, the Great Rift Valley, my home. They flew home to Kenya, when as a child I could not. I suddenly realise that whenever I see them I am haunted with a longing – and now I realise that longing is from my childhood, wanting to go home, to fly as the swallows fly with a homing instinct that cannot be denied.

Through this act of retrieval from the margins, I remember further fragments. My symbolic self was born in my African childhood and sustained me at boarding school, and later working in the bank. As I re-immerse myself in the symbolic awakening that occurred in 1986-87, I can see now that my writings and drawings are inhabited by childhood symbols from Africa. This deep sacramental connection to this lost home, a sacred place in my heart, is picked up in another poem from this period, called 'Absent Without Leaving'.

> Jadini, Kilindini, Malindi
> >Franjipani
> Of Acacia memory,
> Old Nandi man beneath the tree –
> >The road you will no longer see
> To living stone.
> From within me
> Cutting the bone.
> Only the rift valley
> Running in my heart...
> And through the curtains flying

Birds humming
Depart.

My body was at boarding school, but my heart and soul never left Kenya. At this time of spiritual awakening in 1986-87, when I started to go to church and became a Christian, these natural symbols began to speak to me in my new spirituality. Jadini is a beach near the town of Malindi. Kilindini is the harbour for the port of Mombasa. Franjipani is a flowering bush, and acacias are the famous thorn trees of the African plain, their evocative silhouette unmistakeable. Acacia thorns are both beautiful and sharp. The Nandi Hills are where I was born, among the Nandi tribe. The poem suggests that I have been frozen since my experience at boarding school because of being separated from family and place, but I live beneath the surface, cut to the bone. The marrow of my existence is this sacramental connection that feeds me goodness. The Great Rift Valley, where I was born in the province of Uasin Gishu, is mirrored in my heart. The swallows have departed from my soul. It is the remembrance of the symbols and the recognition of meaning they make for me that begins to unfreeze me in the present moment.

If I apply my mindful model of valuing moments of meeting with God that are redemptive and sacramental (implicit relational knowing), then I can reclaim this past, by not just acknowledging the trauma but by remembering the moments of created goodness. I remember as a child diving for silver shillings in a bright aquamarine sparkling pool. They shone and moved at the bottom of the pool, beckoning me to dive in. I realise that I have been beckoned by God to dive again and retrieve the silver shillings of memory that also lie in my boarding school past, which relate to the time I spent in Kenya as a child. Such transcendent moments have value, weight and depth beyond their duration. They also create moments of sacramental goodness in the present.

What about you? Do you need to reclaim good memories from your past? If you take some time to reflect now, what comes into your heart? We often think that to be happy we need to move out of sadness, as if these feelings are on a continuum. Happiness and sadness, difficulty and peace, are different poles that coexist that we need to hold in balance.[285]

Perhaps I am intuitively drawn to this idea of balance because of these lost coins that lie unclaimed in my African childhood, which I have only accessed intermittently. I am aware of the well of sadness within, but I am becoming aware of this stream of incarnated goodness from my childhood that feeds me still. It is often out of awareness, but it is part of my implicit relationship with God.

At boarding school, I had no explicit relationship with God expressed in Christian Trinitarian terms. The insight I have received in reflecting critically on my symbolic self is that the Creator God sustained me through the symbols of my childhood. This insight came in part also from a theological perspective. What kind of God am I encountering in this journey? I have already talked about the compassionate, non-shaming presence of God, but I have also been influenced by the idea of the generous God as outlined by David Brown. David Brown says something akin to my idea of an implicit relationship between myself and God in that God uses symbols to mediate the interaction between human beings and the divine presence because through symbols 'God can act upon us, without destroying our freedom', and this is in the realm of the subconscious.[286]

Another aspect of Brown's argument is that God communicates with us through natural symbols, and this resonates deeply with my experience.[287] These symbols bring

---

[285] See Leslie J Francis, Giuseppe Crea and Patrick Laycock, 'Work-Related Psychological Health among Catholic Religious in Italy: Testing the Balanced Affect Model', *Journal of Empirical Theology* 30, 2 (2017): 236-252, accessed 27th November 2023, dx.doi.org/10.1163/15709256-12341357.

[286] Brown, 'God and Symbolic Action', 116.

[287] Brown, 'God and Symbolic Action', 113-122.

meaning to our lives. God has communicated with me through a whole range of symbols from the created world, and I have felt the divine presence in every dimension of my being. As well as bringing meaning or restoring meaning when we have lost it, these symbols in God's hand bring hope and wonder. Wonder, it must be added, is not just a feeling, but a mode of attention.[288] Some things have a magnetic attraction that draws wonder out of us, but I think as we begin to cultivate attention, wonder can emerge. This is also something the Holy Spirit helps us cultivate.

I have an inkling that the symbols do not act in an isolated way but form patterns. For example, the symbols from childhood form a pattern, a constellation of stars, that guide me in my deep unconscious, my intuitive self. This has been called a 'metaphoric landscape'.[289] I find this language of a metaphoric landscape very helpful, that the symbols are connected and for me can represent the symbolic self I have discovered.

This helps me believe that my life has a God-given plan and purpose. I am a light spoken by the Light, to be light to the world. As discussed earlier, to me this Christian symbolism is an echo of an Eastern Orthodox idea developed particularly by Maximus the Confessor that each of us is a word, a *logos*, spoken by God.

This symbolic self previously on the edge of my life has re-emerged following my immersion in mindfulness, enabling me to access my symbolic childhood. This is another room in my house I am now living in that has become more 'transparent' to me. This also enables me to further reclaim my present moments as I realise my childhood was not all pain and trauma but another sacramental strand. This helps us to answer our third quest question about how to inhabit our whole self more fully – finding our symbolic self is crucial.

---

[288] Torbjörn Gustafsson Chorell, 'Modes of Historical Attention: Wonder, Curiosity, Fascination', *Rethinking History* 25 no. 2 (2021): 244.
[289] James Lawley and Penny Tompkins, *Metaphors in Mind: Transformation Through Symbolic Modelling* (London: The Developing Company Press, 2003), 17-18.

I am also aware from the impact of boarding school that I have a hidden self that I cannot access through my conscious, rational self. I can use psychodynamic techniques, such as free association and the interpretation of symbols, to try to access this dissociated self. Its shadow is looming over the present and is the origin of my anxiety. As I reduce its power as a shadow, I further reclaim my present moments. I position the boat of my life in a better place for the wind of the Spirit.

A symbolic journey using heuristic process

What does natural symbolic interaction look like? I intentionally listened to this natural symbolic interaction while on a family holiday in Rome. I paid attention to symbols that beckoned me to perceive them and the associations that came to mind. This association is grounded in the reality around us, but do bear in mind the warning I gave earlier about free association if you do suffer from trauma, that it doesn't trigger flashbacks or other traumatic reactions. I will give you another symbolic practice to try later in the chapter. I decided to do work with this symbolic interaction through adapting heuristic process.

Heuristic research is about lived experience and includes the use of and cultivation of self-awareness.[290] Self-awareness is a mindful capacity given to us by God that I am looking to cultivate within my mindful formation. Heuristic research uses biographical, autobiographical data and recognises the importance of the lyrical and poetic in the representation of that data.[291] It is a search, a quest, an 'odyssey' that is introspective, attentive and meditative.[292] In such research I need to be personally involved and impacted by the phenomenon I am researching.[293] I had to jump into the water of mindfulness!

To be able to enter mindfulness one must enter one's

---

[290] Moustakas, 9.
[291] Moustakas, 10.
[292] Moustakas, 13.
[293] Moustakas, 11, 14.

mindful capacities, and that is what I am doing. This is working the margins.

Heuristic research has clear phases which help shape the form in which the research is presented. There is an *initial engagement* with a key issue, which for this piece of iterative research is the importance of my symbolic mind, and how that relates to my mindfulness of God.[294] Attending to the symbolic enables us to access what is hidden within us. There follows a period of *immersion* in the research.[295] I have been immersed in mindfulness and mindfulness of God since 2006, but the significance of the symbolic is a more recent insight. I decided to immerse myself for a period of days in the symbolic, and the way it triggers the logic of association in my own mind and spirit.

There follows a period of *incubation,* where thinking can crystallise quietly in the background.[296] Out of these processes comes illumination, insight, awareness and realisations, where the tacit and intuitive can work with critical analysis.[297] Finally, findings and realisations are drawn out of the data, and a creative synthesis of all of the above brings the piece of research to a conclusion.[298] This heuristic approach mirrors our own journeys of discovery and so is a helpful road map to accompany our own contemplative journeys.

While in Rome

While in Rome for three days one summer, if anything presented itself to my consciousness as symbolic (going with my felt sense in the moment), I stopped and immediately wrote whatever associations came to mind. What does that observation of natural symbolic interaction look like? These

---

[294] Moustakas, 27.
[295] Moustakas, 28.
[296] Moustakas, 28-29.
[297] Moustakas, 29-30.
[298] Moustakas, 30-32.

experiences can happen organically when a song or piece of music suddenly takes us back to a past moment , symbolising that period of time in a very powerful, evocative way.

Butterfly
I saw a large butterfly flitting from flower to flower.

The butterfly is my intuitive, symbolic self, flying from symbol to symbol, drinking the nectar they hide.

The river Tiber with no boats
We are walking by the river Tiber and there are no boats.

When anxiety broke the banks and dam that contained it inside me, I was swept down the river, waving and drowning. I had no internal boat that could help me navigate this tidal wave. By grace I landed on the shore of a sabbatical, in a brief respite. Through mindfulness I dragged myself from the shore, beaten and weak. Through mindfulness I built a sailing boat that could navigate the channels of my anxiety.

A spider with a sac of baby spiders
I saw a spider with a sac of baby spiders.

I wanted to see if hundreds of spider babies swarmed from the mother spider, but she ran off. The mother spider for me was boarding school and it spawned a swarm of anxious thoughts. But at the time I did not know I was anxious. I avoided social situations, parties, speaking up in classrooms. I hated having to travel to the airport for holidays on my own, overwhelmed and lost by the terminals and instructions. And then there was the day when the spider thoughts of anxiety all swarmed at once and my body shook, and I had to sit and tremble and fall apart as the spiders span me into a web of trembling confusion.

A series of broken benches
I walked past a series of benches by the river Tiber, each one broken.

I realise that I had no rest places built into my life, nowhere to stop. I was always busy, one step ahead of the spiders hurrying behind me, casting a big shadow over me.

A cloud in a blue sky
It is thirty-three degrees, and a completely blue sky offers no shelter. Suddenly a small cloud blocks out the sun and provides welcome relief.

I suddenly see the cloud as a positive thing. I think of the cloud of anxiety in my life and how I see it as negative. But it has brought me to mindfulness for health and mindfulness of God. It has made me more empathic to those suffering from mental health distress.

Broken mosaic
There is a Roman mosaic with large sections missing.

I am missing large fragments from the mosaic of my life. What is missing might be more important than what I can see. An embodied life has been missing. Instead of an experientially vibrant life which I had as a child in Kenya, my life had become experientially avoidant. An emotionally expressed life has been missing. Awareness has been missing. The symbols may be a way back to access the past that was traumatic, but I am also recognising that there are happy sections of my life I have not been accessing, and the symbols lead to this place.

Vinyl records (LPs) on the wall of a café
Seeing an LP on a wall of a café takes me straight back to our veranda in Nairobi, sitting beneath pepper trees and jacarandas, listening to Paul McCartney. The patio doors are wide open and the music mixes with the breeze and the shade in a poignant memory. These were idyllic moments, paradise, making the separation, not just from my parents, brother and sister, but also from this place, a double cruelty. As I write, a dream that keeps reappearing comes to mind. I am in a car as a child. We drive down a pink road; I know the road and just round the corner is home. But we never leave the road; there is always another corner and I never arrive home. As I remember this right now in the present moment, I remember the intense longing in the dream, so bitter-sweet, to return home.

In a flow of associative logic another memory comes to mind. I would wake up that first morning of the holidays in

Kenya having flown from England with a sense of dread, believing myself still at boarding school. The friendly light coming through the curtains would tell me that I was home in Kenya. The dread would seep away and I would again be filled with joy and a feeling of safety. The first day back at boarding school I would wake up feeling safe and happy... and then as the grey light seeped in through the windows and I looked round at the sleeping boys I would deflate, and sadness would fill me. The feeling of safety seeped away like sand in a timer. As I write this, I am reminded that I have lived on the edge of happiness because of these experiences.

This is a big hole in the mosaic of my life – happiness has been missing. I can fill it one small fragment of mosaic at a time, each moment of happiness that I can recall. In doing so I create a new landscape, which holds together the darkness, with lines of light that hold my fragments together.

The spark of life
In the Sistine Chapel there is the famous painting of the spark of life passing between God and Adam.

The spark of life for my research was 'mindfulness of God'. Something jumped across to me, like a spark of life and sent me on a quest.

Silence
In the Sistine Chapel the guards constantly ask for silence, but no one is silent. I have never silenced my anxious thoughts until recently through mindfulness.

A man and a saluki dog in a café
I saw a man with a white saluki in the Piazza di S Cosimato.

Immediately I was surrounded with ghost hounds as my dead grandmother used to breed salukis. I was taken straight back to my childhood. I especially remembered the sense that I should be seen and not heard, and that decisions like going to boarding school were made for me, without my involvement. This remembrance of things past triggered by the man and his saluki triggered a burst of writing as I allowed this encounter to incubate.

As I sit in the bar, with its golden Brazilian coffee, an inkling floats into my awareness. I realise my anxious thoughts are ghosts from the past trauma of separation, silence and absence, of the unspoken sadness. They are repetitive compulsions, psychic fragments that touch the present. I realise in that moment, with an electric force running through me, that I am running from sadness. I do not ever want to feel as sad as I felt as a child torn from home. I feel the sadness now like a well I was dropped in and have clambered out of, but never live far from. It took a symbolic saluki in the present to raise the ghost hounds of my childhood that led me to the well of sadness that lies within. Anxiety I have named, and shame I circle around, but sadness, sadness is the one that nearly drowned me and can drown me still.

How can we interpret symbolic interaction?

I offer an example below of interpreting symbolic interaction. What attracted my attention as I began my walk in Rome was the fragile hope offered by the butterfly. It is significant that what drew me next were symbols that spoke into my story of brokenness. There were no boats in the river Tiber, and I realised that I had no internal buoyancy when anxiety hit me in 2006. A spider with a sac of babies recalled a particular moment when I felt I was falling apart in 2006, my first experience of conscious brokenness. I saw a series of broken benches, which continued this theme of what was missing – in this case no safe place to stop, rest and be. I must keep moving. I cannot stop. I recognised through a cloud providing relief from relentless sunshine that the cloud of anxiety, although primarily negative, has a silver lining in that I found mindfulness through it and am a more empathetic person because of anxiety.

The symbol of the fragmented mosaic is significant. I am working with fragments. I am gluing together fragments of my own life, especially as it relates to the trauma of separation at boarding school. The method of bricolage is congruent with my lived experience here. I am also made aware that pieces of my life are missing, which I can seek to retrieve. Finding what is missing is an important part of the quest. This includes awareness, embodiment, healthy emotional expression, happiness and the symbols that speak to me and bring freedom.

As well as fragility and hope in the present, and brokenness and fragmentation from the past, memories emerged from my childhood in Africa that are poignant and triggered by the sight of vinyl records. The vinyl records also recall a childhood dream of being driven home in a car but never arriving. The logic of association has enabled memories from the liminal space of transitioning from holiday in Kenya back to boarding school to emerge. In that transitional morning I am either transported to happiness by the African light or transported to despair by the grey light of an English autumn. I am reminded of another insight that because of this experience of consistently having happiness snatched from me I have lived 'on the edge of happiness', not trusting myself to enter that feeling. Using mindful theory, I am aware that this experiential avoidance is as much applied to positive feelings as it is to negative ones. Avoiding the positive feeling of happiness is a way of regulating my emotions and avoiding the crash of disappointment.[299]

The famous painting in the Sistine Chapel of the spark of life passing from God to Adam is a reminder of how one moment of meeting can change your life. For me it was the reading of the phrase by Diadochus of Photike, translated by Olivier Clement as 'mindfulness of God'. This has sparked other moments of new life and transformation, and the process continues in my life now. Although there was no silence in the Sistine Chapel, even though the guards asked for it, it is that practice of mindfulness that has begun to silence my anxiety.

The most evocative moment, unexpected and unsought, was when I saw a man with a white saluki in the Piazza di S

---

[299] Paul Gilbert, and Choden, *Mindful Compassion: Using the Power of Mindfulness and Compassion to Transform Our Lives* (London: Robinson, 2013), 158.

Cosimato. I only realise as I write this that it was probably the colour that also triggered such a strong association, as most of my grandmother's salukis were white, and as a family we had a white saluki called Ty.

Although my anxious thoughts nose me like ghost hounds from the past and are not silent, I became aware of the silence around being sent to boarding school – it was not to be questioned by me as a child. I am aware of my sadness as a child, but again, there is a silence around the sadness; it is not to be spoken of. I am not to speak of the obvious absences from home either. I write, 'I realise my anxious thoughts are ghosts from the past trauma of separation, silence and absence, of the unspoken sadness.' Perhaps in the present moment when I am reminded of, or fear, separation, silence and absence, the sadness I avoid, my anxious thoughts are triggered. The unexpected, deep and terrifying insight is that I am running from the sadness that nearly drowned me as a child. My hope is, drawing on trauma theory, that in the naming of it I can be set free from it. It is significant that the symbol I have intuitively chosen for it is a well of sadness. I have contained it safely, and the well has a lid so that I do not fall in again.

I write about this deep well and what Schaverien calls a 'threshold moment', the moment you realise you are 'alone and in an unsafe place'.[300] This is a different moment of meeting, a moment of dreadful awareness. This was a searing experience of utter aloneness, where all I had was my own self to make a home in. This sense of absolute aloneness has never left me. As I reflect now in the present moment, reliving this threshold moment, I am aware that loneliness has accompanied me ever since.

The pack of hounds became a metaphor for the anxious thoughts that crowd me. I do not have a doorway to shut them out; I cannot close their anxious eyes. They do what anxious thoughts are supposed to do, but in a heightened way, sniffing

---

[300] Schaverien, 52-53.

out every path of worry. I recognise that the quiet whining and barking hide a howling from the past. Perhaps, like the original hounds, I can befriend them and name them.

Coming to some realisations

I knew that I was running from my anxiety, and that I circled around shame. I have been made newly aware of the well of sadness that nearly drowned me at boarding school and that hasn't been drained, and that perhaps its deeper source is loneliness. I am afraid to approach that sadness and loneliness. This symbol of the well of sadness has spoken powerfully to me and emerged from my unconscious. This symbol, along with the other symbols, acts as a bridge between my unconscious, dissociated self and my conscious awareness. Aspects of my boarding school trauma have emerged into the light. My felt sense is that God has been involved in this process as part of the implicit relationship I have identified. In the emergence of these symbols and the associative logic they triggered, there are moments of meeting with God. However, I am aware of how negative thoughts have dominated my mind, and to balance this I can recall moments and symbols of happiness.

A mindfulness of God reading

As I begin to reclaim these aspects of self and self-expression, I become more aware of God. In this sense it is as if I am imaginatively part of Mark 9:15: 'As soon as all the people saw Jesus, they were overwhelmed with wonder and ran to greet him.' My manuductive reading of this verse, which I have memorised and meditated on, is that God transformed their physical sense of sight into a spiritual sense. The crowd sees something (the recently transfigured Jesus), and the Holy Spirit touches their emotions which become wonder, and their bodies are taken up in this wonder and run to Jesus. My reading here is that God can touch our minds, our emotions, our awareness, our senses and our bodies so that we experience the divine presence in a truly incarnated way.

I have found that God has touched all these dimensions in my experience, especially as I have begun to re-inhabit them through mindful awareness. God has communicated with me through a whole range of symbols from the created world, and I have felt the divine presence in every dimension of my being. I am going to continue to reclaim the symbols that represent and contain the happiness from my childhood.

As an alternative to listening to the symbolic interaction of the natural world with your own self, you can ask yourself what experiences or symbols speak to you, in the way swallows speak to me. Try to write in prose what this experience or symbol means to you. Then create a free form of poetry with it. Speak it out, and when there is a natural break for a breath or thought, put a line break in.[301] Then look at the poem and see if any associations emerge from the margins of your life.

Conclusion

In this chapter constructed in heuristic terms and as bricolage, I also draw on mindful theory and implicit relational knowing theory. I retrieve earlier writings, quasi-poetic pieces, lyrical narrative and paintings, and use them as examples of working with the margins.

The African symbols from my childhood have sustained me in times of aridity and anxiety and emerged in times of creative and spiritual awakening. Their surfacing enabled me to see that there has been a narrative of sacramental goodness in my life, which had been hidden because the trauma of boarding school life had been the foreground. As I reflect on this from my sense of being in an implicit relationship with God, I can intuit that God used these symbols to sustain me.

Throughout this chapter I refer to my childhood experiences

---

[301] This is an exercise developed by Denise Levertov in her essays on her poetics. Denise Levertov, *New and Selected Essays* (New York: New Directions Publishing Corporation, 1992), 94.

in Africa as full of sacramental goodness. That is my intuitive sense of them, and my immersion in Roman Catholic monastic life at Worth Abbey and the reading of contemplative texts has also introduced me to the theology of creation as sacramental. Aristotle Papanikolaou makes this point that both Eastern Orthodox and Roman Catholic traditions 'affirm that all of creation is sacramental – that is, it has the power to convey the presence of God'.[302] He extends the sacramental even further to include conversations between one person and another, as he explores the sacrament of confession. It is not just conversation or confession with priests that is sacramental; he goes on to say that 'conversations with friends, parents, and therapists … are all potentially sacramental – that is, potential mediators of the presence of God'.[303] This has implications for the mindful rule, where my desire is that we talk well to each other. I long to have conversations that are sacramental.

The intentional paying attention to symbols in Rome enabled me to see the fragmented mosaic of my life and what was missing. According to embodied trauma theory, the naming of elements of trauma, including the existence of the well of sadness, lessens the shadow of the past on my present moments. I am further able to reclaim my present moments. The discovery of a hidden stream of sacramental goodness feeding me through African symbols from my childhood also further enables me to reclaim my present moments.

I return to our key quest questions. In the reclamation of my symbolic past and my symbolic self I further free up my present moments from the grip of anxiety by redressing the balance between the negative experience of boarding school and the sacramental goodness of my African childhood. We can be in the grip of overly negative interpretations of our early life. I can hold my story more lightly and savour what I experienced as a

---

[302] Aristotle Papanikolaou, 'Liberating Eros: Confession and Desire', *Journal of the Society of Christian Ethics* 26, no. 1 (2006): 125, accessed 11th December 2021, dx.doi.org/10.5840/jsce200626124.
[303] Papanikolaou, 125.

child in Kenya; it sustains and directs me now to live in nature. This chapter also enabled me to add another strand to my idea of mindfulness of God. Part of being mindful of God for me is to be aware of this underground stream of implicit relational knowing, where natural symbols travel as potential moments of meeting, waiting to emerge by God's grace into my conscious awareness. This 'unthought known' is always there and enables me to know that I have not been abandoned or rejected by God and that God's divine presence is always there. In the here and now I can be open to its presence within me and allow it to sustain me in the present.

We now need to draw these strands together in a mindful rule of life that is both personal and relational and which can lead to a mindful formation that is transformational and connected to the world around us. That is where we go next.

Reflection

Intention
I invite you to make an intention to examine the margins of your life. Perhaps ask to remember your dreams. Are there any symbols that are meaningful to you and why? You could wander around where you live and just see what 'beckons you to perceive it'.

Attention
Are there some writings, poems, journals from your past that you could retrieve and pay attention to? Are there some insights about your interests then that help shed light on your journey now?

Attitude
What is your attitude to your own creativity and imagination? Have you internalised negative messages from your childhood that perhaps you are not a creative person? Let go of these negative attitudes and re-immerse yourself in creative pastimes.

Reperceiving
We are all creative beings made in the image of God. Allow yourself to bask in that truth until you can reperceive yourself.

15
The application – the foundation of a mindful rule

Introduction

One of the questions I have been asking about the three models I have created for ethical mindful awareness and mindful formation is, 'So what?' There needs to be an application. As well as leading to a second-person guide for others seeking a mindful spirituality, I see the importance of creating a mindful rule of life as a congruent application for mindful ethical awareness. This ethical awareness is relational and in the service of creating community. This ethical awareness lies at the heart of being like Christ. The mindful rule is to be a framework for a common life together. It's significant that the monastic movement believed the most important contribution they had to make in all their long existence was the creation of a rule of life – living together was impossible without it. In this chapter I explore this motivation and the foundation for such a rule before laying out a provisional framework for a common life, including a confession and a short rule in the following chapter. This mindful rule enables us to lead a mindfully formed life by outlining an intentional pathway to formation. Christian mindfulness in the service of relationship is not easy; it comes at a cost.

Some of the motivation for the application of this came out of the lived experience of the Covid-19 pandemic, where dysfunctional forms of conflict aimed at me and others made me ill and placed a chisel in one of the trauma cracks of boarding school. I experienced a traumatic reaction I had no control over and was left feeling broken, helpless, powerless and overwhelmed. I ended up in A&E with suspected angina, chest pains, trembling, and numbness down my left arm. I was signed off work for six weeks. However, the threads for this idea run back to my childhood and my experience of words used as weapons to harm others at boarding school.

When our life fractures again

The desire for this mindful rule lies in the deeply felt sense that there should be a third way for people to dialogue, between self-justification and blame, and silence. It is based on the realisation that we should have agreed rules of behaviour, clear values of dialogue, before we navigate what we believe. It is also based on the wisdom of community that our first priority is to live out Christlike values.

With the world as I knew it shattered, I was led by God to live in intentional community with my family to seek to glue back together our life and find wisdom to live by my values of awakened language, releasing the creative word in others, and living by a rule of life that recognised others as persons worthy of respect with gracious language in our communication. This direction has been implicit in my life as I have lived in both the world of the local church and the world of contemplation, retreat houses and communities since 2012, when I wrote my first book. The application of mindful ethical awareness to relational living has also been there from the beginning of this contemplative journey.

I had built a life around the Rule of St Benedict and the commitment to stability, change, the conversion of one's whole life, and listening obedience to God.[304] However, as the ground began to shift beneath my feet, I realised I needed other strands of wisdom. I registered that I needed another thread that could

---

[304] Jamison, *Finding Sanctuary*, 116-118, for a short summary of these vows.

help with the more provisional world that was suddenly upon us with the Covid-19 pandemic. I began to read Ignatian spirituality as I wanted to expand beyond the principle of stability into the area of taking more risks for God. I was especially inspired by Ignatius' emphasis on establishing what deep desire God had placed on my heart and to follow it.[305] That deep desire spiralled around mindful formation in community and sacramental conversations. Viewed this way, my desire was to pursue mindfulness in all its depth and move out of the breadth of activities I was involved in as a minister.

As well as navigating the pandemic, I had to negotiate the conflict I found myself in more locally. Psychodynamic theory with its recognition of the distorted dimension of relationships through transference and projection was very helpful in understanding this experience. I expand on this theory later in this chapter. The mindful rule and recognition theory as I apply them are the subversive resistance to all such distortions in relationship. I know from ministering to leaders of all denominations at Scargill House that distorted relationships resulting from projection, transference and dehumanisation are a common experience.

The foundation of the mindful rule

The rule is based on the models I have created for holding values in present moment mnemonic awareness, and for being open to a continuous awareness of God's presence that allows charged and transformative moments of meeting with God. In this model of ethical awareness, scriptural verses that reflect core values can be turned into metacognitive propositions to be meditated on and held in mnemonic awareness – so that the mindful rule becomes a living memory. I have exemplified this earlier in the book with verses from Mark's Gospel, but additional verses can be added. For example, a key principle of

---

[305] Bernadette Miles, 'Ignatian Spirituality, Apostolic Creativity and Leadership in Times of Change', *The Way*, 50, no. 4 (October 2011): 37.

disagreeing well in conflict is to talk to someone face to face (Matthew 18:15). As many people dislike conflict and seek to avoid dealing with it directly, this is an indispensable principle. One of the first things I did when I started as a minister was to have some training in conflict resolution with the former London Mennonite Centre and its Bridge Builders team.[306] The emphasis on the importance of immediate and face-to-face handling of conflict has been the most important principle I have used in reconciling people.

The importance of simple practices like this in conflict is underlined through an analogy made by John Paul Lederach in his book *The Moral Imagination*. Studies have shown that a murmuration of starlings which appears complex is created out of simple moves that the birds all follow.[307] In the same way Lederach argues that, in conflict, 'simplicity precedes complexity'; if simple rules are followed then conflict can be resolved; if they are not, then conflict gets very complicated.[308]

I will come on to the confessional aspect of this mindful rule, but the 'confessional' is also a key element of peace-making.[309] The simplicity of building peace lies in two simple ideas. 'While the justification of violent response has many tributaries, the moral imagination that rises beyond violence has but two: taking personal responsibility and acknowledging relational mutuality.'[310] One of the reasons I am drawn to mindfulness is that it enables us to take personal responsibility. The God-given mindful capacities that were woven in us enable agency in our ethical behaviour. I am also drawn to mindfulness because it recognises our relational mutuality. These mindful capacities of

---

[306] I understand this has now closed, but the work continues through Alastair Mackay and his charity Reconciliation Initiatives, reconciliation-initiatives.org.
[307] John Paul Lederach, *The Moral Imagination: The Art and Soul of Building Peace* (Oxford: Oxford University Press, 2005), 32-33.
[308] Lederach, 33.
[309] Lederach, 35.
[310] Lederach, 35.

self-awareness, self-regulation and self-transcendence are relational.

Lederach adds one other crucial ingredient to peace-making, 'the art of the creative process', which has been 'overshadowed, underestimated and in too many instances forgotten'.[311] He calls this the 'moral imagination', which is the *capacity to imagine something rooted in the challenges of the real world yet capable of giving birth to that which does not yet exist*.[312] This overlaps with my model of ethical awareness in this mindful rule, where I imagine the awakening of the God-given creative word in each person to enable a recognition and reperceiving of them as persons made in the image of God. I return to this idea of creativity, imagination and the moral way of life later in this chapter.

The rule is influenced by Benedictine spirituality and by Ignatian spirituality with its emphasis on imagination. I draw on the lived experience of being in extended community at Scargill House and living by its rule of life, or pathways. I perceive a gap as I do this for a rule that draws on the wisdom of community and mindfulness – especially in utilising mindfulness theory and practice. I make use of the wisdom of other communities that have influenced Scargill, such as Iona, Northumbria and Taizé, influences that have emerged in the oral wisdom of the community.

The wisdom of intentional community

The recognition of the provisional nature of what I am creating here in a mindful rule is influenced by Brother Roger, the founder of the Taizé community. This community did not start 'with a blueprint for their life' but grew 'organically'.[313] Brother Roger himself said, 'Only by living the dynamics of the

---

[311] Lederach, ix.
[312] Lederach, ix.
[313] Susan Rakoczy, 'The Witness of Community Life: Bonhoeffer's *Life Together* and the Taizé Community', *Journal of Theology for Southern Africa* 127 (March 2007): 55.

provisional can we discover, how, time after time, to keep on gaining new momentum.'[314] This recognition of the provisional nature of what we create requires a mindful focus on the present moment. Certainly, in Taizé there appears to be an ethic that could be viewed in recognition terms. Balado says, 'The meetings in Taizé challenge those taking part to enter into a dialogue in which the main thing is to be attentive to one another's essential reality.'[315] This attentiveness to the other's essential reality is a form of recognition. This is expanded in a Christian distinctive: 'Christians are bearers in theory of a unique awareness, that every person in the world is the object of infinite Love.'[316] I believe it is mindfulness of God that can help us cultivate this unique awareness and attentiveness to the other.

I am following another fragment of monastic wisdom that has helped me live with the provisional nature of what I am doing. Fred Bahnson in an essay for *Image Journal* writes, 'You put your body where the question is. Then you walk the question.'[317] I wished to experience the wisdom of intentional community, and so I placed my body where the question is and walked the question. How can I collaborate with others to create mindful community?

Part of that lived experience at Scargill draws on the oral wisdom that forms the implicit heart of community life. One of the wisdom phrases that is repeated, especially by the director of the community, is that every community, if it is to transcend self-focus, needs a 'demanding common task'. The phrase originates with George MacLeod, founder of the Iona Community who stated, 'Only a demanding common task can

---

[314] Quoted in J L G. Balado, *The Story of Taizé* (London, Oxford: Mowbray, 1980), 17.
[315] Balado, 16.
[316] Balado, 17.
[317] Fred Bahnson, 'The Underground Life of Prayer', *Image Journal* 77, accessed 28th February 2022, imagejournal.org/article/underground-life-prayer/.

create community.'[318] The demanding common task at Scargill is hospitality. The demanding common task for mindful community would be the task of awakening kingdom language within to be the words spoken by the Light. The words spoken by the Light will always be light in the world. The language of the kingdom encourages, builds up and seeks to recognise the creative God-given word in each person and awaken it.

In the mindful rule we need each other; we are incomplete without each other. To see this completeness, we need to keep helping others find their purpose or meaning in God.

Ironically, one of the problems of working in a Baptist church that theoretically believes in the priesthood of all believers, namely that everyone is a minister, is living with the projection that as the minister you should do everything (one-person ministry) and be at every event. I never successfully subverted that projection although I involved many others in ministry. My experience of living in intentional community at Scargill is much more that it is not about one person, but about the whole community ministering to others through hospitality. The spirituality of the community also shapes the morning and other prayers, which are led by members of the community. Every member of the community takes a turn to lead morning prayers. This offers me a different model going forward for mindful community as church which will look at everyone participating in the ministry. The question I am wrestling with is, can I create a mindful community in which every participant is a full partner? This leads to a related insight that has deeply moved me: the power of meeting daily.

After twenty-three years of running a church and now having lived in community, some differences have emerged which are helpful and challenging for looking at a new form of mindful community. The church setting was very much based on a weekly rhythm. The community life at Scargill is based on a daily

---

[318] Phyllis Rodgerson Pleasants, 'He Was Ancientfuture Before Ancientfuture Was Cool', *Perspectives in Religious Studies*, 31, no. 1 (2004): 91. See also online at www.iona.org.uk.

rhythm. The community eats together daily, often three times a day. The community prays together daily – morning, lunchtime and evening. These include experiences of silence. The community has daily morning meetings after breakfast. There is also the rhythm of tea and coffee at 11am and tea, coffee and cake at 4pm every day. The community also works together every day in teams. In the lunchtime prayer each day the community is reminded of one of the pathways (rules of life) they seek to follow. This daily rhythm very quickly enables people to work together; it enables a real connection as persons, and an awareness of vulnerability and individual quirks. I have seen that people can show their vulnerability and that vulnerability can be held. The power of the community comes from this daily rhythm as well as having a demanding common task of hospitality to guests.

I am left with the question, could a mindful community that is not living together intentionally have a daily rhythm to distinguish it from the weekly church rhythm I know so well? If this is where the transformative power of community lies, what do I have to give up to make this part of the way of life?

That you must 'give something up' to be part of an intentional community is also one of the strands of oral wisdom at Scargill. Remember that recognition theory states that freedom 'in the sense of independence from others' is illusory. It is in community with others that I find true freedom.

Resistance and recognition

This mindful rule draws on the sacramental goodness of secular mindfulness and the redemptive heart of mindfulness of God. It can be applied to intentional community life, local church life and an individual's walk with God. It subverts and resists the rise of critical and shaming discourse in culture. Seamus Heaney talks about the redress of poetry, how it can tilt 'the scales of reality' in a more 'transcendent' direction and be a 'counter-reality'.[319] My sense is that this idea of awakened language can be democratised and is something many could experience. Awakened language does not have to be poetry or poetic. I hold that God's Spirit can play a part in awakening the language of encouragement in us, the language of our true self, the language of the God-given creative word in us. Such awakened kingdom language can act as a redress to cultural forces that are inimical to wellbeing; it too can be a 'counter-reality'. This awakening requires the recognition of the creative word in one's own self, in others, and the recognition of God as the one who interlaces and transforms us.

The impact of the Covid-19 pandemic

I return to the impact of the Covid-19 pandemic in my life and more widely. The Covid-19 lockdown and pandemic were marked by deep uncertainty and constant change. In my experience, unhelpful forms of conflict were amplified. A mindful rule can act as a trellis, a scaffolding, to enable stability within the uncertainty. It can also help us to keep our attention focused on what is important and openly aware of what is happening around us and in us, living by risk-taking values not fear-based safety. Mindfulness helps me to recognise the provisional nature of my own thought life, as well as life around me. One aspect that I would like to highlight is the further turn to the virtual world because of lockdown and social distancing.

I was already aware of the impact of the virtual world on our capacity to attend deeply prior to the pandemic, as well as how so many in our culture are leading disembodied lives because of digital living. The even more extreme turn to virtual living necessitated by lockdown, while having obvious benefits, amplified the digital distortions of the virtual life, including

---

[319] Heaney, 3.

'online disinhibition'.[320] Online people also wear masks and curate their identities 'with the psychological process of creating imaginary characters'.[321] In this mindful rule, the emphasis will be on being who we truly are, not curating images of our own self. I have seen narcissism rife on Facebook, and Twitter riddled with anger. This narcissism and anger expressed on social media has expanded into other areas of life, and public and community discourse has become far more bitter and angry. This is true of local churches as well. It has led to an inattention to the present moment in our lives, and this mindful rule will focus on the present moment with its ethical choices in everyday life.

Applying the map of mindfulness

This mindful rule uses the groundwork already laid in terms of cultivating a mindful spirituality and ethical awareness of the concerns of God in the present moment. I use the map of mindfulness already outlined as psycho-spiritual education to enable people to understand their whole being and inhabit it. Both secular and spiritual mindful awareness practices are built into the rule, and the rule asks its followers to intentionally train their attention in the present moment through mindful practices. This subverts and resists the capturing and fragmentation of our attentional capacities by the virtual world.

In these practices I am looking to become aware of judgemental attitudes which I would seek to replace with self-compassion and compassion for others. The aim of this is to reperceive God, myself and others. I take the log out of my own eye before I try to take the speck of dust out of someone else's eye (Matthew 7:5). I spiral back to the mindfulness theory we have looked at so far.

---

[320] John Suler, 'The Online Disinhibition Effect', *CyberPsychology & Behaviour*, 7, no.3 (2004): 321, accessed 1st December 2021, dx.doi.org/10.1089/1094931041291295.
[321] Suler, 323.

In this central strand of theory and practice of the mindful rule, I am enhancing self-awareness and self-regulation. This is significant because I am aware that we have a negativity bias, that many of our thoughts are negative, and that our perceptions of others are often biased. I take seriously the commands in Scripture to self-examination and to allow the Holy Spirit to examine me (Romans 8:27). I take seriously the commands to self-regulate my afflictive thoughts – for example, '"In your anger do not sin": do not let the sun go down while you are still angry' (Ephesians 4:26). This might be recognised as a wider form of self-control, one of the fruits of the Holy Spirit (Galatians 5:22-23). As I enhance self-awareness and self-regulation in relationship with others, I can transcend my self-focus – in that moment I can recognise others as persons. Mindfulness theory enables that self-awareness and self-examination and regulation through mindful awareness, not only through practices that will be part of this mindful rule, but also through a well-researched theory of our mindful capacities and sense of self.

As outlined earlier, mindfulness works with three aspects of self: narrative, experiential and witnessing. The mindful rule introduces participants to these aspects. I will ask participants in the mindful rule to try to identify their own relationship to these three aspects of self. The rule would introduce people to the problem of the present moment and introduce them to mindfulness practices such as the body scan and breath practices.

Secular mindfulness shows that we are often not in the present moment, and we are frequently on autopilot, living life out of automaticity – this includes living by automatic cultural, familial and religious scripts. I wish to add to this map of mindfulness the construct of Cultural Intelligence (CQ). Mindfulness is an important element in CQ and is used to help people become aware of what David C Thomas calls 'cultural cruise control'. Cultural cruise control is 'running your life on the basis of your built-in cultural assumptions'.[322] If as a mindful community we are to be multiethnic, then such awareness is very important to cultivate. We are usually not aware that we are not aware and living on autopilot. The mindful rule will help people to become aware of the things they say that come out of these automatic cultural scripts and to discern whether they need to remain unspoken out or need rewriting.

Mindfulness is also employed in secular ethical decision models. This is because 'awareness' is an important precursor to making an ethical decision.[323] Ruedy argues, 'Mindfulness promotes self-awareness, and greater self-awareness curtails unethical behavior.'[324] The language we use to talk to each other is part of our ethical behaviour, and often we say things in unaware ways, not realising the hurt they can cause. I am using mindful awareness as ethical awareness through the intentional cultivation of the things of God, and I am choosing them over the human things jostling for my attention. I have recognised the importance of mindful awareness for my ethical decision-making and built a model around the wisdom of Scripture to enable me to make ethical decisions based on my Christian values.

As already outlined, self-awareness, self-regulation and self-transcendence are God-given mindful capacities that can be enhanced. These will be explored in the rule through both secular mindfulness and scriptural overlap. In Scripture and contemplative history, we are asked to regulate our afflictive thoughts, such as anger, pride, envy, lust, greed, bitterness and

---

[322] David C Thomas & Kerr Inkson, *Cultural Intelligence: Living and Working Globally*, 2nd edition (San Francisco, California: Berrett-Koehler Publishers, 2009), 45-46.

[323] N E Ruedy and M Schweitzer, 'In the Moment: The Effect of Mindfulness on Ethical Decision Making', *Journal of Business Ethics* 95, no. 1 (2010), 73, accessed 13th December 2021, dx.doi.org/10.1007/s10551-011-0796-y.

[324] Ruedy and Schweitzer, 81.

malice.[325] These afflictive thoughts do not just manifest in harmful actions but also in harmful words. Moreover, we are commanded to regulate our tongues and the words that come out of our mouths.

Having experienced over a quarter of a century of church ministry how damaging it is to church and community life when people do not regulate their speech, controlling our tongues is a central aspect of the rule. There is no rule of life in local Baptist churches (or other denominations). This idea of how we speak also has a positive side, not just regulating our shadow side. I have already introduced the idea that mindful spirituality is in part about awakened language.

One strand of that is to awaken kingdom language. In kingdom language we encourage, we build up, we find the God-given creative word in the other and call it out. This leads to the wider principle about how to disagree well and biblical ways of working through conflict. This necessitates spelling out dysfunctional forms of behaviour that are destructive. It also involves working with archetypal dimensions to relationships, including the distorted dimension of transference and projection. I use the word 'distorted' in a non-technical sense, as my way of signalling how transference distorts the way we see the other.

From a theological perspective I have argued that these mindful capacities of awareness and attention, self-awareness, self-regulation and self-transcendence have their origin in God – they are part of our anthropological createdness. This means we can reclaim them and in doing so enable God to redeem them as a graced response. They have a purpose in being created capacities. That purpose is to enable us to focus on God, others, creation and our own self with deep attention.

---

[325] Evagrius of Pontus was the first to fully develop the idea of eight afflictive thoughts, later to become the seven deadly sins, see Simon Tugwell, 'Evagrius and Macarius', in *The Study of Spirituality*, eds Cheslyn Jones, Geoffrey Wainwright and Edward Yarnold, SJ (London: SPCK, 1986), 171.

Transference, projection and other dimensions of relationship

If I am to help others to live together in a mindful rule, then it is important that together we know something about how relationships work. I have outlined the reality that there is a distorted aspect to all relationships where we project and transfer onto others unreal judgements (a psychodynamic insight), sometimes idealistic, often negative, which make working and real aspects of the relationship difficult.[326] Clarkson recognises that there are a 'multiplicity of relationships' in counselling and psychotherapy.[327] I sketch them briefly, as having them in awareness has enabled me to be self-aware and to steer a path with others.

I outline the aspects of theory that have guided me as a minister and psychotherapist; I recognise it is a complex area and more could be said. I have mentioned the working relationship, sometimes called the 'working alliance', which is the 'necessary cooperation' to work together.[328] The real or person-to-person relationship is, says Clarkson, the 'psychotherapeutic relationship most similar to ordinary human relationships'.[329] In moments of meeting that I have drawn on already, it is the real relationship that has emerged. This could be conceptualised as a form of mutual recognition.[330] In my experience these relationships are at play in ordinary relationships; the difference is that in psychotherapy you are working with them in awareness and intentionally.[331] The person-centred counselling approach has 'the realness, or

---

[326] For a brief summary see Petruska Clarkson, *The Therapeutic Relationship* (London: Whurr Publishers Ltd, 1995), 9-11.
[327] Clarkson, *The Therapeutic Relationship*, 3-21.
[328] Clarkson, *The Therapeutic Relationship*, 8.
[329] Clarkson, *The Therapeutic Relationship*, 14.
[330] Clarkson, *The Therapeutic Relationship*, 15.
[331] See Jan Grant and Jim Crawley, *Transference and Projection* (Maidenhead: Open University Press, 2002), xvi, 3, for an acknowledgement of this in relation to transference and projection.

genuineness, or congruence of the counsellor' as one of its core conditions.[332]

Relationship with God, self and other is integral to the mindful rule. Mindful awareness, as a form of relational radar, monitors this multiplicity of relationships which are archetypal, by which I mean they are 'potentially present in any psychotherapeutic encounter', as well as in ordinary relationships.[333] In building relationship and community, I would want to be aware of these dimensions. In counselling, as in life and community, I would want to attend to the working relationship. I have found this is usually where the first stresses of conflict in relationships are revealed.

The second aspect is our real relationship which enables visible trust and vulnerability with each other. We do not have to be friends, but there needs to be a real aspect to each relationship. There may be external circumstances that stress our relationships, but more commonly we need to look inward for distortions. For example, boarding school taught me that being vulnerable was weakness and would get you bullied. Through counselling I have learned that being vulnerable is to be real.

As well as acknowledging the reality of our negativity bias and distorted ways of perceiving, all of us are wounded, and we look at others through the lens of our wounding. Clarkson calls this the '"reparative" or developmentally needed relationship'.[334] In the moment of conflict, we must catch our automatic reactions and see if they are dysfunctional and come out of our wounded self. When I was sent to boarding school, I felt rejected, although this was not the intention or reality behind my family's decision. I still fear rejection.

Because of our life history and experience, we can all enter distortions of relationship – through projection and

---

[332] Dave Mearns and Brian Thorne, *Person-Centred Counselling in Action*, 2nd edition (London: Sage, 2003),15.

[333] Clarkson, *The Therapeutic Relationship*, xii.

[334] Clarkson, *The Therapeutic Relationship*, 11-13.

transference. I have often looked at the Gospels through this lens. As I read and respond to the Gospels, I see in the conflict stories Jesus Himself experienced projection and transference. The Pharisees and teachers of the law saw Him in a distorted way, as someone who would bring the wrath of the Romans down on them (John 11:48). They also saw Jesus as a rival for the support of the crowds – their antagonistic actions toward Him were motivated by self-interest (Matthew 27:18). The disciples possibly believed that Jesus would be the triumphant Messiah who would drive out the Romans, as some other groups at the time commonly believed about the coming Messiah. For example, in Mark 8:31-33; Matthew 16:21-22 Peter rebukes Jesus when He talks about dying on a cross; the way of suffering was not the path he saw for Jesus.

Transference can be defined as 'the client's experience of the therapist that is shaped by his or her own psychological structures and past, and involves displacement onto the therapist, of feelings, attitudes, and behaviors belonging rightfully in earlier significant relationships'.[335] As a minister, whenever I have experienced a person reacting to me negatively, I have often looked for the projection and transference. In recognition theory terms, I am being misrecognised. This transference is usually outside someone's awareness; it is 'largely an unconscious process'.[336] This makes it difficult to work with as I am not being seen as I really am, and the other person is unaware of their distorted perceptions. The main way I have tried to work with transference is to move the person out of a distorted relationship with myself into a real relationship – where they see me as I really am.[337] During the Covid-19 pandemic and lockdown this was very difficult as we could not see people face to face, which was the main way I created real

---

[335] C J Gelso and J A Hayes, *The Psychotherapy Relationship* (New York: Wiley, 1998), 11, as cited in Grant and Crawley, 4.
[336] Grant and Crawley, 5.
[337] Dave Mearns, *Developing Person-Centred Counselling* 2nd edition (London: Sage, 2003), 57.

relationships.

Although transference is projected, Grant and Crawley also further define projection, which can be helpful in further sifting the distortions experienced in relationship. They define projection as 'a psychological process that involves the attribution of unacceptable thoughts, feelings, traits or behaviours to others that are characteristic of oneself'.[338] This relieves the one projecting from 'intolerable' internal 'anxiety and conflict'.[339] In my experience this has a different feel to transference and can be very intense.

There is a body of work that acknowledges the pastoral relationship attracts transference and projection.[340] I have also worked with the realisation that I can be sucked into a countertransference towards the member of my congregation. I have generally worked with the definition that Schwartz uses: 'A second important use of the word countertransference is to describe the responses in the therapist evoked by the patient's transference to him or her; that is to say, your own response to the ways in which a patient insists on mis-perceiving you.'[341] If someone sees me as a punitive authoritative figure projecting someone from the past, I can get drawn into behaving in that way. In my time as a pastor, I worked with a supervisor with whom I could discuss any conflict to examine possible transference and countertransference reactions. In my experience, this transference and countertransference when it is outside of awareness can be one of the most destructive aspects in relationship. Schwartz recognises the stressful weight of transference: 'Most simply put, to be loved, to be hated, to be worshipped, to be despised evokes powerful feelings even in the

---

[338] Grant and Crawley, 18.
[339] Grant and Crawley, 18.
[340] See Richard S Schwartz, 'A Psychiatrist's View of Transference and Countertransference in the Pastoral Relationship', *Journal of Pastoral Care* 43, no. 1 (March 1989): 41-46, accessed 8th December 2021, doi.org/10.1177/002234098904300107.
[341] Schwartz, 42.

healthiest of us.'[342] The main reactions are to attack or withdraw when the transference is negative or lap up the adulation when it is positive.[343]

One piece of advice I was given by my tutor in pastoral care and counselling when I was training as a minister (1994-97) was to stay in difficult relationships if possible. However, in the conflict I experienced in lockdown I realised another piece of wisdom. In this situation I had to withdraw. In envisioning a mindful rule, I must consider the responses that are possible, including when withdrawal is the only option. A mindful rule is, therefore, also about healthy boundaries. One challenge I face is what to do about the reality that the ministerial role attracts a significant burden of transference. This makes a real relationship difficult.

Part of listening to our own self is to ask which part of me is speaking? Am I speaking out of my real self or is it my wounded self that is speaking? Am I speaking out of my working self or is my distorted self projecting onto others here? There is also a spiritual relationship that is there with God and others that is archetypal which can also guide us into wiser living.[344]

In the mindful rule there would be a seeking of a continuous awareness of the presence of God; we can only be mindful of ourselves, others and creation when we are mindful of God. As we seek this awareness as a graced response, we also become aware of God's mindfulness (remembrance) of us (Psalm 8). This compassionate presence which we are invited into enables us to be more compassionate, more Christlike. Although we play our part in living out a mindful rule, we cannot do it on our own self-direction. Under God's direction we are looking to know ourselves.

There is one reality, but we face both the material reality and the reality of God who is present in that reality. Our temptation is to avoid that reality and any difficulties it contains, including

---

[342] Schwartz, 43.
[343] Schwartz, 43.
[344] Clarkson calls this the 'transpersonal relationship', 187.

our own inner conflicts and conflicts with others. In the mindful rule we turn towards the difficulties immediately. Living in the present moment is, therefore, central to the mindful rule. This will include handling our afflictive thoughts so that our present moments are not overwhelmed with anxiety, or self-justification, or other distress.

Reflection

Intention

Having an intention to examine our own life in terms of the five dimensions of relationship outlined above is necessary in mindful formation: working, real, wounded, distorted and spiritual. This can help us navigate conflict and difficulty more clearly.

Attention

It takes time to become attuned to these relationship patterns – but being attentive to the wisdom outlined in these five dimensions is worth the effort. Any training you can undertake that enhances your relational wisdom and self-awareness is worth undertaking. But paying attention is at the heart of relational wellbeing, and this especially includes attentive listening.

Attitude

All our senses are relational and send us immediate messages as we engage consciously and unconsciously with the world. One of the instant reactions is whether we find something pleasant or unpleasant. This can then be a trigger for negative thoughts and feelings.[345] Maybe this feels too much like hard work, so we find an automatic aversion to this self-examination. It is worth trying to catch these primary reactions that are so quick to emerge and influence us out of our awareness. Smell is one way

---

[345] Mark Williams calls this 'feeling tone' in his new book *Deeper Mindfulness: The New Way to Rediscover Calm in a Chaotic World* (London: Piatkus, 2023), 4, Kindle.

we can test these reactions: do you find the smell of coffee pleasant or unpleasant? What about fresh bread? What smells do you find unpleasant? In this work we are trying to become aware of how our more negative attitudes can be influenced by these feeling tones.

Reperceiving

As we develop our self-awareness, we will begin to have a clearer view on reality; we will start to reperceive. Try to notice any insights that emerge for you and write them down in a journal.

16
Other dimensions to the mindful rule

I want to teach the mindful rule in an accessible, participatory and dialogic way, to be congruent with the values of this book. Mindfulness has enabled me to find agency in regulating my mental health and in playing my part in being mindful of God. I have agency or spiritual freedom as I define it, when I exercise self-awareness, self-regulation and transcend my automatic self-focus. To adapt an analogy used by Martin Laird – one that resonates with my symbolic interest in sailing boats – I am the sailing boat, the sail, the rudder and the keel. I can learn to inhabit every part of the boat and develop the skills to sail in life, but I 'cannot produce the necessary wind that moves the boat'.[346] The wind of the Spirit is the graced response of God towards me. I can help others find their agency, both for wellbeing and in mindful spirituality. This clear outline of how I play my part through mindfulness can also be seen as part of my original contribution.

This analogy is an example of an approach that I will adopt in the mindful rule. I have consistently used narrative and the poetic in this spiritual AE. Stories, metaphors, poetry and riddles are also used to teach mindfulness. I will draw on these metaphors, poems and stories, and use stories from my own life. I will encourage those exploring the mindful rule to write their own stories. I will also introduce the idea of listening for the emergence of personal symbols from the underground stream

---

[346] Martin Laird, *Into the Silent Land* (London: Darton, Longman & Todd, 2006), 4.

of implicit relational knowing with God, how the 'unthought known' can be a rich source of interaction with God as moments of meeting emerge from it.

One of the important things I have learned in teaching mindfulness to others is to help them find the motivation to do it. The motivation is the fuel that enables the daily intention. For example, to illustrate the cost of inattentiveness, I often tell the story of how I nearly killed Coco our dog one Christmas morning.

> We had our Christmas service at 10.15am on Christmas Day. We have a member of congregation who always comes for Christmas lunch. It had been a busy festive period and I had led several services, including the late service running past midnight on Christmas Eve. After our lunch it was my turn to do the washing up. Because of anxiety I always like to make sure the sink in the kitchen is clean, so I began to fill it slowly with hot water and bleach. I decided to sit down in the living room for ten seconds just to rest. After a while Coco ran in shaking his paws and rubbing his face on the carpet. I realised I had left the tap running. I ran into the kitchen where the floor was awash with hot bleachy water. I quickly turned the tap off and ran back to check on Coco. Fortunately, the bleach was so diluted he had suffered no harm, but before mopping the floor I ran him upstairs to give him a bath.

I don't want to be on autopilot and so this story motivates me to practise daily. I would then ask, 'What might your intention be in practising mindfulness daily?'

Humour will be an important part of the participatory dialogue and storytelling. Stories can also help bring alive the more technical elements of the mindfulness map as well as distinctives. I am emphasising that mindfulness is not just about personal wellbeing, although I believe it is an important intention to want to move out of anxiety into a place of wellbeing through mindfulness. Another story I often tell is about the relational side of mindfulness as I experienced it first. In this sense the mindful rule is evocative and analytic in its use of mindfulness research and narrative:

> Back in 2006 I was very stressed, anxious and close to burnout. Alongside being a minister, I was studying counselling and psychotherapy part-time at Roehampton University. One day I was on the Tube, and I felt as if I was going to fall apart, and there was nothing I could do about it. It was such an overwhelming feeling that I felt I couldn't ask for help. I reverted to my self-sufficiency. I felt ashamed, that I shouldn't feel like this – that I should be able to cope. One of the lecturers mindfully noticed there was something wrong and took me into her study. She was able to hold me psychically and enabled me to hold myself. She spoke out what was on my heart, even before I knew it was on my heart. I have never forgotten the power of mindful awareness directed to another person. Or that in a busy day of lecturing she lived by her value of putting a student's wellbeing first.

The creation of the mindful rule will also be a participatory and collaborative work. As those who are living the mindful rule immerse themselves in it, they can observe their participation and help to shape communal life. This is a good fit with mindful awareness. We would be participant perceivers of our common life together.

Finally, before I outline the mindful rule, I want to come back to the importance of remembering. My experience of the Benedictine Rule is that it is designed to help us remember how to live a form of mindfulness of God. As I have reflected on living in intentional community at Scargill through its daily rhythms and repetitions, I have learned to remember its rule of life, its pathways, without recourse to a written text. Secular mindfulness is taught in such a way that we remember how to be mindful without recourse to the self-help texts that we started with. The aim with the mindful rule and its intention to create a mindful spirituality that lives in healthy life-giving relationship with others is to enable it to be constructed in such a way that it can be remembered without constant returning to a text.

Another person who has researched the premodern use of memory is Mary Carruthers, and she distinguishes between 'memory understood as the ability to reproduce something exactly ("rote") and memory as recollection'.[347] This is a significant distinction for the mnemonic awareness at the core of my mindfulness of God. She defines recollection as the 'ability to reconstruct such information whether logically, or by a mnemonic scheme'.[348] The repetition and careful construction of mindfulness theory to make it memorable is an implicit form of mnemonic scheme. Carruthers adds that 'recollection occurs consciously through association'.[349] This is another important dimension to association. The mnemonic scheme is created through associative links and can be recollected as part of our mnemonic awareness in the present moment. Mindfulness enables intentional recollection.

In an overlap with mindfulness, *memoria*, the art and craft of memory, is made of designed memories. Mindfulness with its metacognitive propositions, such as 'thoughts are not facts', is also facilitated by such *'designed'* memories.[350] God-designed memories through scriptural propositions are a key part of my ethical mnemonic awareness.

In an aside, Carruthers makes an application of this idea of recollection in discussing monastic *memoria*, especially through *Lectio Divina*. She adds that 'Monastic *memoria* is more like what is now called "mindfulness"' which is 'a discipline of attentive

---

[347] Mary Carruthers, *The Book of Memory: A Study of Memory in Medieval Culture* 2nd edition (Cambridge: Cambridge University Press, 2008), 22.
[348] Carruthers, 22.
[349] Carruthers, 23.
[350] Carruthers, 40.

recollection'.[351] That is, *Lectio Divina* is akin to a discipline of attentive recollection, and this is like mindfulness as described by modern psychologists. The mindful awareness of the things of God I am trying to create through the collection of and meditation on scriptural (and other) propositions can be described as a form of attentive recollection rather than remembering by rote. The revisiting of mindfulness theory in this research is not repetition by rote but an intentional form of attentive recollection in different settings. I wish to make this an explicit part of my theory and practice of mindfulness of God, rather than an implicit part. For this I can draw on the mnemonic structures and ways this attentive recollection was cultivated in the premodern age.

I want to draw some strands together here. This mindful rule based on mindful recognition and reperceiving of the other is made possible by the Holy Spirit's graced attention towards us. It is also a moral and imaginative act, a work of the 'moral imagination'. It can develop in unexpected directions, like a murmuration of starlings, because it seeks to awaken the God-given creative word in each person. In the imagining of such a mindful rule, are there wider cultural and theological connections I can draw on? Walton in her work on poetics outlines the link between *phronesis* and poetics or *poesis* as developed by John Wall.[352]

She defines *phronesis* as the 'capacity to reflect and act well in accordance with a virtuous apprehension of what constitutes the ethical life'.[353] Walton acknowledges the significance of this link when historically philosophy has seen 'creative activity … as fundamentally different from the ethical project of living a good life'.[354] Wall takes up the idea of the possibility of moral imagination and says, 'It seems to me that we ought to be capable of *imagining* each other ever more profoundly,

---

[351] Carruthers, 154.
[352] Walton, *Writing Methods*, 143.
[353] Walton, *Writing Methods*, 143.
[354] Walton, *Writing Methods*, 143.

particularly, lovingly, compassionately.'[355] He argues that this is a created capacity, and that 'despite its impossibility in history, we are ultimately created capable of sympathetic mutuality with others precisely in their otherness'.[356]

Susan F Parsons in her article on the practice of Christian faith and mindfulness argues that '*Phronesis* ... may be translated as mindfulness'.[357] What she means by this is that *phronesis* 'is the way of being mindful, of being prudent, of thinking carefully about what lies ahead'.[358] Mindfulness is used in secular ethical decision models, and so this is a congruent link between *phronesis* and mindfulness. Parsons adds that *phronesis*, or this ethical mindful awareness, is a way of 'letting oneself become aware that the next step to be taken matters, and of understanding *why* this is so'.[359] I am saying something similar in my desire to have in mind the things of God and to choose them over the human things jostling for my attention – I want to know what matters and why in each present moment. So, mindfulness has a connection to ethical awareness, but it also has a connection to enhancing creativity.

It is my experience that since I have practised mindfulness, my creativity has budded, blossomed and flourished. My hypothesis is that mindfulness can help me enhance my 'moral creativity' in the making of a mindful rule with others.[360] This adding of a mindfulness strand to the 'yes but how do I cultivate my moral imagination' may also be a novel application of this theory.

A final point before I outline how the mindful rule comes

---

[355] John Wall, 'The Creative Imperative: Religious Ethics and the Formation of Life in Common', *Journal of Religious Ethics* 33, no. 1, (2005): 55, accessed 21st December 2022, dx.doi.org/10.1111/j.0384-9694.2005.00182.x.
[356] Wall, 'Creative Imperative', 56.
[357] Susan F Parsons, 'The Practice of Christian Ethics: Mindfulness and Faith', *Studies in Christian Ethics* 25, no. 4 (November 2012): 443.
[358] Parsons, 444.
[359] Parsons, 444.
[360] Wall, 'The Creative Imperative', 60.

out of the recognition that I am using different aspects of mindfulness theory which I may be able to connect. I am thinking of narrative, experiential and witnessing selves; mindful capacities as self-awareness, self-regulation and self-transcendence; the importance of intention in training our attention and attitudes non-judgementally so we can reperceive and so on. There is overlap and connection between all these which I would like to find a shape for.

The idea for this came from a mindful walk at night in Wharfedale. There was no light pollution, and the stars were shining like pinpricks of light in a dark velvet expanse of infinity. I could make out constellations that formed part of larger patterns. I see the different aspects of mindfulness I am working with as constellations that are part of a larger pattern or way. I create a metaphoric landscape or map or star chart that holds these different patterns together. I also extend the idea of pilgrimage into the mindful rule to provide shape and direction. I fashion the mindful rule as a pilgrimage, using the elements I have outlined earlier in the research: journey, spiritual magnetism, places, people, practices, pain, the breaking through of healing and transformation into the present. This will not be a franchised pilgrimage but one that can be personally shaped within the patterns and wisdom of mindfulness of God.

Beginning with confession

The rule begins with metacognitive propositions about living mindfully together, which may not be understood fully at the beginning. The aim is for these propositions to become metacognitive insights. Behind each of these propositions lies carefully considered wisdom from mindfulness and the Christian tradition. The rule does not use a rhetoric of persuasion but seeks to help people reperceive their own self, others and God. The desire at the centre of the rule is to enable sacramental conversations that mediate the presence of God, awakening the God-given creative word in each other. The wisdom I have gathered on this pilgrimage towards mindfulness of God is as near to reality and truth as I can get it now – speaking from a perspective of critical realism. It will need constant revision.

In his article on confession as sacramental conversation, Papanikolaou more specifically defines confession as 'speaking truthfully that which one fears most to speak'.[361] In this mindful journey I have been learning to face the reality of who I am and what the world is. What do I fear most to speak out? Because of the shaping of boarding school into self-sufficiency, emotional inexpression and silent unquestioning loyalty, it is to acknowledge that I have needs. It is to recognise that I am not invulnerable, that it is extremely painful to be misrecognised by others and that I need to be recognised as I am. I would like to see this emphasis on speaking what one fears most to speak at the beginning of the rule. It may be that people can add their own variants to the rule to take in their own context.

One question I have asked myself is, why am I drawn to the idea of recognition as a value? In Mark's Gospel there is a pattern of Jesus 'seeing' others (Mark 1:16, 19; 2:5, 14). This is a form of recognition. Joel Marcus in his commentary on Mark puts it like this: 'This seeing is not to be interpreted as passive observation but as an active, "possessive gaze" by means of which Jesus lays claim to something through a thorough inspection of it.'[362] This idea seized me when I read it, that Jesus had seen me, recognised me and called me into ministry back in 1993. This idea has sustained me. Marcus expands on this by saying that the disciples follow Jesus because of '*his* perception of *them*, his prophetic vision of what they will become under the impact of his presence'.[363]

I can reframe this as Jesus calling out the God-given creative word, the little *logos*, in each of them. However, it was its

---

[361] Papanikolaou, 115.
[362] Joel Marcus, *The Anchor Yale Bible Mark 1-8: A new translation with introduction and commentary* (Newhaven, London: Yale University Press, 2000), 183.
[363] Marcus, 2000, 183.

resonance with me that I particularly want to highlight. As I apply it here, the sense I have of it relating to the mindful rule is that all our seeing is first predicated on Jesus' seeing of us – that to have sacramental conversations we need to see and recognise as Jesus sees and recognises. This idea of Jesus seeing and recognising His disciples I can appropriate for my life and is another manuductive moment with a scriptural text.

To come back to the power of telling the truth as far as we can about reality, I begin the mindful rule with such statements. These statements are for us to say and to seek to grasp the reality of them. In the same way participation in Alcoholics Anonymous requires a confession 'that one is a recovering alcoholic', so in the rule we can acknowledge we have a negativity bias, distorted perceptions, and we don't see each other clearly.[364] We begin, therefore, with a form of mindful confession. This confession also recognises our God-given mindful capacities. The research ends as it began, with the strand of the confessional narrative and the idea of confessional theology. I am confessing my own 'personal responsibility' for relationship and the 'relational mutuality' I am part of. The confessional language of responsibility says, 'I am part of this pattern. My choices and behaviors affect it'.[365]

As I move to this mindful confession, the symbol of boats, as it relates to this rule, comes back to mind. The first is a memory of being in Paris with my wife for a few days at a friend's flat. I had bought a ticket to a rare Odilon Redon exhibition as one of his paintings, *The Mystical Boat*, was one of my favourite pieces of art. As I walked around and was drawn into the paintings, I was moved to tears. I once had a dream of the painting about the mystical boat, that there was a flotilla of such boats travelling together. Thinking of each person as a mystical boat underlines our essential aloneness and mystery as a human being made in God's image. However, in my

---

[364] See Papanikolaou, 117, for the confessional element in Alcoholics Anonymous.
[365] Lederach, 35.

experience we also need each other. A flotilla of boats, if it is to sail together, needs rules and boundaries so as not to crash into one another. They need to learn how to tack and catch the wind of the Spirit, not just separately, but together. It is an image of the community that could emerge through a mindful rule.

The second fragment that is magnetically drawn into my memory is that of a 'skin boat'. Apparently a 'skin boat' is a 'curragh', a boat 'made from ox-hide tanned in oak bark and stretched over a rib cage of ash wood'.[366] The term 'skin boat' conveys the fragility of this ancient craft, but for me the association is that I am a fragile skin boat, made for unimaginable voyages. These images help me picture the frailty of a mindful community, made of individual 'skin boats' and yet with the possibility of sailing together.

Reflection

Intention
Have an intention to have a short account with God and an honest practice of confession which acknowledges reactivity in relationships when it happens. Ask God to help you cultivate your moral imagination in relationships.

Attention
Pay attention to the parables, stories, poems, metaphors that have spoken to you. Revisit them or explore new ones and allow them to speak to the margins of your life. Do they somehow encapsulate a value for you?

Attitude
Try to catch your automatic reactions which are almost instantaneous, and in an intentional breathing space try to find a wiser response in your relationships.

---

[366] Samuel Thomas Merton, 'Skin Boat', in *Dark Art Café Blog*, July 7, 2010, accessed 16th March 2022, samuelthomasmartin.wordpress.com/2010/07/07/skin-boat-by-john-terpstra.

Reperceiving
In practising your intention to be mindful of God, training your attention and changing your attitudes, you create the conditions to reperceive God, yourself and others. Perhaps the reperceiving of your own self is that you are beginning to say, 'I can,' rather than, 'I can't.'

17
The mindful rule

A mindful confession

I list below the key metacognitive propositions that begin the mindful rule.

I recognise I am on a pilgrimage journey and never arrive.

This journey will centre around Jesus Christ.

I will seek to fully know myself and others so that I may have sacramental conversations with them.

I aspire to use the wisdom of the mindful rule to map my self-understanding.

I recognise I have a capacity for self-awareness that can be enhanced. Self-awareness is essential in living in community.

I recognise I have a capacity for attention and awareness which is a God-given mindful capacity.

I will work with others.

I recognise I am wounded.

I recognise I have a negativity bias and distorted perceptions.

I realise I can misrecognise other people through projection and transference.

I recognise I have a storytelling self, which is the source of many distorted perceptions of my own self and others.

I recognise I have an embodied, experiential self, and as I step into my body, senses and breath, I can relativise my narrative self and its automatic hold on the centre of my life.

As I make this move, I can more fully inhabit the present moment which is reality.

I recognise I have a witnessing self that can witness my thoughts and feelings, rather than be a victim of them.

I recognise I have a capacity for self-regulation that can be enhanced. Self-regulation is essential in living in community.

I recognise I have a capacity for self-transcendence; this is essential for living in community.

I aim daily to intentionally practise being in the present moment, in mindful awareness.

On this pilgrim journey I plan to use secular mindfulness practices and spiritual mindful awareness practices, such as the Jesus Prayer and *Lectio Divina*, to enhance my mindful capacities.

I will train my capacity for attention and awareness.

I aim to recognise and lay down negative, critical, unhelpful judgements about my own self and others, and to cultivate a compassionate reperceiving.

In conflict with others, I would try to talk to them face to face and use a mediator when necessary. I will work hard to regulate my language. I shall endeavour not to triangulate with others, talking about someone to others rather than talking to them.

I recognise I have a God-given creative word within me that, when awakened, enables me to live life in all its fullness.

I recognise others have a God-given creative word within them.

I hope to create with others a place of spiritual magnetism for those in pain on this pilgrim journey.

The common demanding task of this community is to awaken these words and live them out, being led to other people of peace to help them find their creative word.

In this way the power of the future can break through into our present to bring healing and transformation.

I will use the maps of the mindful rule to understand myself and others.

I recognise the importance of creating a working relationship with others, seeking to be real and authentic in those relationships.

I will work to become aware of my negativity bias and distorted perceptions. I will use mindfulness practices to enhance my self-awareness so that I understand my wounded places, the distorted projections and transference I may put on others.

I recognise that nature is sacramental and is a book that can lead me to God.

I will seek to have sacramental conversations with others, perceiving their essential reality, and will seek that each person I meet is loved with the infinite Love of God.

In summary, then, as part of our confession and as a mindful community, our demanding common task is to recognise the God-given creative word in our own self and in others. In the community, respect does not have to be earned but is given; because each of us is made in the image of God, we have equal dignity. As words spoken by the Light to be light to the world, we will always be looking for people of peace to awaken their creative word. In this we will be led by God's Holy Spirit, and fully respect the person's freedom. I recognise the sacramental goodness of my mindful capacities. I also recognise the gift of the earth, nature, creation.

A star chart of my mindful rule

I have created a short architectural place of memory, a mnemonic structure, that summarises my mindful rule as a star chart. I have drawn on the pattern and mythology of the Orion constellation.

One of the mythological representations of Orion is as a hunter, and in one version he is an archer.[367] I work with this symbol of the archer. I have sketched the constellation of Orion and taken some of the standard features and made them my own symbols. I place the drawing here.

---

[367] Andy Oppenheimer, *Stars of Orion: An Astronomy Special* (2021), 15, Kindle.

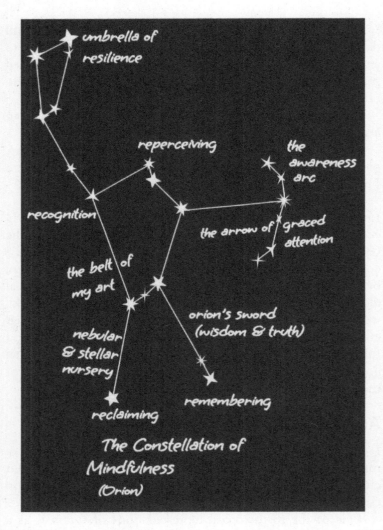

This represents a way of representing and remembering a short version of my mindful rule. Orion as a constellation 'straddles the celestial equator, meaning the constellation is visible, or partly visible, from almost every inhabited region on Earth'.[368] Mindfulness is a universal human capacity accessible to all.

---

[368] Oppenheimer, 2.

The mindful rule

On my pilgrim journey I will watch for the tracings of God's presence all around me as a hunter tracks a deer.

I live within the arc of awareness, openly aware of God, myself, others and creation. Through practices I will sustain, switch and cultivate deep attention.

This arc of attention, like the constellation of Orion, is accessible to most other people; they too can learn to live within it.

My intention is to follow the flight of graced attention. Through that graced attention I will focus on being a word spoken by the Light, shining with others in a community constellation.

In this pilgrimage, I wish this community constellation to be a place of spiritual magnetism for those in pain, seeking healing and transformation.

The belt of 'art' holds me together with others. The three points of light that illumine mindful awareness of self are awareness, regulation and transcendence. I take the log out of my own eye; I do not let the sun go down on my anger, and I transcend the anxious and wounded parts of my self.

Through this 'art' I tell undistorted stories, live an embodied life, fully inhabiting my emotions and witnessing every aspect of my being.

I cultivate ethical mnemonic awareness through meditating on scriptural propositions until they become insights.

I am aware that I am in an implicit relationship of knowing with God, with moments of meeting; this helps me to cultivate an attitude of trust when I am not aware of God. I walk in the dark and trust the stars that guide me.

Mindfulness is my coat and umbrella in the storms of life.

The sword that hangs from the belt is that of wisdom and truth drawn from the wisdom of mindfulness of God.

Within my symbolic self and poetic imagination there is a nebula, a stellar nursery, where creativity, dreams and symbols grow.

I play my part in reclaiming my present moments and remember to come home to God in the present moment. These are the ankles that keep me standing.

I come home to God in the present moment to reperceive God, myself, others and creation. Through reperceiving as a graced response, I mindfully recognise our essential reality and connectedness. Reperceiving and recognition are the shoulders of my archer, enabling me to hold the bow of awareness.

This pilgrimage is a way of wholeness in the here and now.

Reflection

Intention
I invite you to have the intention to work through the mindful confession as a form of self-examination. Try to identify three priorities that you would like to focus on. For example, 'I will endeavour in situations of conflict to talk face to face with the person as quickly as possible.'

Attention
Pay attention for a period to your conversations. Endeavour to make them 'sacramental' conversations where you are looking for the God-given creative word in the other person.

Attitude
Try to become aware of your judgemental thoughts, whether of others or yourself. These are often automatic reactions. Notice them, examine them and let them go. Consider what a wiser response might be on each occasion.

Reperceiving
Endeavour to see what is good in others, their strengths, what could be encouraged. If necessary, try to see them as if for the first time, without any relational baggage.

18
Coming home

An overriding directional image

As we come towards the end of the journey and as I lay out this summary of these themes, one question I want to ask from a wider cultural perspective is whether there is a 'directional image' that also lies within the pilgrimage. As Leigh examined wider cultural patterns in ten spiritual autobiographies in the twentieth century, he identified that these narratives have a directional image often encapsulated in the title, for example, Dorothy Day's *The Long Loneliness*.[369] This can be a helpful quest for anyone – to establish the directional image of their own life.

One such possible directional image is that of home. I have been homesick. Homesickness is a form of loss, a form of bereavement. I am still homesick. Schaverien makes the point that homesickness is a 'totally inadequate description'; it is, she adds, 'actually a symptom of undiagnosed trauma'.[370] I link this feeling of homesickness to the threshold moment already alluded to, where I realised I was completely alone in an unsafe place.

I have reclaimed the African symbols of my childhood that are home for me. My perception is that as a child I fully inhabited the present moment, lived an embodied emotional, imaginative life, immersed in an East African paradise, and all of this was lost. Everything I was at home in was on the other

---

[369] Leigh, 1, Introduction.
[370] Schaverien, 141.

side of the world. I feel like the wandering swallow, or even like the swift we see here at Scargill, which hardly ever lands or nests.

Integral to this quest is that I am trying to find my present moments, which have been lost. There are pragmatic reasons for doing this which mindfulness lists, including finding wellbeing. There are theological reasons for this, the present moment being the point where my time intersects with God's time. I do not picture this quest to fully inhabit my present moments as a purely pragmatic one. I recognise that as a child I experienced beautiful, sacramental moments that I have been able to recall. I have used the word mystical very sparingly, as it is so weighted, but perhaps these moments filled with sacramental goodness, like sunshine, hold a *mystical* charge for me, like Redon's painting, The Mystical Boat.

These were moments of meeting with a mysterious reality that beckoned me to perceive something more. I think my quest casts about to find more such moments of meeting. Because in those moments of meeting, I felt at home. I lost the sense of home and am seeking to find it again, but this time in what is eternal, the presence of God. But the presence of God mediated in the now through my fully inhabited incarnational being.

This directional image of trying to come home resonates with the wider cultural pattern Leigh explores. For example, Thomas Merton's narrative has a 'repeated image of his life as a journey … a journey in search of a permanent "home"'.[371] Nelson Mandela's autobiography is given direction 'by the vision of a harmonious society modelled on the tribal unity of his childhood villages'.[372] This was his experience of home as a child. Leigh identifies in the autobiography of Dan Wakefield, a 'returning home' motif to find redemption.[373] Home can be a problematic concept for many, but it is something that is worth redeeming, even if, like me, you feel you have lost it or never

---

[371] Leigh, 1, Introduction. Leigh is referring to Merton's autobiography, Thomas Merton, *The Seven Story Mountain* (New York: Harcourt, 1948).
[372] Leigh, 2.
[373] Leigh, 215, 217.

had it. The present moment is home in mindfulness of God. I believe that is why many are turning to mainstream mindfulness, trying to return home to their whole self.

Books and attention

Another overlapping theme with this wider cultural picture is with books. Leigh observes that Augustine is obsessed with the '"books" of his childhood'.[374] Leigh also notes that 'the transforming influence of books in the lives of Merton, Day, Lewis, Malcolm X, Gandhi, and Wakefield' is a recurrent theme.[375] In Kenya we had no TV, no computer, no phones. Books were my first love and have been my constant companion since then. English was my favourite subject as I grew up. I went to Leeds university because Tolkien had been a lecturer there. Books became part of my internal home, where I could escape in my imagination, as I could not escape in my body.

A constant focus of my attention since 1986 when I became a Christian was being in charismatic relationship with the Trinitarian God of my faith. This led to a valuing of Scripture as a source of wisdom for my life. That I would be led to study the Book is no surprise to me. This focus on Scripture, but as a living Word, and reading, along with my interest in mindfulness, brought me into contact with biblical commentaries, theological books, articles and different theologies that helped shape the direction of my life and research. I have mainly focused on those elements that led me by the hand to God, but also drawn on my wider reading. In many cases these were theological fragments out of which I have woven together a provisional whole.

I revisit here the work of N Katherine Hayles who links the idea of 'deep attention', which I examined earlier, to books.

---

[374] Leigh, 6.
[375] Leigh, 6.

Deep attention is cultivated through 'close reading' of books.[376] However, with the rise of digital technologies there is continued 'technogenesis', and our capacities for attention and awareness change.[377] Different forms of reading evolve, particularly 'hyper-reading', involving 'skimming, scanning, fragmenting, and juxtaposing texts'.[378] Hayles argues that hyper-reading is linked to 'hyper-attention', where there is a 'low threshold of boredom', where 'different information streams' come at us with a 'high level of stimulation'.[379]

From my personal perspective, I am aware that this necessary inhabiting of a virtual world exacerbates my tendency to live in my head and not my body. The question I am left with is, do we lose the capacity for deep attention? From my experience, mindfulness offers an alternative, where we can have a close focused attention on one thing while being openly aware of other things in our environment. I am left with the sense that the childhood I had which fostered deep attention is an increasingly rare phenomenon. Mindful formation has enabled a deep attention to the idea of mindfulness of God.

This means I have stayed with the quest questions for a long time. When I first encountered mindfulness of God back in 2006, the personal question that became a wider quest question for others was, 'What is mindfulness of God, and how might I cultivate it?' As the journey developed, I realised I needed to ask another question which helped answer the first: 'How can I reclaim my present moments from anxious rumination to be mindful of God?' I discovered that it was not just anxiety that overwhelmed my present moments; it was also the shadow of the past. This led to the third question: 'How could I be fully aware of and at home in my whole embodied self, to further reclaim my present moments?' I needed to reclaim my past self. My whole self also included the underground stream of my

---

[376] Hayles, 11.
[377] Hayles, 10-11.
[378] Hayles, 12.
[379] Hayles, 12.

symbolic self, the 'unthought known', which carried symbols of sacramental goodness that also reclaimed my present moments. These quest questions are applicable to many others. I realised that to be mindful of God I needed to be in the present moment; this was where life in all its fullness was (John 10:10). Life in all its fullness for me is coming home to the present moment. In the present moment we come home to God.

I am able here to bring together our main questions in a creative synthesis, in relation to mindfulness. Mindful awareness enables us to relativise our afflictive thoughts. This is enabled by general mindfulness practice and the cultivation of ethical mnemonic awareness. Through the analogical conceptual model of being in a knowing implicit relationship with God we can cultivate trust in God's providential care even when we are not aware of God's presence.

In the moment we can be mindful of God as a graced response. Through this graced response we can reperceive God, our own self, others and creation. In that reperceiving we can recognise our essential relational reality. To further reclaim our present moments, we need to be fully aware of and at home in our whole embodied self. Through mindfulness we can recognise and relativise the distorted scripts of our past (often the root of our afflictive thoughts). We can cultivate new scripts through scriptural propositions that function as personal values. Interestingly, for the healing and accepting of the past I needed more than mindfulness. It was embodied and sociological trauma theory that brought healing, although mindfulness is incorporated into embodied trauma theory. So, I do not leave mindfulness behind in this wider strand of help.

Mindfulness can also rekindle our creative symbolic self and poetic imagination. The rediscovery and inhabiting of my symbolic self, which originated in the sacramental strand of my childhood, redressed the balance of my narrative. This reduced the anxiety I felt about the past and anchored me in the present moment through a renewed focus on the sacramental world around me.

Alienation

It is plausible that this directional image of coming home but never fully arriving is linked to another insight of Leigh's, where he finds the trait of 'alienation' in the modern autobiographies he analysed. This is 'religious alienation' which 'expresses the decline of religious mediation through a visible church'.[380] Although I was at the centre of a visible church as a minister, I had to go outside the church to find a focus on attention and awareness.

I had to go outside my Protestant, non-conformist Baptist church to access contemplation rather than activism. I first had to find wisdom on attention and awareness, mindfulness, in secular psychology for health before I found it in Christian contemplation. I had to look outside the visible Church to a different Christian expression, a rarer Christian expression, that of intentional community, to rediscover community and a sense of home beyond myself and my nuclear family. Not owning our own home, and living in a 'borrowed' house, a manse, a tied house, added to this sense of alienation. It was difficult to call this house 'home'.

In the cultures I have inhabited, whether boarding school, the bank or church, I have been alienated from awareness, my body and emotions. The virtual culture also alienates us from our true selves. Mindfulness has enabled me to find a home in my awareness, body, emotions and senses, to find a home in God in each present moment. It is in this reinhabiting that I have felt most fully alive, physically and spiritually. It is in this new awareness, a form of reperceiving, that I have felt gratitude for the gift of the skin boat I have been given.

---

[380] Leigh, 3.

Reflection

Intention
It can be a helpful intention to check out the directional image of your life. Can you ask God for a directional image for whatever season of life you are in?

Attention
Our attention is when awareness is stretched towards something. We also have this beautiful capacity for open awareness, where we can observe or witness what is going on. Try to find this big picture perspective to look at the direction(s) of your life. Is there a value you want to reorientate your life around?

Attitude
Again, take a big picture look at your life: what attitudes have you noticed on this journey that you would like to change? Write a summary paragraph outlining this.

Reperceiving
Stay with this metacognitive, big-picture level and gather any insights, any epiphanies, any moments of reperceiving that have emerged on this journey together.

19
Finding a theological home

Finding a home in particular theologies

I also notice that I have found a home in particular theologies: contextual, contemplative, practical, lived, incarnational, sacramental, symbolic, relational, wise and creative. These theologies can help others position themselves in mindful formation. I have asked, as I review my journey, whether there are any implicit theologies in my lived experience. I also asked myself if there was a pattern connecting these theologies. One possible implicit theology to emerge is a theology of attention and awareness.

My lived experience suggests that awareness is the God-given capacity that bridges and holds together the material and the spiritual in the one reality we inhabit. That is why I have been able to say that the same attentional capacities are at work within secular mindfulness and mindfulness of God. The mindful awareness I have cultivated enables me to set up home in the present moment. It is through both a spacious awareness and living in the present moment that I position myself to be in the right place to be aware of God, as God allows by grace. As I become more fully aware of the different aspects of self, as the rooms of the 'house of my being' become more fully transparent, I am more able to sense God at work in all those rooms. It is then that the house of my being becomes a home. Grace is another implicit theology in my work which I will pick up in this section.

However, in terms of any connecting pattern between the

theologies that I have interacted with, awareness has also given me a clue. In a sort of analogical mirroring, I can see a similar process and pattern in the theologies that I have intuitively gathered from. In some sense they could be reframed as aware theologies; they are spacious in their consideration of God and the world. They are mindful in that they can hold different levels of experience in the same theological space.

Context

Contextual theology is aware of multiple contexts that can be synthesised. I see its overlap with practical theology. Another frame has been David Ford's four-fold model of retrieval, bringing up-to-date, accessibility and wisdom, which he calls 'wise creativity', referenced earlier. In this theological space there is room for the past and the future; the non-academic world is accommodated through accessibility and wisdom. I have kept these four points as guiding principles throughout this journey.

Contemplative or spiritual theology has shown me what my place is in the space of God, what is possible for me to do and what only God can do. It has shown me that my spiritual home is in my God-given body; it is in mindful spirituality, a form of kataphatic spirituality, that I come fully alive. Along with mindfulness it has enabled me to examine my other spaces – the past, boarding school, church – and to see the limitations and enclosed nature of these spaces.

Experiential and confessional

My theological approach has not been systematic, but it is open and spacious. It also clears the way for the ordinary and for the transcendent to break through into the ordinary. My theology is experiential, confessional, incarnational and poetic. I examine my own spiritual experience. My open and spacious theology has also cleared the way for me to see the fragments of my life and to work with theological fragments to try to make a whole.

I have found the idea of bricolage and being a bricoleur to be crucial in creating a fragile centre from which I can live and work.

Incarnational and symbolic

There is an incarnational strand running through all these theologies that has magnetised them for me; all of me – body, senses, awareness, imagination, spirit, mind – can participate in the knowing of God. This is also an open and spacious stance. This strand is also sacramental and symbolic. I have drawn on David Brown's idea of the generous God who speaks to us through natural symbols, often subconsciously, to preserve our human freedom. I have drawn on sacramental theology with the whole world being sacramental, moments of meeting with God being sacramental, and the possibility of sacramental conversations. This clears the way for the swallow, and the swift, the stream, the stars, pathways and walking to be woven into my theological reflections. What I perceive with my senses – that is, natural symbols – are somehow 'converted' into the service of the divine.

Spacious relationship

In my theology of relationships, I have room for multiple dimensions of relationships: working, real, wounded, spiritual, distorted. I allow into the space myself, others, God, creation. Although I have had an experience of complete aloneness, and betrayal, and the breaking of trust, I have found that knowing I am in an implicit relationship with God has enabled me to build trust and sustain trust in God. I have made room for a different form of knowing, the unthought known, which is relational. My relational theology allowed me to draw into my space secular mindfulness and integrative and relational counselling and psychotherapy, the wisdom of the world.

My view on things is often small and limited and distorted. In my theological space, however, because I am in an implicit relationship with God, and even though most of the time I am unaware of this relationship, I still participate in a bigger space. As I reflect critically on my life in this research, I can see that God has always been there; I have participated in God's life but been unaware of it much of the time. It is only as I look back and see the providential meetings and moments I have written about that I can see this weaving of my life into God's life. The 'unthought known' has become a stream of knowing that sustains me in the present moment as I practise awareness of it.

I can use an analogy with walking. I walked every day on the Scargill Estate for a few months. It is 90 acres of woodland and limestone terraces that climb up to a ridge. The paths covered in leaves can be slippery, as can the limestone steps. In walking daily, the paths become an unthought known to my body. My steps move from being tentative and stiff to loose limbed, confident and well balanced. When I do slip, I slide with it. When I descend, it is with relaxed awareness, stepping lightly. When I have had a period of not walking the estate, I lose that state of unthought knowing, and the paths become strangers again. It is the same with the stream of unthought known within me. I can inhabit it more fully with practice, or it can be a stranger to me.

I can also use an analogy from the dark night skies above Scargill. I have often walked in the dark there; it is a much more common occurrence than when I was in London with its streetlights. At first it was a strange, even fearful experience, but then it felt normal, and I began to feel at home in the dark. My eyes became more 'dark adapted'.[381] In the dark 'your eyes automatically adapt to try and compensate for the lack of light by dilating the pupil, effectively increasing its aperture. This results in greater light grasp.'[382] My moment of epiphany out of this is that I am much more in the dark with God than I ever realised. There is so much that is out of my awareness, that I

---

[381] Radmila Topalovic and Tom Kerss, *Stargazing: Beginners Guide to Astronomy* (Glasgow: Collins, 2016), 50.
[382] Topalovic and Kerss, 50.

cannot perceive. However, if I accept this and allow myself to become 'dark adapted', my spiritual perceiving can more easily pick up the faintest of traces in my spiritual night sky. My 'Light grasp' grows in the dark. This also helps me to trust as I walk down an almost imperceptible path with God, just as my feet trust my night vision as I walk the paths that take me home. This is a form of creative wisdom.

Contemplative

I draw on early contemplative history, which is anthropological in insight, through the idea of *Logos* theology developed by Maximus the Confessor and others. I am attracted to the idea that I am a little *logos* spoken into being by the *Logos*, Christ. I am a word spoken by the Light to be light, and I recognise that every person is a *logos*. This little *logos* has a capacity that can expand and stretch; it is not limited in nature. It can become a cathedral, a world within me. It has space for others, God and creation. All these theologies enable me to be open, spacious, give meaning to my life and enable me to make sense of it and create a fragile whole within.

The present moment

Another crucial element is the theology of the present moment. I see the present moment as a sacrament, as the point at which my time touches God's eternal present, giving me the possibility of moments of meeting with God that are transformative, those moments of meeting being able to stay in my timeline and not fade away into nothing. Here the present moment expands and grows and is pregnant with possibility. It is the moment that is spacious. It is here I have found my home with God. As I find my home with God, I find my place with others and with creation.

Grace

I return now to the implicit theology of grace. I begin with how I have used the word and will then relate it to a wider understanding of grace within my understanding of the Protestant Church tradition I am part of. The main term I use throughout the research is 'graced response'. Principally, this is in relation to the idea that there is a gap between myself and God that I cannot cross. I cannot find God unless God finds me. I cannot enter a relationship with God until God enters a relationship with me. I cannot be mindful of God unless God is first mindful of me. I draw on contemplative theology for this insight. That this relationship becomes possible is a graced response through the work of the Holy Spirit. For me, it is grace because God does something for me that I cannot do for myself.

I then apply this concept of a graced response to every aspect of my relationship with God: my remembering of God, my spiritual reperceiving, the enabling of my physical senses to perceive spiritually, the possibility of moments of meeting with God, the seeing and transforming of distorted inner narratives, becoming aware of God and God's compassionate presence, the possibility of my playing a part in being mindful of God, my cooperation with God – all these things are graced responses in which I play my part.

I also apply the concept of graced response to God's providential care, the convergences between myself, secular mindfulness and mindfulness of God, that brought healing and transformation. In this sense grace has often been hidden, and I have found it in the symbolic interaction between myself and God, the 'unthought known'. This grace is patient, and the swallows keep returning to me until I catch up with them. The underground stream that brings natural symbols to me in my intuitive self keeps flowing regardless of whether I am aware of it or not. This links to the idea of the sacramental nature of creation as an act of God's grace, 'that the physical, material stuff of creation and embodiment is the means by which God's grace meets us and gets hold of us'.[383] This grace, as I have experienced it, is also spacious and open and generous.

I have found that mindfulness has enabled me to have a realistic sense of my negativity bias and distorted perceiving, and my absolute need for God's transforming grace, recognising that need, even though I have some agency to reclaim my life from anxiety. I repeatedly argue I cannot redeem my own life; only God can do that.

Grace needs to inhabit our spoken and written language. I come back to my childhood and ministerial experiences of how critical words, wrongly spoken, shatter and fragment trust, identity and life itself. I do not wish to manipulate anyone into belief in God or use a rhetoric of persuasion. I am to be a word spoken by the Light that can, as a graced response, enable others to freely reperceive their life in relationship to God. My mindful rule is based on a realistic sense of how both myself and others need transforming, how we can take personal responsibility for our part in creating a common life, always recognising we live in relational mutuality. I have learnt about the need for boundaries and assertiveness, but I find myself, at the end of this journey, in a non-negotiable stance when it comes to deliberately using words to harm or to hurt. I know I can do this unintentionally or out of transferential feelings, but I am always seeking to show grace, as I have been shown grace. I am also aware that it is gratitude for God's grace that motivates me to seek the divine presence rather than guilt or shame.

I have found these theologies, or they have found me. They have mediated God's presence to me. But not just for me. I believe my research is a 'spiritual journal' that desires to be a second-person guide for others seeking to be mindful of God. If I look to summarise the theology that has emerged from this research, then perhaps it is lived theology, transcendent and contextual, aware and spacious, seeking to be accessible, wise

---

[383] Smith, 141.

and creative, *made out of the 'dark adapted', 'Light grasping' lived experience of my spiritual journey.*

Reflection

Intention
The moment we reflect on our own spiritual experience in the light of God, we are theologians. At a big-picture level, have an intention to explore what theologies you are drawn to or are implicit in your life. Are there any that I mention here that resonate with you? Has your theology changed over the course of your spiritual journey?

Attention
What has your theological stance, churchmanship, spirituality made you inattentive to?

Attitude
Can you cultivate a mindful attitude as you look at the world, aware of its complexity and able to hold different views in your head as you navigate your way forward?

Reperceiving
Are there fragments of your life that you can reperceive and create a fragile whole out of? Meditate on the story of Elijah running away in 1 Kings 19:1-18 to open yourself up to insight from God.

20
The onward journey

Introduction

This chapter is a final crystallisation as I step back and look at the patterns and shapes of the whole journey of mindful formation. I use a heuristic term, 'creative synthesis', to weave together the essential strands of mindful formation.

I am aware of the different cultural contexts I inhabit and how the past still influences the present. In the voyage to reclaim my present moments I discovered that the anxiety that holds me to ransom in the present has its genesis in my boarding school past and the trauma of separation from my family and beloved Africa. Many others share this story of present moment anxiety and a traumatic past and need an understanding of the cultural contexts they inhabit.

In mindful formation we need to be aware of the family or cultural forces that have shaped us. Through mindful awareness and God's grace we can be reformed: because of neuroplasticity we are not fixed in personality and behaviour. We can be transformed and renewed (Romans 12:2). It was a timely sabbatical, and discovering mindfulness for health and mindfulness of God, that led me into the culture of attention and awareness, of contemplation, both secular and spiritual. This was the turning point. I learned the language of attention and awareness and how to inhabit it. In immersing myself in mindfulness I was going against the flow and being mindfully formed. I found freedom.

Remembrance, reperceiving, reclaiming, redeeming and recognition

I have noticed five main connected themes in mindful formation.

Remembrance

The first is the idea of the remembrance or mindfulness of God. I have retrieved this strand of contemplative history and recontextualised it for the twenty-first century. How to remember in a culture where I do not need to remember has led to a model for remembering the things of God in each ethical moment of choice and choosing them over the anxious human things jostling for my attention. What we pay attention to is our life, and I am choosing to pay attention to my values. It is remembering in the present moment that is central to us being mindful of God. The intention to help others remember the key tenets of mindful spirituality is also at the centre of the construction of the mindful rule. This is a participative spirituality, and the remembering at its heart comes through repetition and intentional mnemonic practice.

Reperceiving

Second, as we cultivate this mindfulness of God, we begin to reperceive God, our own self and others. This is the work of God, as my part of being mindful is taken up in the life of God. Secular mindfulness enables a reperceiving in a narrower sense, as a 'shift in perspective' through being able to 'disidentify' from my thoughts.

This is important, but I am talking here about my wider use of the word, a spiritual reperceiving through the same capacities that are used in secular mindfulness, but capacities transformed and inhabited by the divine presence. I liken this reperceiving to the *diorasis*, the clear seeing in the early Church that was cultivated through contemplative practices. Through the influence of disability studies, I move away from the idea of clear seeing to 'reperceiving', which includes the perceiving of all my senses, my body, awareness, imagination, emotions and thinking. In this reperceiving I recognise others as made in the image of God. This is made possible by the graced awakening of the God-given creative word within me. This reperceiving is, therefore, ethical, mnemonic and aware. It enables the exercise of my moral and creative imagination. Mindful formation leads to reperceiving.

This awareness is also crucial to my anthropology. Only as we cultivate this awareness, and it is taken up and inhabited by the divine presence, is it possible for us to inhabit every aspect of our being more fully, and for those aspects to become transparent to us. As we do this, we are better able to reclaim our present moments, so that there is the graced possibility for God to redeem them. Before I participated in mindfulness for health and mindfulness of God, I was working with a reduced capacity for awareness. Through participating in mindfulness for health and mindfulness of God I have expanded my capacity for awareness. This is a possibility for others.

Reclaiming

The third main theme is the need to reclaim our present moments from the anxiety or other factors that overwhelm our present moments. I have found a way to reclaim my present moments through mindfulness, and I have developed an incarnational mindful spirituality drawing on the wisdom of secular mindfulness and Christian contemplation. This is an original pathway to kataphatic spirituality. I suggest that this pathway, as with kataphatic spirituality generally, is more accessible right now with the cultural interest in mindfulness. As well as an ethical mnemonic awareness, there is an awareness of moments of meeting with God that are transformative. This is based on a conceptual model that we are in an implicit relationship with God. Most of that relationship happens out of our awareness; it can play out in our unconscious, in dreams, using symbols. In cultivating a more continuous present moment awareness we are open to the graced offering of moments of meeting with God. The influence of such moments lasts a lifetime. Each of us needs to discover what keeps us out of the present moment.

The key moment of meeting with God for me was reading the Olivier Clement translation of Diadochus of Photike: 'Let us keep our eyes always fixed on the depths of our heart with an unceasing *mindfulness* of God.' I circle around it again here. A doorway opened in that moment that I could not have opened, and I stepped through. The doorway has never closed, and even when my mind and body are tired and I have felt cleft by conflict, the energy of this moment has never left me. That moment is why this book has happened.

I have used the word sacramental to describe the natural symbols of my African childhood that have redressed the balance of trauma in my memory. I recognise that all of creation is sacramental. Papanikolaou adds, 'Although all of creation is sacramental, not all of creation is sacramental to the same degree.'[384] James K A Smith takes this idea to illustrate the difference between the sacramental and what have been called the sacraments in the history of the Church. He develops this further by saying, 'While the whole world is a sacrament, we might say that *the* sacraments and the liturgy are unique "hot spots" where God's formative, illuminating presence is particularly "intense."'[385]

In this sense, I can say that my moment of meeting with God through the phrase 'mindfulness of God' is sacramental. While not having the status of a sacrament, I can use the analogy of intensity and hot spots to say that it has been the intense hot spot of God's presence in my life. This moment of meeting spoke to me, gave me direction cognitively, emotionally, spiritually, physically and imaginatively. I have learned to value moments, to treasure them in my heart and ponder them as Mary did (Luke 2:19). Each of us is offered moments of meeting with God that can be charged with recognition or missed altogether.

---

[384] Papanikolaou, 126.
[385] Smith, 148.

I am also aware that many of us need to reclaim our past, as I needed to reclaim my past from the shadow of boarding school trauma, trauma caused by separation from my parents and the home I loved in Kenya. In turning to face the shadow of anxiety and my boarding school past, I have found a measure of healing through mindfulness and its affinity with trauma theory. I have been able to name it as trauma and find a voice to speak it out. This has helped further free up the grip of anxiety on my present moment consciousness. I was a talkative child who became silent through the trauma of boarding school. I have found a voice and been able to piece together a narrative of the past from fragments and the story of another boarding school witness, who with the help of a therapist was able to tell his story.

I learned that the traumatic responses I experienced at boarding school and during the pandemic were out of my control. This knowledge helps me to be more self-compassionate. In the trauma of boarding school, I had a threshold moment, a searing recognition that I was utterly alone, that I could only rely on myself. I understood that I needed to make my home in my own self. From Kai Erikson's sociological theory of trauma, I became aware that this damaged my ability to trust. This made me even more self-sufficient. The blow that triggered a traumatic response in me during the Covid-19 pandemic, a blistering personal assault, also damaged my ability to trust. I think trauma is more widespread than is often realised.

Redeeming

In using the precise word 'reclaim' as my part in being mindful of God, I am aware theologically that only God can redeem those present moments. What does it mean for those moments to be redeemed by God? The redemption of our present moments means we are enabled to be fully present to our whole incarnated being, the world, others and God's presence by the grace of God. This is coming home. This is the goal of mindful formation. I am aware that we cannot be fully free in the present moment through our own effort. We are dependent on 'something more' coming from God. I am aware that redeeming can be further defined as the releasing of the God-given creative word within us, our little *logos*, the awakening of that word in the now and not yet of our life's experience. This redeeming goes beyond me to the calling together, by God, of others into that redemption.

In distinguishing between my part, which is reclaiming my present moments through my God-given mindful capacities, and the redeeming that is God's graced response, I answer the theological problem of the 'gap between the Creator and myself as a created being'. The entering into a relationship with God is a graced response through the Holy Spirit. However, I have acknowledged, through the wisdom of spiritual theology, that human beings have an 'affinity' to interact with God, which God himself has placed within us. These mindful capacities have a *telos*, a purpose, to reperceive, and God redeems this purpose.

Recognition

I began this pilgrimage with the ideas of remembrance (mindfulness), reperceiving and redeeming, and on the journey understood that I can reclaim my present moments but not redeem them myself. Perhaps the most surprising word that I didn't expect as the last major theme is the idea of recognition. It is a word I used intuitively in my writing, but found a resonance with recognition theory, or the ethics of recognition. Recognition theory is a mainly secular approach, but it has been used more recently within a spiritual framework.[386] Principally it is about recognising others as persons, giving them respect and esteem simply for being human, without having to earn that recognition. From my Christian perspective, the equal dignity of all human beings is conferred on them through being made in the image of God. In my own personal experience, there is great power in being recognised for my true self, and great pain

---

[386] Kahlos, Koskinen and Palmen, 8.

when I have been misrecognised. It is a common theme in conversations I have with people who feel ignored, unrecognised, seen in a distorted way. All these themes overlap and converge into a central stream.

In mindfulness of God, through graced attention, we remember to come home to the present moment to reperceive God, our own self and others; in reperceiving we recognise our essential relational reality and the God-given creative word within – our true identity. In that moment we begin to be mindfully formed.

In this novel application of mindfulness and recognition with its ethical mnemonic awareness, I cultivate a moral imagination; I allow moral creativity to emerge as I recognise the God-given creative word in others, the little *logos* within them. I also reclaim my symbolic self which anchors me in the present moment and rebalances my past.

I can see why remembering is important to me: remembering is connected to my sense of what is real. The reperceiving I am seeking through mindfulness is about seeing reality as it is, in a fresh and not distorted way. When I recognise someone else, I even say that I am perceiving their 'essential reality'. I want to reclaim my present moments because I have found the nearest thing to reality in those present moments. I recognise I need God, the ultimate in realness, to redeem those present moments. Home was most real for me and that is what I lost. I am aware in the moment now, I remember that home, before I lost it, felt real; it was real; I was very happy.

I recognise that my personal journey could be adapted to be a second-person guide, and that is what this book is.

The journey as a second-person guide

My journey can help others to be spiritually autoethnographic, to be participant perceivers of their own participation in mindfulness of God and the context of their culture. I can encourage them to create their own spiritual journal that is both evocative and analytic. The methods I used have been simplified further. People can take their own pilgrimage walks of any length, literal or metaphorical. They can establish how present they are to the here and now as they walk, and what their mind wanders to. I have created an exercise where they listen to the different parts of their own self and carry out a self-interview, asking themselves intuitive questions, seeking to be discovery-based in orientation. These interviews can help show if they, too, have a shadow from the past blocking the light in the present. These interviews are a simple form of *examen*. Simple exercises for noticing the symbolic, what beckons one to perceive it, can be created. My story can rehumanise others' stories and help them find a directional image in their story.

The models I develop are applicable to others. I can ask what pieces of wisdom can become metacognitive propositions that would help someone live by their values in their context. Using the idea of being in an implicit relationship with God, the reader can examine their own life for moments of meeting with God and cultivate an attentiveness and awareness of the graced possibility of other such moments.

I have used the language of secular mindfulness. I have translated my gospel understanding of mindfulness of God into secular language that is accessible to those who are seeking God but have not yet found God. I hold the tension that gives them access to mindfulness for health and mindfulness of God, allowing them to trace one path or both paths.

Another aspect of Leigh's analysis that I want to draw attention to is that 'what makes the conversion sequence of most modern autobiographers notably different from that of Augustine is that they explicitly include a societal dimension to their moral and religious conversions'.[387] The application of my developed theory and practice is a societal application, how we dialogue with each other with awakened language, how we can release the God-given creative word in others, to facilitate dialogue and a sense of community between those who are different. The essential centre of this application is a novel

---

[387] Leigh, 17.

application of recognition theory actualised through mindfulness and the theology of the *logos*, the creative word in each of us that is our true identity. It is a mindful recognition of myself, God and others. My societal application is a mindful rule. Our spirituality within this framework is contemplation in action. It is doing out of being, and its foundation is awareness.

I am calling this mindful spirituality kataphatic spirituality. It is how we are mindfully formed. My experience is that the same embodied senses are at work in a secular mindfulness exercise that are at work in mindfulness of God. Here I find Balthasar's theological rationale for this a plausible explanation for my experience. Balthasar takes up the patristic idea of assumption and exchange of states: 'God participated in our life to let us share in the divine life. In the process of incarnation, cross and resurrection the human senses are assumed, and opened to a redeeming transformation.'[388] As it was for Jesus, so it becomes possible for me that my human senses are also assumed, taken up into the divine life of the indwelling Holy Spirit, becoming spiritual senses but always mediated through my body as 'something more'. There is an exchange. It is not just my senses that are assumed, but my mindful capacities for attention and awareness, self-awareness, self-regulation and self-transcendence. It is not just my mindful capacities that are assumed but also my imagination and creative capacity.

Those parts of me that I dissociated from, the traumatised parts, can also be assumed and healed. All this is in the service of enabling me to live out as fully as possible the God-given creative word within me, that only I can inhabit and manifest in the world. This is a non-dualistic incarnational spirituality.

In writing a spiritual formation book and detailing moments of meeting with God and my encounters with secular mindfulness and mindfulness of God as divinely providential, I offer two analogies that help me discern where I sense God at work. The first is the idea of 'hot spots', which I borrow from

---

[388] De Maeseneer, 281.

sacramental theology. Some moments have a greater intensity, are 'hot spots', which enable me to discern God's presence without claiming them in certainty but in humble faith. The second is the idea of my life as a tapestry that is being stitched in each moment in time.

A summary of mindful formation

This creative path home to God in the present moment is a retrieval of a strand of historic mindfulness of God in the Christian contemplative tradition, recontextualised with the theory, practice and language of secular mindfulness.

In my experience, the general direction of Christian mindfulness is about importing secular mindfulness into a Christian worldview for therapeutic reasons. As a practitioner and researcher of mindfulness of God and secular mindfulness, my aim is to move in the other direction and translate mindfulness of God into accessible secular mindfulness language, theory and practice, so that mindfulness of God features in our cultural marketplace as a transformational option, which also makes this a piece of original contextual theology.

Although mindfulness of God is a historical concept in Christian contemplation, I have identified a gap in 'how to' cultivate and recontextualise mindfulness of God through translating it into the language of secular mindfulness theory and practice. The Christian distinctives I draw out include the intentional focus on God and the cultivation of ethical mindful awareness, culminating in the creation of an original mindful rule of life.

My evidence is that my immersion in secular mindfulness led to the creation of an aware and embodied mindful spirituality more deeply attuned to the presence of God. In this original model of mindful spirituality my God-given mindful capacities of awareness, embodied self, physical senses, emotions and imagination play a central role as I open myself to the grace of the Holy Spirit at work in the integral unity of my being. This brings an ethical dimension to this mindful spirituality that seeks to create a present moment ethical awareness, to have in mind the concerns of God and choose them over the human concerns jostling for my attention. As well as developing self-awareness of our bodies, I emphasise the necessity of becoming self-aware of our thoughts and emotions.

I have also created an original method for cultivating this continuous ethical awareness. Secular mindfulness depends on holding key metacognitive propositions in present moment awareness to reperceive thoughts as passing mental events rather than facts. With practice, these propositions become insights – I reperceive my thoughts in the present moment as passing mental events and can let them go. I have turned scriptural verses that I have identified with, such as Mark 8:35, 'whoever wants to save their life will lose it', into metacognitive propositions. Because present moment awareness has this ability to remember these propositions (figures) at ethical points of choice, I can notice when anxiety wants me to experientially avoid a situation. Using my resculpted scriptural proposition, which becomes an insight, I hold that automatic reaction of avoidance and choose a wiser, more biblical response – to face the situation with God. In this way, instead of my present moments being overwhelmed by anxiety, through this form of mindfulness of God I can redeem them and in the moment be more mindful of God. This basic practice and tentative model can be placed at the centre of a mindful rule of life.

I have drawn on the secular concept of implicit relational knowing to create an original analogical conceptual model for psychological and spiritual experience of God in the present moment. The Boston Change Process Study Group presents evidence that a therapist and client are in an implicit relationship out of which emerge missed moments, and moments of meeting where change and transformation happen. By way of analogy, I am saying that I am in an implicit relationship with God (God is always present). Most of the time I am not present, but when I (as a graced response that I cooperate with) am present then I have the graced possibility of moments of meeting with God which are also transformational. As I cultivate mindfulness of God, my hypothesis is that I will experience more moments of meeting with God, thus redeeming my present moments. I can also use this conceptual model to sustain and cultivate my trust in God.

I have not drawn on mainstream apophatic Christian contemplative tradition, which has been seen as elitist, inaccessible and anti-incarnational, with its Platonic roots. I have discovered that secular mindfulness theory and practice in the service of mindfulness of God is an original gateway to embodied, incarnational kataphatic spirituality. I would also like to suggest that my experience where my senses, body, emotions and awareness become aware of God can be seen as evidence for natural senses becoming spiritual senses through the grace of the Holy Spirit. My experience is that the same God-given mindful capacities are at work in secular mindfulness and mindfulness of God.

This pattern of mindful spirituality, with its core of ethical awareness, lies at the centre of a mindful rule of life I have created, which involves the intentional cultivation of self-awareness, self-regulation and self-transcendence through mindful awareness practices to have in mind the concerns of God and to choose them over the human things jostling for my attention. This mindful rule of life has mindful awareness practices at its centre and can be a second-person guide for others seeking a similar incarnational spirituality.

I have amended the Jesus Prayer and *Lectio Divina* to make them mindful awareness practices. I have also combined mindfulness and recognition theory to suggest that mindful recognition enables us to reperceive others in their essential God-given reality. This includes an awareness of the God-given creative word at the centre of their being, which is to be awakened. This is a novel application of mindfulness and recognition theory with *Logos* theology to enable moral creativity and the release of moral imagination. Through the idea of reclaiming my present moments, which as a graced response God can redeem, I offer a solution to what is my part in mindfulness of God.

A 'Holway'

The pilgrimage of mindfulness continues for me. I am fascinated by holloways, literally a 'hollow way', a 'sunken path, a deep and shady lane. A route that centuries of foot-fall, hoof-hit, wheel-roll & rain-run have harrowed into the land.'[389] I have been harrowed by falls and hits and rolls, but in this I have been reshaped into something mysterious, like a holloway. A holloway seems to me a portal to new awareness, and this is where I find myself. These holloways in the land are 'old ways', where one might find new things, 'rifts' which allow one to '*slip back out of this world*'.[390] The old ways I have retrieved have helped me find new things and slip back into the world, into a new level of awareness, mindful of God, myself, others and creation.

An earlier rendering of the word holloway is 'Holway'.[391] When I say this word, I hear 'whole-way'. Mindfulness for me has been a path, a holway, a way to wholeness. It is the path where I can slip out of my head and the weight of my thoughts into my body, senses and breath, and then slip again into an open, witnessing awareness where I hold all of me, and sense the presence of God holding all of me. Holloways have been shaped by walking, and walking has been a key practice for me, and walking has led to the poetic.

It is also symbolically important to me that some holloways have been made by pilgrims.[392] This holway is a path that is a here-path, a here and now path. Mindfulness, like the holloway,

---

[389] Robert Macfarlane, Stanley Donwood and Dan Richards, *Holloway*, paperback edition (London: Faber & Faber, 2013, 2014), 3.
[390] Macfarlane, Donwood and Richards, 4.
[391] Macfarlane, Donwood and Richards, 2.
[392] Macfarlane, Donwood and Richards, 36.

is 'a way amongst ways'.[393] Mindfulness has been a whole way that has led me by a path to the here and now Way.

> An angel touched me...
> And still I limp.
> And yet I am made like a honey dipper,
> Turned like wood,
> To bear the viscous presence of God.
> And still I limp,
> On the holway home,
> Here and now is the Way.

---

[393] Macfarlane, Donwood and Richards, 36.

Bibliography

Adams, Tony E, Holman Stacy Jones and Carolyn Ellis. *Autoethnography: Understanding Qualitative Research*. Oxford: Oxford University Press, 2015.

Alford, Lucy. *Forms of Poetic Attention*. New York: Columbia University Press, 2020. Kindle.

Anderson Leon, and Bonnie Glass-Coffin. 'I Learn by Going.' In *Handbook of Autoethnography* edited by Stacy Holman Jones, Tony E Adams and Carolyn Ellis, 57-83. Walnut Creek, California: Left Coast Press Inc, 2013.

Atkinson, Paul, et al. 'Editorial Introduction.' In *Handbook of Ethnography*, edited by Paul Atkinson, et al. 1-8. Los Angeles, London: Sage, 2001.

Avakian, Sylvie. 'Christian Spirituality: Maximus the Confessor A Challenge to the 21st Century.' *International Congregational Journal* 14, no. 2 (Winter 2015): 67-83.

Bahnson, Fred. 'The Underground Life of Prayer.' Image 77. Accessed 28th February 2022. imagejournal.org/article/underground-life-prayer.

Balado, J L G. *The Story of Taizé*. London, Oxford: Mowbray, 1980.

Balthasar, Hans Urs von. *The Glory of the Lord: A Theological Aesthetics 1: Seeing the Form*, edited by Joseph Fessio, SJ and John Riches, translated by Erasmo Leiva-Merikakis. San Francisco, California: Ignatius Press, 1982.

———. *Prayer*. Translated by Graham Harrison. San Francisco, California: Ignatius Press, 1986.

Bevans, Stephen B. *Models of Contextual Theology*. Maryknoll,

New York: Orbis Books, 1992.

Bishop, Scott R, et al. 'Mindfulness: A Proposed Operational Definition.' *Clinical Psychology: Science and Practice* 11, no. 3 (2004): 230-241. Accessed 18th July 2014. doi.org/10.1093/clipsy.bph077.

Bourgeault, Cynthia. *Centering Prayer and Inner Awakening.* Lanham, Maryland: Cowley Publications, 2004.

Bourgeault, Cynthia. 'Centering Prayer and Attention of the Heart.' *Cross Currents* 59 no. 1, (2009): 15-27.

Bretherton, Roger. 'Mindfulness: What's All the Fuss About?' In *Being Mindful, Being Christian: A Guide to Mindful Discipleship*, edited by Dr Roger Bretherton, Revd Dr Joanna Collicutt and Dr Jennifer Brickman, 13-24. Oxford: Monarch Books, 2016.

Brown, David. 'God and Symbolic Action.' In *Divine Action: Studies Inspired by the Philosophical Theology of Austin Farrer*, edited by Brian Hebblethwaite and Edward Henderson, 103-122. Edinburgh: T&T Clark, 1990.

———. *Divine Generosity and Human Creativity*. London, New York: Routledge, 2017.

Brown, Kirk Warren, Richard M Ryan and J David Cresswell. 'Mindfulness: Theoretical Foundations and Evidence for its Salutary Effects.' *Psychological Inquiry* 18, no. 4 (2007): 211-237. Accessed 20th March 2022. dx.doi.org/10.1080/10478400701598298.

Brown, Kirk Warren, and Richard M Ryan. 'The Benefits of Being Present: Mindfulness and its Role in Psychological Well-being.' *Journal of Personality and Social Psychology* 84, no. 4 (2003): 822-848. Accessed 18th September 2017. dx.doi.org/10.1037/0022-3514.84.4.822.

Burch, Vidyamala and Danny Penman. *Mindfulness for Health – A Practical Guide to Relieving Pain, Reducing Stress and Restoring Wellbeing.* London: Piatkus, 2013.

Candler Jr, Peter M. *Theology, Rhetoric, Manuduction, or Reading Scripture Caruth Together on the Path to God.* London: SCM

Press, 2007.

Carruthers, Mary. *The Book of Memory: A Study of Memory in Medieval Culture*. 2nd edition. Cambridge: Cambridge University Press, 2008.

Casey, Michael. 'Mindfulness of God in the Monastic Tradition.' *Cistercian Studies Quarterly* XVII, no. 2 (1982): 111-126.

Casiday, A M. *Evagrius Ponticus*. London, New York: Routledge, 2006.

Caussade, Jean-Pierre de. *Self-Abandonment to Divine Providence*. Translated by Alger Thorold. London: Collins, 1977.

Cazalet, Mark. 'Walking Man: The Art of Thomas Denny.' *Image Journal* 86. Accessed 18th October 2019. imagejournal.org/article/walking-man-art-thomas-denny.

Chopp, Rebecca S. 'Theology and the Poetics of Testimony.' In *Converging on Culture: Theologians in Dialogues with Cultural Analysis and Criticism*, edited by D Brown, S G Davaney and K Tanner, 56-70. Oxford: Oxford University Press, 2001.

Chorell, Torbjörn Gustafsson. 'Modes of Historical Attention: Wonder, Curiosity, Fascination.' *Rethinking History* 25 no. 2 (2021): 242-257.

Clarkson, Petruska. *The Therapeutic Relationship*. London: Whurr Publishers Ltd, 1995.

———. *Gestalt Counselling in Action*. 3rd edition. Los Angeles, California: Sage, 2004.

———. *Gestalt Counselling in Action* 4th edition. Updated by Simon Cavicchia. Sage Counselling in Action Series. Series editor Windy Dryden. London: Sage, 2014. Kindle.

Clement, Olivier. *The Roots of Christian Mysticism*. 7th edition. London: New City, 2002.

Cobb, David. *The British Museum: Haiku*. London: The British Museum Press, 2002.

Daffern, Megan I J. 'The Semantic Field of "Remembering" in the Psalms.' *Journal for the Study of the Old Testament* 41, no. 1,

(2016): 79-97.

Deikman, Arthur J. *The Observing Self: Mysticism and Psychotherapy*. Boston, MA: Beacon Press, 1982.

Denny, Tom. *Gloucester Cathedral: Stained Glass Windows*. Chapter of Gloucester Cathedral, 2016.

Denzin, Norman K. 'Interpretive Autoethnography.' In *Handbook of Autoethnography*, edited by Stacy Holman Jones, Tony E Adams and Carolyn Ellis, 123-142. Walnut Creek, California: Left Coast Press Inc, 2013.

———. *Interpretive Autoethnography*. Los Angeles, California: Sage, 2014.

Dhammarakkhita, Ven Dr. 'Prayer and Meditation.' In *The Gethsemani Encounter*, edited by Donald Mitchell and James A Wiseman OSB. New York: Continuum, 1998, 34-67.

Doehring, Carrie. *Taking Care: Monitoring Power Dynamics and Relational Boundaries in Pastoral Care and Counselling*. Nashville, Tennessee: Abingdon Press, 1995.

———. *The Practice of Pastoral Care: A Postmodern Approach*. Louisville, Kentucky: Westminster John Knox Press, 2006.

Diadoque de Photice. *Oeuvres Spirituelles*. Translated by Edouard des Places. Les Editions du Cerf, 2011.

Dreyfus, George. 'Is Mindfulness Present-Centred and Non-Judgmental? A Discussion of the Cognitive Dimensions of Mindfulness.' In *Mindfulness: Diverse Perspectives on its Meaning, Origins, and Applications*. Edited by J Mark, G Williams and Jon Kabat-Zinn, 41-54. London: Routledge, 2013.

Dubisch, Jill. *In A Different Place: Pilgrimage, Gender and Politics at a Greek Island Shrine*. Princeton, New Jersey: Princeton University Press, 1995.

Duffell, Nick. *The Making of Them: The British Attitude to Children and the Boarding School System*. London: Lone Arrow Press, 2010.

Ellis, Carolyn, Tony E Adams and Arthur P Bochner. 'Autoethnography: An Overview.' Forum: *Qualitative Social*

Research 12, no. 1 (2011): 345-357. Accessed 26th August 2016. www.qualitative-research.net/index.php/fqs/article/view/1589.

Epstein, Andrew. *Attention Equals Life: The Pursuit of the Everyday in Contemporary Poetry and Culture.* Oxford: Oxford University Press, 2016. Kindle.

Ermatinger, Cliff. *Following the Footsteps of the Invisible: The Complete Works of Diadochus of Photike.* Vol. 239. Collegeville, Minnesota: Liturgical Press, 2010.

Erikson, Kai. *A New Species of Trouble: The Human Experience of Modern Disasters.* New York, London: W W Norton & Company, 1994.

Fields, Stephen. 'Balthasar and Rahner on the Spiritual Senses.' *Theological Studies* 57, no. 2 (May 1996): 224-41. Accessed 12th April 2020. dx.doi.org/10.1177/004056399605700202.

Ponticus, Evagrius. *The Praktikos: Chapters on Prayer.* Translated by John Eudes Bamberger OCSO. Spencer, Massachusetts: Cistercian Publications, 1970.

Farb, Norman A S, et al. 'Attending to the Present: Mindfulness Meditation Reveals Distinct Neural Modes of Self-Reference.' *Social Cognitive and Affective Neuroscience (SCAN)* 2 (2007): 313-322. Accessed 13th March 2019. dx.doi.org/10.1093/scan/nsm030.

Ford, David F. *The Future of Christian Theology.* Chichester, West Sussex: Wiley-Blackwell, 2011.

Francis, Leslie J, Giuseppe Crea and Patrick Laycock. 'Work-Related Psychological Health among Catholic Religious in Italy: Testing the Balanced Affect Model.' *Journal of Empirical Theology* 30, 2 (2017): 236-252. Accessed 27th November 2023. http://dx.doi.org/10.1163/15709256-12341357.

Funk, Mary Margaret. *Thoughts Matter.* New York: Continuum, 1998.

———. *Tools Matter for Practicing the Spiritual Life.* New York:

Continuum, 2004.

Furman, Rich. (2005) 'Autoethnographic Poems and Narrative Reflections: A Qualitative Study on the Death of a Companion Animal.' *Journal of Family Social Work* 9, no.4 (2005): 23-38. Accessed 14th June 2020. dx.doi.org/10.1300/j039v09n04_03.

———. 'Poetic Forms and Structures in Qualitative Health Research.' *Qualitative Health Research* 16, no. 4 (April 2006): 560-66. Accessed 14th June 2018. dx.doi.org/10.1177%2F1049732306286819.

Gibson, Jonathan. 'Mindfulness, Interoception, and the Body: A Contemporary Perspective.' *Frontiers in Psychology* 10 (September 2019): 1-18. Accessed 2nd November 2021. dx.doi.org/:10.3389/fpsyg.2019.02012.

Gilbert, Paul and Choden. *Mindful Compassion: Using the Power of Mindfulness and Compassion to Transform Our Lives.* London: Robinson, 2013.

Gilligan, Carol, et al. 'On the Listening Guide: A Voice-Centered Relational Method.' In *Emergent Methods in Social Research*, edited by Sharlene Nagy Hesse-Biber and Patricia Leavy, 253-272. London: Sage, 2006.

Gilligan, Carol and Jessica Eddy. 'Listening as a Path to Psychological Discovery: An Introduction to the Listening Guide.' *Perspectives on Medical Education* 6, (2017): 76-81. Accessed 16th February 2019. dx.doi.org/10.1007/s40037-017-0335-3.

Grant, Jan and Jim Crawley. *Transference and Projection.* Maidenhead: Open University Press, 2002.

Grosch Miller, Carla A. *Trauma and Pastoral Care.* Norwich: Canterbury Press, 2021.

Grossman, Paul. 'Mindfulness for Psychologists: Paying Kind Attention to the Perceptible.' *Mindfulness* 1, (2010): 87-97. Accessed 20th March 2022. dx.doi.org/10.1007/s12671-010-0012-7.

Gurney, Ivor. *Severn & Somme and War's Embers.* Edited by R K

R Thornton. Manchester, Carcanet Press, 1997.

Gurney, Ivor. *Rewards of Wonder*. Edited by George Walter. Manchester: Carcanet Press, 2000.

Gurney, Ivor. *Collected Poems*. Edited by P J Kavanagh. Manchester: Carcanet Press, 2004.

Harden, R M. 'What is a spiral curriculum?' *Medical Teacher* 21, no. 2 (1999): 141-143. Accessed 28th September 2023. dx.doi.org/10.1080/01421599979752.

Harris, Thomas A. *I'm OK – You're OK*. London: Arrow, 2012.

Hasenkamp, Wendy, et al. 'Mind Wandering and Attention During Focused Meditation: A Fine-grained Temporal Analysis of Fluctuating Cognitive States.' *Neuroimage* 59 (2012): 750-760. Accessed 20th March 2022. dx.doi.org/10.1016/j.neuroimage.2011.07.008.

Haussher, Irenee. *Spiritual Direction in the Early Christian East*. Spencer, Massachusetts: Cistercian Publications, 1990.

Hayes, Steven C. *Get Out of Your Mind and Into Your Life*. Oakland, California: New Harbinger Publications Inc, 2005.

Hayles, N Katherine. *How We Think: Digital Media and Contemporary Technogenesis*. Chicago, London: The University of Chicago Press, 2012.

Heaney, Seamus. *The Redress of Poetry*. London: Faber & Faber, 2006.

Hoffman, Julian. *The Small Heart of Things: Being at Home in a Beckoning World*. Athens, Georgia: The University of Georgia Press, 2014.

———. *Irreplaceable: The Fight to Save Our Wild Places*. London: Hamish Hamilton, 2019.

Holt, Nicholas L. 'Representation, Legitimation, and Autoethnography: An Autoethnographic Writing Story.' *International Journal of Qualitative Methods* 2, no. 1 (1 March 2003): 18-28. Accessed 22nd December 2021. dx.doi.org/10.1177%2F160940690300200102.

Holman Jones, Stacey, Tony Adams and Carolyn Ellis. 'Introduction: Coming to Know Autoethnography as More than a Method.' In *Handbook of Autoethnography*, edited by Stacy Holman Jones, Tony E Adams and Carolyn Ellis, 17-48. Walnut Creek, California: Left Coast Press Inc, 2013.

Howells, Edward. 'Apophatic Spirituality.' In *The New SCM Dictionary of Christian Spirituality*, edited by Philip Sheldrake, 117-119. London: SCM Press, 2005.

Ikaheimo, Heikki. 'Causes for Lack of Recognition: From the Secular to the Non-Secular.' In *Recognition and Religion: Contemporary and Historical Perspectives*, edited by Maijastina Kahlos, Heikki J Koskinen and Rita Palmen, 51-68. London: Routledge, 2019.

Ison, Hilary. 'Working with an embodied and systemic approach to trauma and tragedy.' In *Tragedies and Christian Congregations: The Practical Theology of Trauma*, edited by Megan Warner, et al, 47-63. London, New York: Routledge, 2020.

Jamison, Christopher. *Finding Sanctuary: Monastic Steps for Everyday Life*. London: Phoenix, 2006.

Jha, Dr Amishi P. *Peak Mind*. London: Piatkus, 2021. Kindle.

Johnsén, Henrik Rydell. 'The Early Jesus Prayer and Meditation in Greco-Roman Philosophy.' In *Meditation in Judaism, Christianity and Islam*, edited by Halvor Eifring, 93-106. London: Bloomsbury, T&T Clark, 2013.

Kabat-Zinn, Jon. *Wherever You Go, There You Are: Mindfulness Meditation for Everyday Life*. New York: Hyperion, 1994.

———. *Full Catastrophe Living: Using the Wisdom of Your Body and Mind to Face Stress, Pain, and Illness*. London: Piatkus, 2008.

Kahlos, Maijastina, Heikki J Koskinen and Rita Palmen. 'Introduction.' In *Recognition and Religion: Contemporary and Historical Perspectives*, edited by Maijastina Kahlos, Heikki J Koskinen and Rita Palmen, 1-14. London: Routledge, 2019.

Kardong, Terrence G. *Benedict's Rule: A Translation and*

Commentary. Collegeville, Minnesota: The Liturgical Press, 1981.

Kiegelmann, M. (2009). 'Making Oneself Vulnerable to Discovery. Carol Gilligan in Conversation With Mechthild Kiegelmann.' Forum Qualitative Sozialforschung / Forum: *Qualitative Social Research*, Vol. 10, no. 2 (2009). Accessed 3rd June 2020. dx.doi.org/10.17169/fqs-10.2.1178.

Koehler, Margaret. *Poetry of Attention in the Eighteenth Century.* London: Palgrave Macmillan, 2012.

Laird, Martin. *Into the Silent Land.* London: Darton, Longman & Todd, 2006.

Lambert, Shaun. *A Book of Sparks: A Study in Christian Mindfullness.* 2nd edition. Watford: Instant Apostle, 2014.

———. *Putting On the Wakeful One: Attuning to the Spirit of Jesus through Watchfulness.* Watford: Instant Apostle, 2016.

———. 'The Present Moment as Home in Mindfulness of God.' PhD diss. University of Middlesex, 2022.

Langer, Ellen, J. *Mindfulness.* Cambridge: MA: Merloyd Lawrence, 1989.

———. *The Power of Mindful Learning.* Reading, Massachusetts: Addison-Wesley Publishing Company Inc., 1997.

Lawley, James and Penny Tompkins. *Metaphors in Mind: Transformation Through Symbolic Modelling.* London: The Developing Company Press, 2003.

Lawrence, Louise Joy. *An Ethnography of the Gospel of Matthew: A Critical Assessment of the Use of the Honour and Shame Model in New Testament Studies.* Tübingen: Mohr Siebeck, 2003.

———. 'Exploring the Sense-scape of the Gospel of Mark.' *Journal for the Study of the New Testament* 33, no. 4, 2012: 387-397.

———. *Sense and Stigma in the Gospels.* Oxford: Oxford University Press, 2013.

Le Guin, Ursula. *A Wizard of Earthsea.* Bath: Chivers Press, 1986.

———. *Earthsea: The First Four Books*. Penguin Books, 2016.
Leavy, Patricia. *Method Meets Art: Arts-Based Research Practice*. New York, London: The Guilford Press, 2015.
Lederach, John Paul. *The Moral Imagination: The Art and Soul of Building Peace*. Oxford: Oxford University Press, 2005.
Leigh, David, J. *Circuitous Journeys: Modern Spiritual Autobiography*. New York: Fordham University Press, 2000. Kindle.
Levertov, Denise. *New and Selected Essays*. New York: New Directions Publishing Corporation, 1992.
Levine, Peter, A. *Healing Trauma*. Boulder, Colorado: Sounds True, 2008.
Lewis, C S. *The Screwtape Letters*. London: Fount, 1991.
Lomas, Tim. *Masculinity, Meditation and Mental Health*. London: Palgrave Macmillan, 2014.
———. 'A Meditation on Boredom: Re-Appraising Its Value through Introspective Phenomenology.' *Qualitative Research in Psychology* 14 (1): 1-22. Accessed 12th March 2018. dx.doi.org/10.1080/14780887.2016.1205695.
Louth, Andrew. 'Denys the Areopagite.' In *The Study of Spirituality*, edited by Cheslyn Jones, Geoffrey Wainwright and Edward Yarnold, SJ. London: SPCK, 1986.
———. 'Evagrius on Prayer.' In *'Stand up to Godwards' – Essays in Mystical and Monastic Theology in Honour of the Reverend John Clark on his Sixty-fifth Birthday*, edited by James Hogg, 163-172. Salzburg: University of Salzburg, 2002.
Macfarlane, Robert, Stanley Donwood and Dan Richards. Paperback edition. *Holloway*. London: Faber & Faber, 2013, 2014.
Marcus, Joel. *Mark 1-8: Anchor Bible*. New York: Doubleday, 2000.
Maeseneer, Yves de. 'Retrieving the Spiritual Senses in the Wake of Hans Urs von Balthasar.' *Communio Viatorum* 55 (2013): 277-290.

Mark, J, G Williams and Jon Kabat-Zinn. 'Mindfulness: Diverse Perspectives on its Meaning, Origins, and Multiple Applications at the Intersection of Science and Dharma.' In *Mindfulness: Diverse Perspectives on its Meaning, Origins, and Applications*, edited by J Mark, G Williams and Jon Kabat-Zinn, 1-18. London: Routledge, 2013.

McGrath, Alister E. *The Open Secret: A New Vision for Natural Theology*. Oxford: Blackwell Publishing, 2008.

McInroy, Mark J. 'Karl Rahner and Hans Urs von Balthasar.' In *The Spiritual Senses: Perceiving God in Western Christianity*, edited by Paul L Gavrilyuk and Sarah Coakley, 257-274. Cambridge: Cambridge University Press, 2013.

McIntosh, Mark A. *Mystical Theology: The Integrity of Spirituality and Theology*. Blackwell Publishing, 1998.

McLeod, John. *Qualitative Research in Counselling and Psychotherapy*. London: Sage, 2001.

Mearns, Dave and Brian Thorne. *Person-Centred Counselling in Action*. 2nd edition. London: Sage, 2003.

Mearns, Dave. *Developing Person-Centred Counselling*. 2nd edition. London: Sage, 2003.

Michene, Ronald T. 'Theological Turns Toward Theopoetic Sensibilities: Embodiment, Humility, and Hospitality.' *Evangelical Quarterly: An International Review of Bible and Theology* 89, no. 1 (2018): 21-23. Accessed 22nd November 2023. dx.doi.org/10.1163/27725472-08901002.

Miles, Bernadette. 'Ignatian Spirituality, Apostolic Creativity and Leadership in Times of Change.' *The Way*, 50, no. 4 (October 2011): 35-41.

Mitchell, Donald and James A. Wiseman OSB. 'Introduction.' In *The Gethsemani Encounter*, edited by Donald Mitchell and James A. Wiseman OSB, xvii-xxiii. New York: Continuum, 1998.

Moustakas, Clark. *Loneliness*. New York: Prentice Hall, 1961.

———. *Heuristic Research: Design, Methodology and Applications*. London: Sage, 1990.

Oppenheimer, Andy. *Stars of Orion: An Astronomy Special.* 2021. Kindle.

Palmer, G E H, P Sherrard and K Ware, eds. *The Philokalia.* London: Faber & Faber, 1979.

Papanikolaou, Aristotle. 'Liberating Eros: Confession and Desire.' *Journal of the Society of Christian Ethics* 26, no. 1 (2006): 115-36. Accessed 11th December 2021. dx.doi.org/10.5840/jsce200626124

Parsons, Susan F. 'The Practice of Christian Ethics: Mindfulness and Faith.' *Studies in Christian Ethics* 25, no. 4 (November 2012): 442-53.

Pattison, Stephen. *Shame: Theory, Therapy, Theology.* Cambridge: Cambridge University Press, 2000.

Penman, Danny. *Mindfulness for Creativity: Adapt, Create and Thrive in a Frantic World.* London: Piatkus, 2015.

Pink, Sarah. *Doing Sensory Ethnography* 2nd edition. Los Angeles, London: Sage, 2015.

Pleasants, Phyllis Rodgerson. 'He Was Ancientfuture Before Ancientfuture Was Cool.' *Perspectives in Religious Studies*, 31, no. 1 (2004): 83-97.

Podles, Mary Elizabeth. 'A Thousand Words: Kintsugi Bowl.' *Touchstone: A Journal of Mere Christianity* 34, no. 5 (Sep/Oct 2021): 62-63.

Rakoczy, Susan. 'The Witness of Community Life: Bonhoeffer's Life Together and the Taizé Community.' *Journal of Theology for Southern Africa* 127 (March 2007): 43-62.

Rhoads, David, Joanna Dewey and Donald Michie. *Mark As Story.* 2nd edition. Minneapolis: Fortress Press, 1999.

Rhoads, David. *Reading Mark – Engaging the Gospel.* Minneapolis, Minnesota: Fortress Press, 2004.

Rubin, David C, ed. *Remembering Our Past: Studies in Autobiographical Memory.* Cambridge: Cambridge University Press, 1995.

Ruedy N E and M Schweitzer. 'In the Moment: The Effect of Mindfulness on Ethical Decision Making.' *Journal of Business Ethics*, 95, no. 1 (2010): 73-87. Accessed 13th December 2021. http://dx.doi.org/10.1007/s10551-011-0796-y.

Ruffing, Janet. K. 'The World Transfigured: Kataphatic Religious Experience Explored through Qualitative Research Methodology.' *Studies in Spirituality* 5 (1995): 232-259.

———. 'Kataphatic Spirituality.' In *The New SCM Dictionary of Christian Spirituality*, edited by Philip Sheldrake. London: SCM Press, 2005.

Schaverien, Joy. *Boarding School Syndrome: The psychological trauma of the 'privileged' child*. London, New York: Routledge, 2015.

Schwartz, Richard S. 'A Psychiatrist's View of Transference and Countertransference in the Pastoral Relationship.' *Journal of Pastoral Care* 43, no. 1 (March 1989): 41-46. Accessed 8th December 2021. dx.doi.org/10.1177/002234098904300107.

Sedighimornani, Neda, Katherine A Rimes, and Bas Verplanken. 'Exploring the Relationship Between Mindfulness, Self-Compassion, and Shame.' *Sage Open* (July-September 2019): 1-9. Accessed 7th December 2021. dx.doi.org/10.1177/2158244019866294.

Segal, Zindel V, J Mark, G Williams and John D Teasdale. *Mindfulness-Based Cognitive Therapy for Depression*. New York: The Guilford Press, 2002.

Sennett, Richard. *Respect: The Formation of Character in an Age of Inequality*. London: Penguin Books, 2003.

Shapiro, Shauna L, et al. 'Mechanisms of Mindfulness.' *Journal of Clinical Psychology* 62, no. 3 (2006): 373-386. Accessed 18th July 2014. dx.doi.org/10.1002/jclp.20237.

Sheldrake, Philip F. *Explorations in Spirituality: History, Theology, and Social Practice*. New York: Paulist Press, 2010.

Siegel, Daniel J. *The Mindful Brain*. New York: W W Norton & Company, 2007.

———. 'Mindfulness Training and Neural Integration: Differentiation of Distinct Streams of Awareness and the Cultivation of Well-being.' *Social Cognitive and Affective Neuroscience (SCAN)* 2, no. 4 (2007), 261. Accessed 12th March 2022. dx.doi.org/10.1093/scan/nsm034.

Smith, J A, P Flowers and M Larkin. *Interpretative Phenomenological Analysis: Theory, Method and Research.* London: Sage, 2009.

Smith, James, K A. *Desiring the Kingdom: Worship, Worldview, and Cultural Formation.* Grand Rapids, Michigan: Baker Academic, 2009.

———. 'The Scandal of Sheer Grace: When Mercy Offends.' *Calvin Theological Journal* 56 no. 2(2021): 309-319.

Spidlik, Tomas. *The Spirituality of the Christian East.* Collegeville, Minnesota: Liturgical Press, 1986.

Stein, Howard F. 'A Window to the Interior of Experience.' *Families, Systems and Health.* 22, no. 2 (2004): 178-179. Accessed 8th May 2019. dx.doi.org/10.1037/1091-7527.22.2.178.

Stewart, Columba OSB. *Prayer and Community: The Benedictine Tradition.* London: Darton, Longman & Todd, 1998.

Stewart, Ian., & Vann Joines. *TA Today: A New Introduction to Transactional Analysis.* Nottingham & Chapel Hill: Lifespace Publishing, 1987.

Strobel, Kyle. 'In Your Light They Shall See Light: A Theological Prolegomena for Contemplation.' *Journal of Spiritual Formation and Soul Care* 7, no. 1 (May 2014): 85-106. Accessed 12th May 2020. dx.doi.org/10.1177/193979091400700109.

Suler, John. 'The Online Disinhibition Effect.' *CyberPsychology & Behaviour*, 7, no. 3 (2004): 321-326. Accessed 1st December 2021. dx.doi.org/10.1089/1094931041291295.

Swales Michaela A, and Heidi L Heard, *Dialectical Behaviour Therapy.* The CBT Distinctive Features Series. Series editor Windy Dryden. London, New York: Routledge, 2009.

Teasdale, John D, and Philip J Bernard. *Affect Cognition and Change: Re-modelling Depressive Thought.* Hove: Lawrence Erlbaum Associates, 1993.

Teasdale, J D. 'Metacognition, Mindfulness and the Modification of Mood Disorders.' *Clinical Psychology & Psychotherapy* 6 (1999): 146-155.

Teasdale, John D, et al. 'Metacognitive Awareness and Prevention of Relapse in Depression: Empirical Evidence.' *Journal of Counselling and Clinical Psychology* 70, no. 2 (2002): 275-287. Accessed 26th December 2017. dx.doi.org/10.1037//0022-006X.70.2.275.

Tedloch, Barbara. 'From Participant Observation to the Observation of Participation: The Emergence of Narrative Ethnography.' *Journal of Anthropological Research* 47, no. 1 (1991): 69-94.

———. 'Braiding Evocative with Analytic Autoethnography.' In *Handbook of Autoethnography*, edited by Stacy Holman Jones, Tony E Adams and Carolyn Ellis, 358-362. Walnut Creek, California: Left Coast Press Inc, 2013.

The Boston Change Process Study Group. Change in *Psychotherapy: A Unifying Paradigm.* New York, London: W W Norton & Company, 2010.

Thibodeaux, Mark E, SJ. *Reimagining the Ignatian Examen.* Chicago, Illinois: Loyala Press, 2015.

Thomas, David C. 'Domain and Development of Cultural Intelligence: The Importance of Mindfulness.' *Group & Organization Management* 31, no. 1 (February 2006): 78-99. Accessed 28th November 2018. dx.doi.org/10.1177/1059601105275266.

Thomas, David C, and Kerr Inkson. *Cultural Intelligence: Living and Working Globally.* 2nd edition. San Francisco, California: Berrett-Koehler Publishers, 2009.

Topalovic, Radmila and Tom Kerss. *Stargazing: Beginners Guide to Astronomy.* Glasgow: Collins, 2016.

Treleaven, David A. *Trauma-Sensitive Mindfulness: Practices for Safe and Transformative Healing.* New York, London: W W Norton & Company, 2018. Kindle.

Tugwell, Simon. 'Evagrius and Macarius.' In *The Study of Spirituality*, edited by Cheslyn Jones, Geoffrey Wainwright and Edward Yarnold, SJ. London: SPCK, 1986.

Vago, David R. PhD, and David A Silbersweig. 'Self-Awareness, Self-Regulation, and Self-Transcendence (S-ART): A Framework for Understanding the Neurobiological Mechanisms of Mindfulness.' *Frontiers in Human Neuroscience* 6 (2012): 1-30. Accessed 16th September 2017. dx.doi.org/10.3389/fnhum.2012.00296.

van der Kolk, Bessel. *The Body Keeps the Score: Mind, Brain and Body in the Transformation of Trauma.* London: Penguin Books, 2014.

Varela, Francisco J, and Jonathan Shear. 'First-Person Methodologies: What, Why, How?' In *The View from Within: First-person approaches to the study of consciousness*, edited by Francisco J Varela and Jonathan Shear, 1-14. Imprint Academic, 1999.

Veling, Terry A. 'Poetic License', *International Journal of Practical Theology* 23, no. 1 (2019): 39-48. Accessed 7th December 2021. dx.doi.org/10.1515/ijpt-2018-0029.

Wall, John. 'The Creative Imperative: Religious Ethics and the Formation of Life in Common.' *Journal of Religious Ethics* 33, no. 1, (2005): 55. Accessed 21st December 2022. dx.doi.org/10.1111/j.0384-9694.2005.00182.x.

Walton, Heather. *Writing Methods in Theological Reflection.* London: SCM Press, 2014.

———. 'A Theopoetics of Practice: Re-forming in Practical Theology: Presidential Address to the International Academy of Practical Theology, Eastertide 2017.' *International Journal of Practical Theology* 23, no. 1 (2019): 3-23. Accessed 7th December 2021, http://dx.doi.org/10.1515/ijpt-2018-0033.

Ward, Frances and Richard Sudworth. 'Introduction.' In *Holy*

Attention: Preaching in Today's Church. Edited by Frances Ward and Richard Sudworth. Norwich: Canterbury Press, 2019. Kindle.

Ward Barrington, Simon. *The Jesus Prayer*. Oxford: The Bible Reading Fellowship, 2007.

———. *The Jesus Prayer: A Way to Contemplation*. Boston, Massachusetts: Pauline Books & Media, 2011.

Ware, Kallistos. 'The Origins of the Jesus Prayer: Diadochus, Gaza, Sinai.' In *The Study of Spirituality* edited by Cheslyn Jones, Geoffrey Wainwright and Edward Yarnold, SJ, 175-183. London: SPCK, 1986.

Warner, Megan, et al. 'Introduction.' In *Tragedies and Christian Congregations: The Practical Theology of Trauma*. Edited by Megan Warner, et al, 1-9. London, New York: Routledge, 2020.

Watkins, Mary. 'Seeding Liberation: A Dialogue Between Depth Psychology and Liberation Psychology.' In *Depth Psychology: Meditations in the Field*. Edited by D Slattery and L Corbett, 204-225. Daimon Verlag, 2001.

Wax, Ruby. *Sane New World: Taming the Mind*. London: Hodder & Stoughton, 2013.

Wiebe, Kate. 'Toward a Faith-Based Approach to Healing after Collective Trauma.' In *Tragedies and Christian Congregations: The Practical Theology of Trauma*, edited by Megan Warner, et al. London: Routledge, 2020.

Williams, James. *Stand Out of Our Light: Freedom and Resistance in the Attention Economy*. Cambridge: Cambridge University Press, 2018.

Williams, Mark, et al. *The Mindful Way through Depression: Freeing Yourself from Chronic Unhappiness*. New York, London: The Guilford Press, 2007.

Williams, J M G. (2010). 'Mindfulness and psychological process.' *Emotion*, 10, no. 1 (2010): 1-7. Accessed 3rd June 2020. dx.doi.org/10.1037/a001836.

Williams, Mark and Danny Penman. *Mindfulness: A Practical*

Guide to Finding Peace in a Frantic World. London: Piatkus, 2011.

Williams, Mark, and Danny Penman. *Deeper Mindfulness: The New Way to Rediscover Calm in a Chaotic World*. London: Piatkus, 2023, Kindle.

Williams, Rowan. *Silence and Honey Cakes*. Oxford: Lion, 2003.

Willis, Peter. 'Don't Call it Poetry.' *The Indo-Pacific Journal of Phenomenology* 2, no. 1 (April 2002): 1-14.

Wire, Antoinette Clark. *The Case for Mark Composed in Performance*. Eugene, OR: Cascade Books, 2011.

Wiseman, James A OSB. 'The Contemplative Life.' A subsection of 'Prayer and Meditation.' In *The Gethsemani Encounter*, edited by Donald Mitchell and James A. Wiseman OSB. New York: Continuum, 1998, 54-59.

Woodward, Russell. 'The Spiral Curriculum in Higher Education: Analysis in Pedagogic Context and a Business Studies Application.' In *E-Journal of Business Education and Scholarship of Teaching* 13, no. 3 (2019): 14-26.

Wright, Andrew. *Christianity and Critical Realism: Ambiguity, Truth and Theological Literacy*. London: Routledge, 2013.

Yarnold, Edward. 'The Theology of Christian Spirituality.' In *The Study of Spirituality*, edited by Cheslyn Jones, Geoffrey Wainwright and Edward Yarnold, SJ, 9-16. London: SPCK, 1986.